Journal of the Early Republic

VOLUME 32, NUMBER 4
WINTER 2012

The *Journal of the Early Republic* (ISSN 0275-1275) is published quarterly
by the University of Pennsylvania Press
for the Society for Historians of the Early American Republic

Journal of the Early Republic

VOLUME 32, NUMBER 4 (WINTER 2012)

ISSN 0275-1275

Published by the University of Pennsylvania Press, 3905 Spruce Street, Philadelphia, PA 19104.
The *Journal of the Early Republic*, its publishers, and its sponsors disclaim responsibility for statements of fact or opinion appearing in the pages of the journal. Printed in the U.S.A. on acid-free paper.

The *Journal of the Early Republic* is a quarterly journal committed to publishing the best scholarship on the history and culture of the United States in the years of the early republic (1776–1861). Contributors should prepare their manuscripts following the *Chicago Manual of Style*. All articles should be submitted to the editor for consideration. Complete preparation and submission information is available at http://jer.pennpress.org.

INDEXED IN: *Historical Abstracts*, *America: History and Life*, *JSTOR*, *Current Contents/Arts & Humanities*, *The American Humanities Index*, and *Arts & Humanities Citation Index*.

2013 ANNUAL MEMBERSHIP/SUBSCRIPTION INFORMATION (USD)

Individuals/Members:		Institutions:	$120.00
Income above $45,000:	$70.00	Single Issues:	$30.00
Income to $45,000:	$40.00		
Community College faculty:	$40.00		
K–12 teachers:	$35.00		
Students:	$30.00		

Please add $17.00 for shipment to addresses outside the U.S.

Friends of SHEAR: Provide SHEAR with additional support by becoming a Friend of SHEAR. Send a check for $500.00, $300.00, or $150.00, to SHEAR, 3355 Woodland Walk, Philadelphia, PA 19104-4531. This check will cover your SHEAR membership, including your *JER* subscription. If you become a Friend of SHEAR, the SHEAR office will subscribe to the *JER* for you and your support will be acknowledged in the *JER*.

Memberships/subscriptions are valid January 1 through December 31. Memberships/subscriptions received after October 31 in any year become effective the following January 1. Members/subscribers joining mid-year receive immediately copies of all issues of the *JER* already in print for that year.

Please direct all subscription orders, inquiries, requests for single issues, address changes, and other business communications as follows: *Journal of the Early Republic*, c/o SHEAR, 3355 Woodland Walk, Philadelphia, PA 19104-4531. Phone: 215-746-5393. Fax: 215-573-3391. Email: info@shear.org.

Prepayment is required. Checks and money orders should be made payable to "Society for Historians of the Early American Republic," and sent to the address printed above. To subscribe online visit http://www.shear.org.

Postmaster: Send address changes to *Journal of the Early Republic*, c/o SHEAR, 3355 Woodland Walk, Philadelphia, PA 19104-4531.

Journal of the Early Republic

VOLUME 32, NUMBER 4 (WINTER 2012)

CONTENTS

ARTICLES

REVIEWS

S.C.
N.C.
P
M.
N.J.
N.Y.
N.E.
Unite and Conquer

"A Dangerous Set of People"

British Captives and the Making of Revolutionary Identity in the Mid-Atlantic Interior

KEN MILLER

During their fall 1775 incursion into Canada, rebel forces under the command of Brigadier General Richard Montgomery captured the British garrisons manning Forts Chambly and St. John's, just southeast of Montreal. Claiming few American lives and netting nearly seven hundred prisoners, the victories raised Whigs' spirits but posed a serious problem for the new Continental Congress. Having just commenced hostilities with Britain, Whigs lacked both a coherent policy and the necessary institutions to hold hundreds of enemy captives. In the years ahead, the revolutionaries would disperse upwards of thirteen thousand prisoners—both British regulars and their so-called Hessian auxiliaries—in isolated communities in Virginia, Maryland, and Pennsylvania. The captives fell under the immediate jurisdiction of local officials in makeshift detention camps loosely supervised by state and national

Ken Miller is an assistant professor of history at Washington College and the author of *Dangerous Guests: Enemy Captives and Revolutionary Communities During the War for Independence*, forthcoming from Cornell University Press. He gives special thanks to Alan Taylor, Karen Halttunen, John Smolenski, Brett Rushforth, Fredrika Teute, David Waldstreicher, Karin Wulf, Paul Mapp, Douglas Winiarski, Robert Parkinson, Donna Whicher, and Michael McGandy for their valuable feedback on earlier versions of this article. He is also grateful to the editor and the three anonymous readers of the *Journal of the Early Republic* whose insightful comments and criticisms substantially improved the piece. This project received generous financial support from the University of California, Davis, the Library Company of Philadelphia, the Historical Society of Pennsylvania, the David Library of the American Revolution, the Colonial Williamsburg Foundation, the German Historical Institute, and Washington College.

Journal of the Early Republic, 32 (Winter 2012)

authorities. In late 1775, however, the prisoners remained under the informal control of Congress and General George Washington.[1]

Eighteenth-century European military conventions furnished Continental officials with several precedents for managing their new captives. Belligerents customarily bore the expense of their own soldiers in captivity. To reclaim their troops, nations negotiated formal cartels, exchanging rank for rank, with officers receiving priority over the enlisted men. Captured officers were paroled on their honor as gentlemen, affording them more freedom than their men, who were typically confined pending their exchange. To reduce the costs and burdens of a long confinement, the combatants occasionally permitted their rank-and-file prisoners to hire their labor until exchanged. These conventions had informed the treatment of European captives as recently as the Seven Years' War.[2]

---

1. An Officer at La Prairie, Nov. 3, 1775, *American Archives, Consisting of a Collection of Authentick Records, State Papers, Debates, and Letters and Other Notices of Publick Affairs*, ed. Peter Force (Washington, DC, 1837–53), Fourth Series, 3: 1342 (hereafter *AA*); Colonel Bedel to New Hampshire Committee of Safety, Oct. 27, 1775, Force, *AA*, Fourth Series, 3: 1207; An Officer of the New York Forces, Nov. 3, 1775, Force, *AA*, Fourth Series, 3: 1343; An Officer at Fort St. John's, Nov. 3, 1775, Force, *AA*, Fourth Series, 3: 1344; Extracts of Letters Received in England from Quebec, Nov. 9, 1775, Force, *AA*, Fourth Series, 3: 1418; Richard Henry Lee to Catherine Macaulay, Nov. 29, 1775, *Letters of Delegates to Congress, 1774–1789*, ed. Paul H. Smith (Washington, DC, 1976–2000), 2: 405–406; Don Higginbotham, *The War of American Independence: Military Attitudes, Policies, and Practice, 1763–1789* (New York, 1971), 106–12; General Montgomery to General Schuyler, Oct. 20, 1775, Force, *AA*, Fourth Series, 3: 1132. For Continental prisoner policy, see Charles H. Metzger, *The Prisoner in the American Revolution* (Chicago, 1971); Martha W. Dixon, "Divided Authority: The American Management of Prisoners in the Revolutionary War, 1775–1783" (PhD diss., University of Utah, 1977); Robert C. Doyle, *The Enemy in Our Hands: America's Treatment of Prisoners of War from the Revolution to the War on Terror* (Lexington, KY, 2010), 11–31; Paul J. Springer, *America's Captives: Treatment of POWs from the Revolutionary War to the War on Terror* (Lawrence, KS, 2010), 13–41; Kenneth Miller, "'Dangerous Guests': Enemy Captives and American National Identity in Revolutionary Lancaster, Pennsylvania, 1760–1783" (PhD diss., University of California, Davis, 2006); Daniel Krebs, "Approaching the Enemy: German Captives in the American War of Independence, 1776–1783" (PhD diss., Emory University, 2007).

2. *Journals of the Continental Congress, 1774–1789*, ed. Worthington C. Ford et al. (34 vols.; Washington, DC, 1904–37), 4: 361 (hereafter *JCC*); Doyle, *The Enemy in Our Hands*, 11–12; Springer, *America's Captives*, 9–12; Krebs,

North America's latest conflict was no ordinary war, however, but a colonial revolt against imperial authority. Complicating matters for Continental officials, their prisoners were fellow Britons seized in an unlawful rebellion. British officials refused to bow to conventions in a war against domestic rebels, fearing that any recognition of the Americans' belligerent status might legitimize the insurgency. The Americans also briefly enjoyed a favorable balance of prisoners following their initial success in Canada and felt little urgency to press for a general exchange, particularly with their new captives providing potential leverage in future deliberations. After carefully weighing their options, Continental officials elected to detain their captives pending negotiations with the British. Officials hoped their new prisoners would ensure both the recognition of Americans' status as formal combatants and the good treatment and safe return of Americans held by the British.[3]

To ensure the prisoners' safekeeping, Congress dispatched them to York, Carlisle, Reading, and Lancaster, Pennsylvania, four inland towns well removed from potentially threatening military operations along the coast. Boasting some three thousand inhabitants during the War for Independence, Lancaster received nearly four hundred prisoners and quickly became the Continentals' leading detention center. Nestled in Pennsylvania's bountiful agricultural hinterland and equipped with a large barracks constructed during the Seven Years' War, Lancaster answered the immediate needs of Continental officials. The town's inhabitants had already demonstrated their enthusiasm for the cause by mobilizing abundant men and materiel, and Congressional officials now trusted them faithfully to execute Continental policy.[4]

"Approaching the Enemy," 191–93; Ian K. Steele, "When Worlds Collide: The Fate of Canadian and French Prisoners Taken at Fort Niagara, 1759," *Journal of Canadian Studies* 39 (Fall 2005), 9–39.

3. Dixon, "Divided Authority," 3–4; Linda Colley, *Captives: Britain, Empire, and the World, 1600–1850* (London, 2002), 203–38; Caroline Cox, *A Proper Sense of Honor: Service and Sacrifice in George Washington's Army* (Chapel Hill, NC, 2004), 199–235; Edwin G. Burrows, *Forgotten Patriots: The Untold Story of American Prisoners during the Revolutionary War* (New York, 2008).

4. Continental Congress, Nov. 17, 1775, Force, *AA*, Fourth Series, 3: 1921; *JCC*, 3: 358, 404; George Washington to President of Congress, Nov. 8, 1775, *The Writings of George Washington, from the Original Manuscript Sources, 1745–1799*, ed. John C. Fitzpatrick (39 vols., Washington, DC, 1931–44), 4: 73; Dixon, "Divided Authority," 115–37; John B. Frantz and William Pencak, eds., *Beyond*

But for Lancaster's insurgents the British captives constituted an unwelcome addition to an anxious and a divided community. In late 1775, amid the growing frictions with Britain and the mounting vicissitudes of war, locals retained vivid memories of the brutal frontier violence of the 1750s and 1760s, when vicious encounters between natives and settlers had scarred the Pennsylvania backcountry. Years after the bloodshed, residents continued to dread the "horrors of an Indian War," and local security remained their overriding concern. The region's Indians maintained a precarious neutrality in the escalating conflict with Britain, but the uncertainties surrounding their future commitments placed Lancaster at the crossroads of a potentially explosive frontier.[5]

The British captives also added a volatile ingredient to the community's simmering wartime divisions and dizzying cultural diversity. German, English, Welsh, and Scots-Irish emigrants of widely divergent faiths, from Quaker and Presbyterian to Lutheran and Mennonite, had flocked to Lancaster County through the mid-1700s in search of religious freedom and economic opportunity. Ethnocultural divisions bred tensions in the dynamic, bustling community, reinforcing settlers' particular ethnic identities. Lancaster's diverse inhabitants generally identified with and congregated among their own, clinging to their peculiar languages and customs and privileging specific ethnic and religious interests. Even as they mobilized for war, the community's English- and German-speaking insurgents divided along familiar ethnocultural lines. The struggle with Britain heightened local divisions as supporters and

Philadelphia: The American Revolution in the Pennsylvania Hinterland (University Park, PA, 1998), xx; Franklin Ellis and Samuel Evans, *History of Lancaster County, Pennsylvania; With Biographical Sketches of Many of Its Pioneers and Prominent Men* (Philadelphia, 1883), 33–69; Jerome H. Wood, Jr., *Conestoga Crossroads: Lancaster, Pennsylvania, 1730–1790* (Harrisburg, PA, 1979), 79–89; Charles H. Kessler, *Lancaster in the Revolution* (Lititz, PA, 1975); Miller, "'Dangerous Guests.'"

5. Jasper Yeates to Joseph Swift, Jan. 30, 1768, Burd–Shippen Family Collection, 1704–1900, Reel 2, Film 707, David Library of the American Revolution, Washington Crossing, PA (hereafter DLAR); Peter Silver, *Our Savage Neighbors: How Indian War Transformed Early America* (New York, 2008); Kevin Kenny, *Peaceable Kingdom Lost: The Paxton Boys and the Destruction of William Penn's Holy Experiment* (New York, 2009); Colin Calloway, *The American Revolution in Indian Country: Crisis and Diversity in Native American Communities* (New York, 1995).

opponents of the resistance chose sides and split into hostile camps. The prisoners' arrival in late 1775 threatened to multiply the challenges already confronting the internally divided community. As both imperial kinsmen and enemy combatants, the British prisoners could conceivably exacerbate local tensions.[6]

Lancaster—as the Whigs' principal detention site for enemy prisoners of war—soon stood at the nexus of two vastly different revolutionary worlds: one national, the other intensely local. Before 1776, Lancaster's wartime experience paralleled broader patterns in the Pennsylvania interior, as supporters of the resistance mobilized men and materiel and harried the disaffected minority from their newly formed militias and extralegal committees. Continental policy brought the war to the town's insurgents by depositing the enemy on their doorsteps. Lancaster's peculiar vulnerability raised the stakes for local militants and fueled their growing enmity for the British. The continuing infusion of prisoners reaffirmed locals' status as revolutionaries embroiled in an irreconcilable conflict with their imperial antagonists.

Through 1776, locals came to know their prisoners intimately as hard-boiled combatants devoid of sympathy for their erstwhile kindred. Embittered by the enemies' disdain for their cause, militants developed a corresponding revulsion for the imperial fold. The prisoners promptly inflamed Lancaster's wartime divisions while consolidating the ranks of hardline insurgents. As the captives defied their hosts and cultivated subversive associations, militants policed the community, sorting friend from foe. The new dangers rallied Lancaster's English- and German-speaking insurgents, encouraging them to transcend their cultural differences as they distinguished themselves from their British enemies and identified with a broader revolutionary community. But the prisoners also revealed the boundaries of locals' patriotism by exposing competing communal and Continental agendas.[7]

---

6. Wood, *Conestoga Crossroads*, 1–20, 79–89, 181–215; Mark Haeberlein, *The Practice of Pluralism: Congregational Life and Religious Diversity in Lancaster, Pennsylvania, 1730–1820* (University Park, PA, 2009), 15–188.

7. Gregory T. Knouff, *The Soldiers' Revolution: Pennsylvanians in Arms and the Forging of Early American Identity* (University Park, PA, 2004). The historiography of Revolutionary Pennsylvania has emphasized the ways in which the Revolution exacerbated social differences. See, for example, David Freeman Hawke, *In the Midst of a Revolution* (Philadelphia, 1961); Richard Alan Ryerson, *The Revolution Is Now Begun: The Radical Committees of Philadelphia, 1765–1776* (Philadel-

Lancaster's first British captives arrived during early December 1775. On Saturday, December 9, 250 members of the British 7th Regiment of Foot, Royal Fusiliers, marched into the borough under military escort accompanied by sixty women and children. Another 130 prisoners, members of the 26th Regiment of Foot, followed two days later. Lancaster's new Committee of Observation faced an immediate crisis when Egbert Dumond, commander of the American escort, announced that the prisoners had only two days' provisions. Dumond added that he had received no specific orders concerning the captives and could offer local officials no more guidance than to "take such measures . . . as they may think most conducive to the Publick Service."[8]

Lacking instructions from Philadelphia, Lancaster's committee had to determine how to house and provision the prisoners while ensuring their

phia, 1978); Steven Rosswurm, *Arms, Country, and Class: The Philadelphia Militia and "Lower Sort" During the American Revolution, 1775–1783* (New Brunswick, NJ, 1987); Anne M. Ousterhout, *A State Divided: Opposition in Pennsylvania to the American Revolution* (Westport, CT, 1987); Frantz and Pencak, *Beyond Philadelphia*; Francis Fox, *Sweet Land of Liberty: The Ordeal of the American Revolution in Northampton County, Pennsylvania* (University Park, PA, 2000); Liam Riordan, *Many Identities, One Nation: The Revolution and Its Legacy in the Mid-Atlantic* (Philadelphia, 2007), 43–81. For examples of American identity formation during the Revolution, see Charles Royster, *A Revolutionary People at War: The Continental Army and American Character, 1775–1783* (Chapel Hill, NC, 1979); David Waldstreicher, *In the Midst of Perpetual Fetes: The Making of American Nationalism, 1776–1820* (Chapel Hill, NC, 1997), 17–52; Colley, *Captives*, 203–38; Carroll Smith-Rosenberg, *This Violent Empire: The Birth of an American National Identity* (Chapel Hill, NC, 2010), 1–54.

8. Lancaster County Committee of Safety, Dec. 9, 1775, Peter Force Papers, Series 7E, reel 16, film 559, DLAR; Continental Congress, Nov. 17, 1775, Force, *AA*, Fourth Series, 3: 1921; *JCC*, 3: 358, 404; "Notes from Letters of Judge Yeates, December 9, 1775," *Notes and Queries, Historical and Genealogical, Chiefly Relating to Interior Pennsylvania*, ed. William Henry Egle (Baltimore, 1894–1900), 2: 382; "Extracts from Moravian Diaries at Bethlehem," *Papers Read Before the Lancaster County Historical Society* 27, no. 5 (1923), 91 (hereafter *PLCHS*); *The Pennsylvania Archives* (hereafter *PA*), ed. Samuel Hazard et al. (9 series, 119 vols., Philadelphia and Harrisburg, PA, 1852–1949), Second Series, 1: 440–48; "List of the Officers Taken at St. John's," Egle, *Notes and Queries* (Annual Vol., Harrisburg, PA, 1900), 171–72.

safekeeping and the security of the inhabitants. Local officials moved the British enlisted men and their families into the empty barracks but permitted the officers to rent private lodgings at their own expense. The German innkeeper and committeeman Matthias Slough volunteered to supply the captives until Congress appointed a permanent provisioning agent. Congress quickly sent word that the captives should draw their provisions from David Franks, a prominent Philadelphia-based merchant contracted to supply Pennsylvania's British prisoners "at the expence of the crown." Having resolved the matters of lodging and subsistence, local officials soon found themselves saddled with new responsibilities.[9]

The captives stood in dire need of warm clothing after arriving without their baggage with the winter season threatening. Moved by the prisoners' plight and eager to please the Congress, Lancaster's officials furnished their visitors with blankets and linen "on the Public Account." The committee encountered a more serious problem in early January when the new provisioning agent David Franks refused to provide food for the prisoners' wives and children. The wives implored the committee for assistance, insisting "they must inevitably perish, unless relieved from their present distress." Local officials arranged to supply the families at the public expense until Congress issued orders for their future subsistence.[10]

As the committee's chairman Jasper Yeates explained to Congress: "Being mindful that humanity ought ever to distinguish the sons of America, and that cruelty should find no admission amongst a free people, we could not avoid considering the situation of their women and children as pitiable, indeed." Thus, "we were strongly inclined . . . to assist them in their distress." The captive officers thanked the committee and the town for "raising a subscription for the women and children, and, likewise, for other civilities." Congress, too, voiced its warm

9. *JCC*, 3: 398–99, 359, 434, 435; Lancaster County Committee of Safety, Dec. 9, 1775, Peter Force Papers, Series 7E, Reel 16, Film 559; "Notes from Letters of Judge Yeates," Egle, *Notes and Queries*, 382.

10. Lancaster County Committee of Safety, Dec. 27, 1775, Peter Force Papers, Series 7E, Reel 16, Film 559; Lancaster Committee to President of Congress, Jan. 10, 1776, Force, *AA*, Fourth Series, 4: 619; Lancaster Committee to President of Congress, Dec. 21, 1775, Papers of the Continental Congress (hereafter PCC), Reel 83, National Archives, Washington, DC; "Notes from Letters of Judge Yeates," Egle, *Notes and Queries*, 382.

approval of the "civility" and "humane sentiments" displayed by the town's inhabitants. Locals' generosity mirrored Continental officials' broader concerns for their British captives.[11]

But Whigs' magnanimity deviated sharply from Britain's treatment of American prisoners. Following Lexington and Concord, the British approached their captives as treasonous rebels unworthy of the privileges of formal combatants. Disregarding conventions, they refused to distinguish between American officers and enlisted men and subjected both to a rigorous confinement. Washington rebuked General Thomas Gage as early as August 1775 for detaining captured American officers in "a common jail appropriated for felons" without consideration for the "most respectable rank." Many British officials felt a more fitting punishment awaited their prisoners on the scaffold. Authorities warned the rebels captured at Quebec during December 1775 that "they deserved nothing but death; for they had taken up arms against their own country." The British ultimately consigned most of their American prisoners to a long and severe confinement in cramped and dingy jails, churches, warehouses, sugar refineries, and transport ships.[12]

Even after receiving reports of the harsh treatment meted out to American prisoners, however, Washington and Congress urged Whigs to treat their captives with civility and compassion and thereby avoid Britain's "unworthy example." In September 1775, Washington issued instructions for the care of British prisoners held by the Hartford, Connecticut, Committee of Correspondence: "Allow me to recommend a gentleness, even to forbearance, with persons so entirely in our power. We know not what the chance of war may be; but . . . the duties of humanity and

11. Lancaster Committee to President of Congress, Jan. 10, 1776, Force, *AA*, Fourth Series, 4: 619; British Officers to Continental Congress, Jan. 20, 1776, Force, *AA*, Fourth Series, 4: 801–802; President of Congress to Lancaster Committee, Jan. 18, 1776, Force, *AA*, Fourth Series, 4: 761–63; *JCC*, 4: 21.

12. George Washington to Thomas Gage, Aug. 11, 1775, Force, *AA*, Fourth Series, 3: 245; Kenneth Roberts, ed., *March to Quebec: Journals of the Members of Arnold's Expedition* (New York, 1938), 591; Thomas Gage to George Washington, Aug., 13, 1775, Force, *AA*, Fourth Series, 3: 246. Larry Bowman, *Captive Americans: Prisoners during the American Revolution* (Athens, OH, 1976); Francis D. Cogliano, *American Maritime Prisoners in the Revolutionary War: The Captivity of William Russell* (Annapolis, MD, 2001); Cox, *A Proper Sense of Honor*, 199–235; Burrows, *Forgotten Patriots*. The British eventually placed most captured American officers under parole.

kindness will demand from us such a treatment as we should expect from others, the case being reversed."[13]

Influencing early Continental policy were the informal conventions governing the humane treatment of European prisoners of war. Washington and leading Continental officials recognized that American prisoner policy needed to remain above reproach. The neglect or abuse of British prisoners could discredit the American resistance and alienate potential supporters. By contrast, a policy of humane treatment could enable Whigs to seize the moral high ground by bolstering their image as injured innocents, particularly in light of Britain's continuing neglect of American captives. Indeed, pursuing a humanitarian policy could legitimize, even sanctify, the American rebellion, while potentially alleviating the distress of rebel prisoners.

Along with such practical considerations, early Continental policy sprang from a persistent cultural affinity to Great Britain. In late 1775, when envisioning their British adversaries, many Continental officials still felt the faint tug of kinship borne of a sense of common identity. Following nearly a year of hostilities, the colonies had yet to declare their independence, and reconciliation with the mother country remained the hope of many Americans. Mindful of their shared British heritage and their enduring cultural affiliation with their overseas brethren, authorities on both sides continued to situate their opponents within a collective imperial identity. This feeling of common kinship informed Continental officials' approach to their British captives.[14]

---

13. George Washington to Major Christopher French, Sept. 26, 1775, Force, *AA*, Fourth Series, 3: 810–11; George Washington to Hartford Committee, Sept. 26, 1775, Force, *AA*, Fourth Series, 3: 810. See also Robert Harrison to Springfield Committee, Feb. 9, 1776, Force, *AA*, Fourth Series, 4: 973; Joseph Reed to Major Christopher French, Sept. 3, 1775, Force, *AA*, Fourth Series, 3: 639; Joseph Reed to Hartford Committee, Sept. 3, 1775, Force, *AA*, Fourth Series, 3: 639–40.

14. Michael Zuckerman, "Identity in British America: Unease in Eden," in *Colonial Identity in the Atlantic World, 1500–1800*, ed. Nicholas Canny and Anthony Pagden (Princeton, NJ, 1987), 115–57; John Murrin, "A Roof without Walls: The Dilemma of American National Identity," in *Beyond Confederation: Origins of the Constitution and American National Identity*, ed. Richard Beeman, et al. (Chapel Hill, NC, 1987), 333–48; T. H. Breen, "Ideology and Nationalism on the Eve of the American Revolution: Revisions *Once More* in Need of Revising," *Journal of American History* 84 (June 1997), 13–39; Smith-Rosenberg, *This Violent Empire*, 1–18; Stephen Conway, "From Fellow-Nationals to Foreigners:

Major General Philip Schuyler, the commander of the Americans' Canadian expedition, articulated this sense of shared identity rooted in a common past in his instructions to the prisoners' military escort. "You will be particularly attentive," he directed, "that no person, who may have forgotten the rights of mankind, and the principles of Englishmen, offer the least insult to any of the gentlemen, their soldiers, their wives, or children." Similarly, in August 1775, Washington assured General Gage that despite the many abuses American prisoners suffered under the British, the colonists treated their captives "with a tenderness due to fellow-citizens and brethren." "As men, they have a claim to all the rights of humanity," observed John Hancock of Lancaster's prisoners in January 1776. "As countrymen, though enemies," he added, "they claim something more."[15]

Even the British found occasion to praise American policy. A British officer captured at Fort Chambly reported shortly after surrendering that he and his fellow prisoners had "been treated with the greatest civility and politeness." Everywhere he went his hosts faithfully adhered to "the benevolent principles on which they wish this unnatural contest may be conducted." Impressed by Whigs' charitableness, he concluded it was "the sincere sentiment of the generality of the Americans, that a happy and honourable accommodation between Great Britain and her colonies may speedily take place." While the officer misjudged his hosts' commitment to a hasty reconciliation, he astutely grasped the persistent ties of affection binding some Britons and Americans.[16]

British Perceptions of the Americans, circa 1739–1783," *William and Mary Quarterly* 59 (Jan. 2002), 65–100; Colley, *Captives*, 203–38.

15. Philip Schuyler to Captain Hulbert, Nov. 1, 1775, Force, *AA*, Fourth Series, 4: 816; George Washington to General Thomas Gage, Aug. 19, 1775, Force, *AA*, Fourth Series, 3: 246–47; President of Congress to Lancaster Committee, Jan. 18, 1776, Force, *AA*, Fourth Series, 4: 761–63. See also Edward Shippen to James Burd, Apr. 11, 1774, Shippen Family Papers, 7, Historical Society of Pennsylvania, Philadelphia (hereafter HSP); James Burd to Edward Shippen, Dec. 4, 1774, Shippen Family Papers, 7, HSP; Edward Shippen to Joseph Shippen, May 13, 1775, Shippen Family Papers, BSh6lf.1, American Philosophical Society, Philadelphia (hereafter APS); "Lancaster Committee to York Committee, March 19, 1776," Egle, *Notes and Queries* (First and Second Series, 2 vols., Harrisburg, PA, 1894), 1: 428; "Eberhart Michael to John Andre, April 26, 1776," *PLCHS* 18, no. 6 (1914), 134–35.

16. Unknown British Officer, Nov. 19, 1775, Force, *AA*, Fourth Series, 3: 1608.

Some of Lancaster's leading moderates, hopeful of eventually reconciling with the mother country, continued to envision the British as reluctant antagonists loath to wage a fratricidal war against their American cousins. The wealthy committeeman Edward Shippen ranked among Lancaster's most influential inhabitants and brought a distinguished record of public service to the Whig resistance. But while he supported the colonists' resort to arms, Shippen had obtained wealth and position under British rule and longed for a quick peace, dreading a permanent rupture with the empire. Weeks after Lexington and Concord, he sharply distinguished between the British and American troops while acknowledging their common bond. Pondering the distinct motives that brought combatants to the field, Shippen concluded: "The Americans fight for every thing that are most dear to them—their lives Liberty and fortunes; whereas the Regulars, poor fellows, fight for six pence a day, and with reluctancy against their own brethren." In early spring 1776, the wealthy German shopkeeper and secretary of Lancaster's Committee Eberhart Michael informed Lieutenant John Andre, one of the British officers captured at Fort St. John's, of his sincere hope that "peace will again reign and inhabitants and soldiers will again enjoy brotherly association. These colonies and Great Britain—a people mighty and famous in the world." Even after a year of armed conflict, such sentiments continued to shape American prisoner policy.[17]

By mid-1776, however, Pennsylvania's diversity, the escalating hostilities, and the mounting antagonisms between local insurgents and their British captives combined to complicate and frustrate Continental policy. In Lancaster, English and German speakers' tense face-to-face, day-to-day encounters with their captives facilitated the break with Britain and nurtured an emerging revolutionary identity. For locals, the prisoners magnified dangers both real and imagined. Residents' fears, in turn, fed simmering resentments of their enemies and anxious attachments to their friends. As Lancaster's prisoners grew in number and became more difficult to control, pressures radiated outward into the diverse Pennsylvania hinterland. Local pressures helped to redefine Continental perceptions of the British and to transform American prisoner policy.

---

17. Edward Shippen to Joseph Shippen, May 13, 1775, Shippen Family Papers, BSh6lf.1, APS; "Eberhart Michael to John Andre," *PLCHS*, 134–35; Wood, *Conestoga Crossroads*, 141, 175–76; Haeberlein, *The Practice of Pluralism*, 45, 48, 125–26.

As several historians have shown, the Revolutionary War rendered the combatants' identities ambiguous and contested. At the onset of hostilities, the antagonists faced each other ambivalently across ill-defined lines. Captivity initially muddled but later clarified identities by widening the breach between the combatants and heightening their sense of difference. In Lancaster, captors and captives met as mutually diverse communities bound by cords of empire. The prisoners, for example, formed a motley assortment of officers and enlisted; raw recruits and disciplined veterans; English, Irish, Welsh, and Scots. Collectively, they contributed to the bewildering blend of languages and dialects resounding through the Pennsylvania interior. Hardening battle lines overrode divisions within the warring camps by underscoring their shared military and political commitments. For most British prisoners, captivity reinforced perceptions of their enemies as renegades threatening the stability and sanctity of empire. For their American hosts, captivity exposed the British as devoted agents of tyranny sent to trample cherished rights and liberties. The escalating military crisis fractured and reconfigured prevailing identities and allegiances, slowly transforming the combatants' views of themselves and of their enemies.[18]

With no well-defined policy or established apparatus with which to administer their prisoners, Americans had to improvise. And Lancaster soon became a veritable laboratory for the revolutionaries' evolving prisoner policy. When the first British captives arrived in Lancaster, the local committee asked Congress whether they should "be kept constantly confined to the Barracks under a Guard." Local officials hoped to preserve the "peace of the Borough" and to ensure residents' security by

---

18. According to Linda Colley, the War for Independence was "always about different and shifting constructions of identity." Colley, *Captives*, 203–38, especially 233. For other examples of the Revolution's dislocating effects on preexisting identities and attachments, see Liam Riordan, "Identity and Revolution: Everyday Life and Crisis in Three Delaware River Towns," *Pennsylvania History* 64 (Winter 1997), 56–101; Wayne Bodle, *The Valley Forge Winter: Civilians and Soldiers in War* (University Park, PA, 2002); Knouff, *The Soldiers' Revolution*; Smith-Rosenberg, *This Violent Empire*, 1–18. For the condition of the British Army at the beginning of the War for Independence, see J. A. Houlding, *Fit for Service: The Training of the British Army, 1715–1795* (Oxford, UK, 1981).

fencing in the barracks and restricting the prisoners' movement. Congress instead preferred a policy of enlargement that would enable the British captives to mix freely with their local hosts. As the Lancaster Committeeman George Ross indicated, by encouraging fluid interactions between the town's inhabitants and prisoners, Congress hoped to cultivate kindred relations and elicit the captives' sympathy for Americans and their cause. To render the British enlisted prisoners more amenable to Whig influence, Congress ordered their officers relocated to neighboring towns. Congress also insisted the officers sign paroles, which prohibited them from traveling more than six miles from their residence and from engaging in any correspondence concerning the dispute between Great Britain and the colonies.[19]

Continental policy posed immediate problems, as the proximity between captors and captives bred not mutual understanding but antipathy and mistrust. Nine months of hostilities had frayed whatever bonds remained between the combatants. Indeed, if most Americans continued to see themselves as equal Britons, invested with the same rights and privileges as their imperial cousins, their enemies disagreed. As the British demonstrated their determination to humble the colonies and to suppress the rebellion by force of arms, growing numbers of Americans began earnestly contemplating independence. Thus, whatever the expectations of Continental officials, in their daily encounters in American host communities, captors and captives eyed each other with suspicion.

Most British regulars bitterly resented the indignities of captivity under colonial insurgents. Paroled officers routinely derided Whigs as "rascals" and "vagabonds," whose unnatural rebellion, railed one lieutenant, "branded the name of America with an odium, that no time can obliterate, no merit expunge." After he and his men surrendered during the summer of 1776, Captain Alexander Campbell grieved, "I cannot well express how my Soul is affected at the disagreeable manner by

19. Lancaster County Committee of Safety, Dec. 9, 1775, Peter Force Papers, Series 7E, Reel 16, Film 559; "Notes from Letters of Judge Yeates," Egle, *Notes and Queries*, 382; President of Congress to Lancaster Committee, Jan. 18, 1776, Force, *AA*, Fourth Series, 4: 761–63; *JCC*, 4: 22; George Ross to President of Congress, July 7, 1776, Force, *AA*, Fifth Series, 1: 103–04; *JCC*, 3: 359, 398–99, 434, 435. For the improvised nature of and tensions associated with Continental prisoner policy, see Dixon, "Divided Authority"; Springer, *America's Captives*, 13–41; Miller, "'Dangerous Guests.'"

which my Friends and other trusty Associates have fallen into the hands of a rebellious and tumultuous enemy." From London, British officials vented similar frustrations. In February 1776, Lord George Germaine, the British Secretary of State for America, bemoaned the plight of "his Majesty's officers and loyal subjects" now "in the disgraceful situation of being prisoners to the Rebels."[20]

Many locals approached their British guests with similar disdain. Lancaster's older residents recalled their troubles with the British troops who had garrisoned the community over a decade earlier when the Seven Years' War left Pennsylvania's backcountry vulnerable to the French and their Indian allies. Though locals had initially welcomed their defenders, the pressures of quartering soldiers in private homes soon brought mounting protests from disgruntled inhabitants, and the royal forces who lingered through the 1760s stirred latent fears of standing armies. Worse troubles loomed a decade later when the King's troops returned not as custodians of the frontier but as captives in an increasingly bitter colonial rebellion, with the very barracks that had housed imperial forces during the 1760s now serving as quarters for hundreds of restlessly defiant British prisoners. Roving the streets in their scarlet regimentals, the regulars offered locals a grim daily reminder of their escalating difficulties with the mother country and their corresponding insecurity at home.[21]

Indeed, by 1776 the county's troops had already traded blows with the British. In December 1775, local riflemen participated in the disastrous assault on Quebec, numbering among the more than four hundred

---

20. Thomas Hughes, *A Journal by Thos Hughes, for His Amusement and Designed Only for His Perusal by the Time He Attains the Age of 50, If He Lives So Long* (Cambridge, UK, 1947), 19–20, 31, 37, 71, 75; Thomas Anburey, *Travels Through the Interior Parts of America* (2 vols., 1789; repr. New York, 1969), 2: 313; Alexander Campbell, "A Narrative of the Loss of the Ship Glasgow Packet," July 22–31, 1776, Sir Henry Clinton Papers, 17: 39, William Clements Library, Ann Arbor, MI; Lord George Germaine to Major General Howe, Feb. 1, 1776, Force, *AA*, Fourth Series, 4: 902–903. See also Matthew H. Spring, *With Zeal and With Bayonets Only: The British Army on Campaign in North America* (Norman, OK, 2008), 124–37; Richard Archer, *As If an Enemy's Country: The British Occupation of Boston and the Origins of Revolution* (New York, 2010).

21. Wood, *Conestoga Crossroads*, 77–79; Kenny, *Peaceable Kingdom Lost*, 140; John Shy, *Toward Lexington: The Role of the British Army in the Coming of the American Revolution* (Princeton, NJ, 1965), 207–209. See also Archer, *As If an Enemy's Country*.

Americans killed or captured during the engagement. Several dozen of the county's riflemen still languished in captivity with the approach of spring. Nursing bitter grievances sharpened on the battlefield, local volunteers returned home only to find their enemies haunting their neighborhoods. British officers reaped the particular scorn of local militiamen, who despised their enemies' privileged status and haughty demeanor. One paroled officer, for example, testified that he and his colleagues "were not only insulted but threat'ned," while another reportedly felt "in Danger of his Life."[22]

Continental policy faced particular challenges in the diverse Pennsylvania hinterland, where Germans intermingled with their English and Scots-Irish neighbors, multiplying and complicating identities. Immigrants from Northern Ireland and southwestern Germany had accounted for most of Lancaster County's growth since the 1730s. Though members of Lancaster's English minority might identify their British guests as cultural kinsmen, the Germans and Scots-Irish were more inclined to see them as menacing intruders. Many of the county's German clans had traded the chronic warfare and cumbersome military obligations of central Europe for the promised peace and prosperity of Pennsylvania. Legions of Scots-Irish emigrants, meanwhile, had borne their longstanding grievances against the English to the Pennsylvania backcountry. Following Lexington and Concord, they supplied many of the county's most zealous recruits.[23]

---

22. Captain Home's Narrative of His Treatment When Prisoner, N.D., Sir Guy Carleton Papers, Records of British Army Headquarters in America, 1775–1783, Reel 3, Film 57, DLAR; Philip Greenwalt to Lancaster Committee, June 16, 1776, Jasper Yeates Papers, Correspondence, 1762–1786, HSP; Frederic Shriver Klein, *Fighting the Battles* (Lititz, PA, 1975); J. Samuel Walker, *The Perils of Patriotism: John Joseph Henry and the American Attack on Quebec, 1775* (Lititz, PA, 1975); Ellis and Evans, *History of Lancaster County, Pennsylvania*, 42–43; Howard Peckham, ed., *The Toll of Independence: Engagements and Battle Casualties of the American Revolution* (Chicago, 1974), 11.

23. For the region's ethnocultural diversity, see Wood, *Conestoga Crossroads*, 1–20, 181–215; Michael Zuckerman, ed., *Friends and Neighbors: Group Life in America's First Plural Society* (Philadelphia, 1982); Sally Schwartz, *"A Mixed Multitude": The Struggle for Toleration in Colonial Pennsylvania* (New York, 1987); Alan Tully, *Forming American Politics: Ideals, Interests, and Institutions in Colonial New York and Pennsylvania* (Baltimore, 1994); Haeberlein, *The Practice of Pluralism*; A. G. Roeber, "The Origin of Whatever Is Not English among Us: The Dutch-speaking and the German-speaking Peoples of Colonial British

Trouble followed within a few weeks of the prisoners' arrival when the British officers balked at Congress's order to separate them from their men. The officers complained that the order violated the terms of their capitulation and that the absence of their baggage, combined with their poor health during the severe winter season, required them to remain in Lancaster. The officers insisted that they had signed their paroles believing that Congress would honor the terms of their surrender and permit them to remain with their troops. They then issued a thinly veiled threat, hinting that they would regret having to break their paroles.[24]

Congress agreed to postpone the officers' relocation but denied their claim that separating them from their men constituted a breach of the capitulation. As the President of Congress John Hancock explained, while "all the stipulations of a capitulation ought, undoubtedly, to be held sacred, and faithfully fulfilled . . . no such stipulation is to be found in the capitulation upon which those gentlemen surrendered." Then Hancock issued a warning of his own, promising that Congress would "be extremely sorry to be reduced to the necessity of confining them in prison, if they cancel their parole." The officers' obstinacy fed local anxiety. In late January, committee chairman Jasper Yeates informed a friend,

---

America," in *Strangers within the Realm: Cultural Margins of the First British Empire*, ed. Bernard Bailyn and Philip D. Morgan (Chapel Hill, NC, 1991), 220–83; Aaron Spencer Fogleman, *Hopeful Journeys: German Immigration, Settlement, and Political Culture in Colonial America, 1717–1775* (Philadelphia, 1996); Hartmut Lehmann, Herman Wellenreuther, and Renate Wilson, eds., *In Search of Peace and Prosperity: New German Settlements in Eighteenth-Century Europe and America* (University Park, PA, 1999); David Doyle, *Ireland, Irishmen, and Revolutionary America, 1760–1820* (Cork, IRE, 1981); Maldwyn Jones, "The Scotch-Irish in British America," in *Strangers within the Realm*, 284–313; Patrick Griffin, *The People with No Name: Ireland's Ulster Scots, America's Scots Irish, and the Creation of a British Atlantic World, 1689–1764* (Princeton, NJ, 2001); Henry C. Peden, Jr., *Revolutionary Patriots of Lancaster County, Pennsylvania, 1775–1783* (Westminster, MD, 2002); John Andre to Mary Louise Andre, Dec. 17, 1776, as quoted in Robert McConnell Hatch, *Major John Andre: A Gallant in Spy's Clothing* (Boston, 1986), 60; "John Andre to Eberhart Michael, April 10, 1776," *PLCHS* 18, no. 6 (1914), 133.

24. Lancaster Committee to President of Congress, Dec. 21, 1775, PCC, Reel 83; Lancaster Committee to President of Congress, Jan. 22, 1776, Force, *AA*, Fourth Series, 4: 801; British Officers to Continental Congress, Jan. 20, 1776, Force, *AA*, Fourth Series, 4: 801–802.

"We fear something disagreeable will happen before those gentlemen leave their privates."[25]

Most troubling to local authorities, however, were the hundreds of rank-and-file prisoners, whose wanderings bred tensions with the town's leery inhabitants. Since emerging during the 1740s as a key trading and manufacturing center linking the coast and frontier, Lancaster had attracted a diverse mix of artisans, laborers, merchants, and professionals. By the mid-1770s, the visibly stratified community contained a conspicuous number of laboring poor, and anxious residents now dreaded mingling with the volatile dregs of a conventional standing army. Lancaster's Committee promptly established formal regulations to govern the prisoners' conduct along with a night watch consisting of a dozen associators to guard the public magazine, patrol the streets, and preserve the peace. A half measure, the night watch proved unequal to the task of curbing disorder. One resident grumbled on January 10 that the "many soldiers here, more than four hundred, create disturbances." Tensions escalated during early February following the arrival of several dozen fresh enlisted prisoners from New Jersey. On February 10, Lancaster's Committee received complaints of captives roaming the town antagonizing the residents. The prisoner John Wilson, for instance, ran afoul of local authorities for voicing inflammatory sentiments, which led to his confinement in the town jail.[26]

Lancaster's prisoners had become so unmanageable by late February

---

25. President of Congress to Lancaster Committee, Jan. 18, 1776, Force, *AA*, Fourth Series, 4: 761–63; Congress to Lancaster Committee, Jan. 20, 1776, Force, *AA*, Fourth Series, 4: 801; Jasper Yeates to Colonel Wilson, Jan. 20, 1776, Simon Gratz Manuscripts, Case 2, Box 13, Supreme Court of Pennsylvania, HSP; Lancaster Committee to President of Congress, Jan. 22, 1776, Force, *AA*, Fourth Series, 4: 801.

26. "Items from Letters," *PLCHS* 27, no. 5 (1923), 96; Wood, *Conestoga Crossroads*, 139–80; John Carmichael, *A Self-defensive War Lawful, Proved in a Sermon, Preached at Lancaster, before Captain Ross's Company of Militia, in the Presbyterian Church, on Sabbath Morning, June 4th*, 1775 (Philadelphia, 1775), Early American Imprints, Series I: Evans, 1639–1800, no. 13862, 18; Lancaster Committee to President of Congress, Jan. 3, 1776, Force, *AA*, Fourth Series, 4: 561; *PA*, Second Series, 1: 440–48; Samuel Miller Sener, *The Lancaster Barracks: Where the British and Hessian Prisoners were Detained During the Revolution* (Harrisburg, PA, 1895), 20; John Wilson to Lancaster Committee, Feb. 24, 1776, Sol Feinstone Collection, 1685, Reel 3, Film 1, DLAR.

that Pennsylvania's Council of Safety petitioned Congress for their relocation. The situation in Lancaster had become increasingly precarious, warned the council, with the captives growing more insolent by the day. According to the council's chairman John Nixon: "The kind treatment given them meets with very improper and indecent return . . . they often express themselves in most disrespectful and offensive terms, and openly threaten revenge whenever opportunity shall present." Current conditions also furnished opportunities for escape. As Nixon explained, with Lancaster "but a day's march from navigable water, and their prisoners stout and numerous, there may be a danger that should the enemy effect a landing on the upper part of Chesapeake-Bay, a daring spirit might lead them off." The council therefore recommended dispersing the captives throughout the Pennsylvania interior, "in different towns, or . . . among the farmers in the country, where their opportunities of doing mischief will less correspond with their inclinations."[27]

Congress preferred to consolidate the enlisted prisoners in Lancaster, but ordered their officers immediately relocated to York and Carlisle, across the Susquehanna River, "for the greater safety of the publick." Congress authorized local authorities to closely confine officers who refused to comply. On March 22, the officers, accompanied by their servants and a small military escort, bid farewell to their men and set off for York and Carlisle. While Lancaster's insurgents welcomed the officers' departure, their enlisted prisoners remained a source of continuing anxiety. Borough officials notified Pennsylvania's Council of Safety on March 29 of their "utmost Concern" at the small "Number of good Arms in the Hands" of local associators. "The fatal Consequences which may arrive from the Want of arms amongst us are too obvious to be insisted on," warned Jasper Yeates, "particularly in this Town, where we have about four hundred Prisoners, and most of them of active, restless and uneasy Spirits."[28]

---

27. Pennsylvania Council of Safety to President of Congress, Feb. 20, 1776, Force, *AA*, Fourth Series, 4: 1213–14; Pennsylvania Council of Safety, Feb. 20, 1776, Force, *AA*, Fourth Series, 4: 1573.

28. *PA*, Second Series, 13: 512–15; Continental Congress, Feb. 26, 1776, Force, *AA*, Fourth Series, 4: 1690; Pennsylvania Committee of Safety, Mar. 2, 1776, Force, *AA*, Fourth Series, 5: 718; *The Colonial Records of Pennsylvania* (hereafter *CR*), ed. Samuel Hazard (16 vols., Philadelphia, 1838–53), 10: 515; Lancaster County Committee of Safety, Mar. 19, 1776, Peter Force Papers, Series

County officials faced new pressures in mid-April following the arrival of nearly a half dozen paroled British officers to the small town of Lebanon, more than twenty miles north of Lancaster. British officers found captivity especially onerous, chafing under the resentments and restrictions of their grudging hosts. Ever solicitous of their honor and the customary privileges of their rank and status, they registered a gentleman's contempt for the provincial upstarts who flouted imperial authority and abused their newfound influence. From York, parolees protested the "ill treatment which our characters as British officers . . . has not merited." "Outrage hath succeeded insult," they complained, "and a violation of every law of humanity been dignified by the name of authority." Lieutenant Andre, in turn, damned Carlisle's "greasy committee of worsted stocking knaves," who took pains "to humiliate us and exalt themselves."[29]

Lebanon's newly arrived parolees, frustrated by their poor accommodations, promptly petitioned provincial officials for relocation. Obtaining no redress following several appeals, the officers took matters into their own hands. On the night of June 15, Lancaster's Committee received alarming news that the officers had escaped. Lebanon authorities reported that the fugitives had left town the day before to go fishing, but never returned to their lodgings. The county committee quickly dispatched riders "to alarm the Country" and to warn officials in York and Carlisle to take immediate precautions lest their prisoners attempt a similar escape. "It cannot but be obvious that the public is intimately interested to prevent practices of this nature," exhorted committee chairman Adam Reigart, "as well as to apprehend the Prisoners who have meditated their escape." Dismayed authorities failed to recapture the fugitives, who fled north through Northumberland County, eventually arriving in British-held New York City.[30]

7E, Reel 16, Film 559; Edward Shippen to Joseph Shippen, Mar. 23, 1776, Shippen Family Papers, 10, HSP.

29. British Officers to President of Congress, July 12, 1776, Force, *AA*, Fifth Series, 1: 222–23; John Andre to Mary Louise Andre, Dec. 17, 1776, as quoted in Hatch, *Major John Andre*, 67. See also *PLCHS* 18, no. 6 (1914), 139. For officers and assumptions of honor, see Cox, *A Proper Sense of Honor*, 199–235; Burrows, *Forgotten Patriots*, 27–28, 45.

30. *PA*, Second Series, 13: 525–26; "Lancaster Committee to York and Cumberland Committees, June 16, 1776," Egle, *Notes and Queries*, First and Second Series, 2: 380–81; *PA*, Second Series, 13: 520, 522–23; *CR*, 10: 546; *PA*, Second

The officers' escape confirmed locals' suspicions that their prisoners required closer supervision. Officials were especially vexed that the fugitives had violated their sworn parole. Though the officers had been openly critical of the American resistance, county officials trusted them to behave as gentlemen. Instead, the officers rejected Whigs' authority as illegitimate and underlined their contempt by breaking their parole. Most distressing, however, was how they had managed their escape. Evidence indicated that the fugitives had shed their regimentals and donned American dress, assuming the guise of "Virginia gentlemen" to avoid suspicion and elude their captors. This particular detail alarmed residents of Lancaster, some of whose enlisted prisoners had recently taken to dressing as American riflemen.[31]

Months before, the sight of British prisoners in American dress might have seemed an encouraging sign to local insurgents eager to win British converts to their cause. Now, however, with the war intensifying and with relations between the belligerents growing increasingly strained, anxious militants worried that the prisoners' novel choice of apparel revealed less an affinity for their hosts than a cleverly disguised but sinister intent. During the spring of 1776, the lines separating Britons and Americans remained ambiguous and ill-defined. Cultural and linguistic ties blurred the divisions between friend and foe, creating a permeable boundary between the combatants. Consequently, while the riflemen's garb vividly distinguished the Americans from their enemies, it readily obscured distinctions when appropriated by the British. The British captives shared enough in common with their English-speaking hosts that they could conceal their Britishness beneath a veneer of American dress. Most British enlisted prisoners, lacking the polish of their officers, could scarcely pass as Virginia gentlemen. Cloaked in the homespun

---

Series, 1: 477; Philip Greenwalt to Lancaster Committee, June 16, 1776, Jasper Yeates Papers, HSP; Lebanon Committee to Lancaster Committee, July 16, 1776, Peter Force Collection, Series 9, Reel 102, Library of Congress, Washington, DC (hereafter LOC).

31. Examination of William Poor, July 26, 1776, Force, *AA*, Fifth Series, 1: 597–98; Examination of John White, July 26, 1776, Force, *AA*, Fifth Series, 1: 597–99; George Ross to President of Congress, July 7, 1776, Force, *AA*, Fifth Series, 1: 103–104. See also Cumberland Committee to President of Congress, July 14, 1776, Force, *AA*, Fifth Series, 1: 328; List of Prisoners in Gaol, Nov. 14, 1776, Peter Force Collection, Series 9, Reel 103, LOC.

attire of the riflemen, however, they could easily pose as backcountry associators. If so inclined, they could exploit this fluidity for subversive ends, assuming a friendly guise to mask hostile aims.[32]

The riflemen provided the perfect cover for British fugitives clandestinely negotiating American lines. Specially recruited from the Pennsylvania, Maryland, and Virginia backcountry for their deadly accuracy with a rifle, they formed an elite corps in the Continental ranks. For many of their compatriots, they embodied the American cause. During the summer of 1775, as the riflemen wound through the towns of Pennsylvania en route to joining the growing force assembling in Cambridge, Massachusetts, they met with adoring crowds and thrilled spectators with dazzling feats of marksmanship. Clothed in fringed hunting frocks, leggings, and moccasins, and armed with long rifles, tomahawks, and hunting knives, they breezed through American checkpoints. Pennsylvania's poorly supplied British prisoners mostly donned frontier dress to supplement their badly worn uniforms. But Lancaster's insurgents feared the rifleman's garb provided their captives a virtual "passport," enabling them to move about the country undetected with the presumable design of thwarting American interests.[33]

The sharpening hostilities and Pennsylvanians' conflicting allegiances afforded the captives fertile ground for subversion. By spring 1776, the deepening crisis had eroded Whigs' hopes for an early end to the conflict. Parliament's Prohibitory Act of December 1775 sealed the colonies' ports and declared open war on American shipping. Ominous overseas intelligence warned that the British had launched a massive military mobilization to crush the rebellion, even commencing negotiations with German princes to enlist the aid of thousands of foreign auxiliaries. Throughout the backcountry rumors hinted that British agents were

---

32. For the blurred lines separating the combatants, see also Colley, *Captives*, 203–38.

33. George Ross to President of Congress, July 7, 1776, Force, *AA*, Fifth Series, 1: 103–104; Henry J. Young, "The Spirit of 1775: A Letter to Robert Magaw, Major of the Continental Riflemen to the Gentlemen of the Committee of Correspondence in the Town of Carlisle," *John and Mary's Journal* 1 (Mar. 1975), 1–60; *Pennsylvania Packet* (Philadelphia), Aug. 28, 1775; Royster, *A Revolutionary People at War*, 33–35; Knouff, *The Soldiers' Revolution*, 135–36; Linda Baumgarten, *What Clothes Reveal: The Language of Clothing in Colonial and Federal America* (New Haven, CT, 2002), 18, 20, 66, 69, 72, 74.

busy recruiting Indian allies. From Lancaster, Edward Shippen fumed that while Lord North lulled the "ignorant people of Great Britain to sleep" the "MONSTEROUS MURDERER is ordering our throats to be cut." Thomas Paine's *Common Sense* and King George III's spurning of the conciliatory Olive Branch Petition, meanwhile, further undercut the provincial proponents of reconciliation.[34]

Staunch Lancaster County Whigs like Shippen's son-in-law James Burd now realized they faced the likelihood of a long and bitter struggle. Only two decades earlier during the Seven Years' War, Burd had proudly fought alongside the British as an officer in the provincial forces. By May 1776, however, he ruled out any possibility of a peaceful return to the imperial fold. "There is too much Hatred and Bitterness towards us in the Court of Britain," he concluded, "to leave us any Hopes of Reconciliation. The Devil is in them and with them wherever they or their murderous Agents go." But Burd remained assured of Whigs' eventual triumph. "Murders, indeed, we shall hear of in great number. But they will rouse us out of our Supineness," he predicted, "and we shall unite and disperse our Enemies."[35]

Burd's optimistic forecast of a unified resistance discounted the deep divisions polarizing Pennsylvanians. British resolve fueled the radical advocates of independence. The push for independence, in turn, fractured the fragile provincial resistance, as despairing conservatives abandoned the cause to join the swelling ranks of the disaffected. With divisions multiplying daily, Pennsylvania's militants struggled to curb dissent. Insurgents in Lancaster and neighboring host communities faced not only these mounting pressures, but the machinations of their British prisoners, who threatened to exacerbate the province's growing internal fissures.[36]

Indeed, if congressional officials had hoped to seduce their captives,

---

34. Edward Shippen to James Burd, Mar. 4, 1776, Shippen Family Papers, 7, HSP; Lancaster Committee to Alexander McKee, Jan. 15, 1776, Peter Force Collection, Series 9, Reel 102, LOC; Lancaster Committee to George Ross, Jan. 15, 1776, Peter Force Collection, Series 9, Reel 102, LOC.

35. James Burd to Edward Shippen, May 18, 1776, Shippen Family Papers, 7, HSP.

36. For Pennsylvania's growing divisions, see Ousterhout, *A State Divided*; Ryerson, *The Revolution Is Now Begun*; Knouff, *The Soldiers' Revolution*, 195–231; Frantz and Pencak, *Beyond Philadelphia*.

their enemies promptly turned the tables by tempting the wavering and rallying support for the crown. Persistent rumors warned of captives gathering intelligence, fomenting dissent, and inciting violence. In early April 1776, Cumberland County's Committee accused Lancaster's prisoners of carrying illicit correspondence between local loyalists and the British officers in Carlisle. Committee chairman John Montgomery later cautioned Congress that the paroled officers had corrupted "many weak and ignorant persons." Their servants, moreover, were "dressed with hunting-shirts and trousers, the uniform of our people, which might facilitate their escape." By summer, locals worried that their captives harbored deadly intentions. The Paxton resident John Harris, for example, reckoned that the fleeing officers from Lebanon had incited the Indians "to take up the Hatchet agt us."[37]

As stray prisoners prowled the interior, locals labored to curtail subversive activity within their neighborhoods. Lancaster's enlisted prisoners soon required passes for travel outside the borough, and county committees began inspecting the paroled officers' correspondence. In York and Carlisle, the officers fell under an evening curfew, with a handful eventually winding up in the Cumberland County jail. Tempers flared during early summer when militants accused local loyalists of assisting the officers' escape from Lebanon. Charged with aiding the fugitives, John White was clapped in irons and thrown in the Lancaster jail, where he languished for over a year. Even friends of the resistance in Pennsylvania's host communities risked censure for their casual associations with the enemy. The American Major Edward Burd, for instance, antagonized Reading's militants by dining with paroled officers and refusing to impose a curfew. "I feared that the people . . . were possessed of the idea of my being that monster a tory," Burd reported.[38]

---

37. Cumberland Committee to President of Congress, July 14, 1776, Force, *AA*, Fifth Series, 1: 328; *PA*, First Series, 4: 789; *JCC*, 3: 402; *PA*, Second Series, 1: 593–95; Lebanon Committee to Lancaster Committee, July 24, 1776, Peter Force Collection, Series 9, Reel 102, LOC.

38. Edward Burd to Jasper Yeates, Apr. 15, 1776, Jasper Yeates Papers, HSP; Lancaster County Committee of Safety, Dec. 27, 1776 and Mar. 25, 1776, Peter Force Papers, Series 7E, Reel 16, Film 559, DLAR; Jasper Yeates to Colonel Wilson, Jan. 20, 1776, Simon Gratz Manuscripts, Case 2, Box 13, Supreme Court of Pennsylvania, HSP; Hatch, *Major John Andre*, 67; Examination of William Poor, July 26, 1776, Force, *AA*, Fifth Series, 1: 596–97; Examination of John White, July 26, 1776, Force, *AA*, Fifth Series, 1: 597–99; Petition of James White,

The mounting complaints from provincial officials and the widening rift with the British soon prompted Continental authorities to rethink their policies and to introduce a more rigorous system of controls. In late February, Congress empowered local committees to superintend their prisoners' "conduct, and, in cases of gross misbehaviour, to confine them." A month later, Congress gave provincial officials discretion to relocate their captives "from place to place" within their particular provinces as often as "shall seem proper." With this new authority, however, came new responsibilities. Provincial officials now had to furnish Congress with general returns of their captives. Congress also recirculated all the previously enacted resolves concerning the prisoners to ensure their uniform management.[39]

Not until summer, however, after persistent pressure from provincial authorities and British officials' continuing neglect of American prisoners, would Congress finally embrace a policy of confinement in Lancaster. Lancaster's exasperated officials renewed their pleas for stricter controls following the officers' escape from Lebanon. Adding to locals' sense of urgency was an order from Philadelphia summoning the town's militia for service in New Jersey. Residents feared the militia's absence would place them at the mercy of their vengeful prisoners. Lancaster's Committee complained to Congress on July 7, emphasizing the shortcomings of Continental policy and the need for enhanced security. Committee chairman George Ross stressed the "dangerous situation of the town," which stood "exposed to the fury and ravages of near four hun-

Oct. 9, 1777, Records of Pennsylvania's Revolutionary Governments, 1775–1790 (hereafter PRG), Clemency Files, Reel 36, DLAR; Petition of John White, Oct. 16, 1777, PRG, Clemency Files, Reel 36, DLAR; Lancaster Committee to Captain John Henry, June 6, 1776, Jasper Yeates Papers, HSP.

39. Continental Congress, Feb. 28, 1776, Force, *AA*, Fourth Series, 4: 1689–90; Continental Congress, Apr. 12, 1776, Force, *AA*, Fourth Series, 5: 1670–71; Pennsylvania Council of Safety, Apr. 13, 1776, Force, *AA*, Fourth Series, 5: 738–39; Continental Congress, Apr. 9, 1776, Force, *AA*, Fourth Series, 5: 1662; Continental Congress, May 21, 1776, Force, *AA*, Fourth Series, 6: 1675–77; Pennsylvania Assembly, May 30, 1776, Force, *AA*, Fourth Series, 6: 854–55. See also George Washington to President of Congress, May 11, 1776, Force, *AA*, Fourth Series, 6: 423–25; Minutes Respecting the Mode of Treating Prisoners in England, Force, *AA*, Fourth Series, 6: 425–26.

dred" prisoners who roamed at will because of the "open state of our barracks."[40]

Ross reminded Congress that it had refused the committee's earlier request to enclose the barracks and post a guard over the captives, assuming that by their "mixing and working with the inhabitants, they would learn and be convinced of the justness of our cause, and become rather the friends than enemies of the rights of America." Instead, "by their mixing with the people they have done much mischief," as they "adhere, with an extraordinary degree of firmness, to their tyrannical master and his cause, and every action and expression convinces us that they would seize every opportunity to promote it and distress us." The committee therefore recommended having the prisoners "in some manner secured, so as to prevent their straggling, carrying intelligence, or insulting or injuring the inhabitants." For "while at liberty, they are a dangerous set of people."[41]

Much to locals' relief, on July 10, Congress ordered Lancaster's Committee to confine and guard the captives and to enclose their barracks with a stockade. The committee quickly rounded up the prisoners under its jurisdiction, issuing a circular to neighboring towns to assemble and forward all their British captives under armed guards for confinement in Lancaster's barracks. Meanwhile, officials raised a town guard of 150 men and began construction of the stockade. "They say it is to be boarded fifty feet high," reported one relieved resident. Developments in Lancaster had far-reaching implications. The town's newly stockaded barracks became the working Continental model, literally furnishing the blueprint for corresponding wartime detention facilities throughout the states. With the new emphasis on confinement, Whig policy also became a closer approximation of British prisoner policy.[42]

---

40. George Ross to President of Congress, July 7, 1776, Force, *AA*, Fifth Series, 1: 103–104; *PLCHS* 27, no. 5 (1923), 91–92.

41. George Ross to President of Congress, July 7, 1776, Force, AA, Fifth Series, 1: 103–104.

42. Sarah Yeates to Jasper Yeates, July 15, 1776, Jasper Yeates Papers, HSP; Continental Congress, July 10, 1776, Force, *AA*, Fifth Series, 1: 1571; President of Congress to Lancaster Committee, July 12, 1776, Force, *AA*, Fifth Series, 1: 219; Lancaster Committee to Committee Members and Militia Officers, Lancaster County, July 14, 1776, Force, *AA*, Fifth Series, 1: 327; Lancaster Committee, July 11, 1776, Force, *AA*, Fifth Series, 1: 188; William Atlee to President of Congress,

But Congress's revamped security measures came with unexpected consequences for Lancaster. The residents of Reading who had quartered enlisted prisoners in their homes since early 1776 now recommended their confinement so "they may be more easily restrained from mischief." Continental officials obligingly relocated several hundred of Reading's loosely supervised prisoners to Lancaster's freshly secured barracks, placing new pressures on the borough and raising local anxiety. The sight of one of Reading's newly relocated captives arriving in Lancaster under armed guard "damning the Congress all the way" only affirmed locals' misgivings. By July 18, the number of British prisoners in Lancaster had nearly doubled, with close to seven hundred occupying the barracks. Days later, a resident put the total at roughly one thousand, and local officials realized that they would have to expand the facility.[43]

Lancaster's officials reduced the pressure on their rapidly overcrowding barracks by hiring out skilled captives to local employers as wage laborers. The hiring of prisoners was a familiar wartime practice that offered authorities the dual benefit of mobilizing laborers for local needs while reducing the risks and burdens of consolidating hundreds of enemy captives. Keen to capitalize on their prisoners' labor, provincial officials had considered putting them to work as early as spring 1776. Pennsylvania's Council of Safety asked Lancaster's Committee in early

July 13, 1776, Force, *AA*, Fifth Series, 1: 255; "Extracts from Moravian Diaries," *PLCHS*, 91–92; *PA*, Second Series, 13: 349–50; Matthias Slough to Jasper Yeates, Aug. 22, 1776, Historical Society of Pennsylvania Miscellaneous Collection, 1676–1937, HSP; James Ewing to Lancaster Committee, 1776, Peter Force Collection, Series 9, Reel 103; William Atlee to George Ross, Mar. 12, 1777, Reel 74, PCC; *JCC*, 6: 184, 190.

43. Inhabitants of Reading to Pennsylvania Assembly, Mar. 6, 1776, Force, *AA*, Fourth Series, 5: 675; Sarah Yeates to Jasper Yeates, July 15, 1776, Jasper Yeates Papers, HSP; Continental Congress, July 10, 1776, Force, *AA*, Fifth Series, 1: 1571; President of Congress to Lancaster Committee, July 12, 1776, Force, *AA*, Fifth Series, 1: 219; Henry Haller to President of Congress, July 13, 1776, Force, *AA*, Fifth Series, 1: 254; Lancaster Committee to Council of Safety, July 18, 1776, Force, *AA*, Fifth Series, 1: 411; "Extracts from Moravian Diaries," *PLCHS*, 92; Lancaster Committee, July 23, 1776, Force, *AA*, Fifth Series, 1: 533; William Atlee to Board of War, July 23, 1776, Force, *AA*, Fifth Series, 1: 535; James Burd to Edward Shippen, July 15, 1776, Shippen Family Papers, 7, HSP; Lancaster Committee, Aug. 24, 1776, Force, *AA*, Fifth Series, 1: 1135; Lancaster Committee, Sept. 17, 1776, Force, *AA*, Fifth Series, 2: 365.

March to inquire whether any of their prisoners wished to come to Philadelphia to "work, upon wages, at their respective Occupations." Taking a quick inventory of the prisoners' skills, the committee compiled a list of ninety-eight craftsmen with trades ranging from mason and weaver to tailor and cordwainer.[44]

With many of Lancaster County's able-bodied males committed to distant military service and with labor increasingly scarce, the hiring of prisoners answered a pressing local need. A small proportion of the captives, in turn, welcomed the opportunity to escape the constraints of the barracks, ply their particular trades, and supplement their meager wages. The local committee's records suggest that upwards of one hundred prisoners hired out through the summer and fall of 1776. On July 25, for example, Samuel Eaton hired out as a stocking weaver. Daniel Allen and William Sutherland of the 26th Regiment entered the employ of the Lancaster tailor Michael Shirdle. William Frenniman hired out twice, first with the Lancaster apothecary Christian Voght and subsequently with the gunsmith Jacob Graeff. As a member of Lancaster's Committee explained, because "hands were scarce," many of the tradesmen commanded handsome wages.[45]

---

44. Council of Safety to Lancaster Committee, Mar. 6, 1776, Peter Force Collection, Series 9, Reel 102, LOC; Lancaster County Committee of Safety, Apr. 10, 1776, Peter Force Papers, Series 7E, Reel 16, Film 559, DLAR; Lancaster County Committee of Safety, Apr. 12, 1776, Peter Force Papers, Series 7E, Reel 16, Film 559, DLAR; Report of Subcommittee respecting Tradesmen among the Prisoners, Apr. 11, 1776, Peter Force Collection, Series 9, Reel 102, LOC. For hiring out during the Seven Years' War, see Steele, "When Worlds Collide," 9–39.

45. *PA*, Second Series, 13: 536; British Soldiers Permitted to Work List, July 15, 1776, Peter Force Collection, Series 9, Reel 102, LOC; Lancaster Committee, July 23, 1776, Force, *AA*, Fifth Series, 1: 534; Lancaster Committee, July 25, 1776, Force, *AA*, Fifth Series, 1: 572–73; Lancaster Committee, July 26, 1776, Force, *AA*, Fifth Series, 1: 596; *PA*, Second Series, 1: 486; Council of Safety to Lancaster Committee, July 29, 1776, Peter Force Collection, Series 9, Reel 102, LOC; Lancaster Committee, July 30, 1776, Force, *AA*, Fifth Series, 1: 673; Examination of Peter Schoecker, August 2, 1776, Force, *AA*, Fifth Series, 1: 760–61; Lancaster Committee, Aug. 5, 1776, Force, *AA*, Fifth Series, 1: 760; Lancaster Committee, Aug. 16, 1776, Force, *AA*, Fifth Series, 1: 947–48; Lancaster Committee, Aug. 19, 1776, Force, *AA*, Fifth Series, 1: 1062; Lancaster Committee, Aug. 24, 1776, Force, *AA*, Fifth Series, 1: 1135; Lancaster Committee, Sept. 11, 1776, Force, *AA*, Fifth Series, 2: 287; Lancaster Committee, Sept. 17, 1776, Force, *AA*, Fifth Series, 2: 365; Lancaster Committee, Oct. 12, 1776, Force, *AA*,

Hiring out the captives also promised to enhance local security. With the prisoners privately employed and earning generous wages, provincial officials hoped they would prove less inclined to flee or to endanger residents' lives or property. Lancaster's Committee held employers responsible for the prisoners' safekeeping and prompt return, demanding bonds as security for their good behavior. Contrary to the expectations of provincial authorities, however, hiring out created additional problems.[46]

Freed from the confines of the barracks, laborers found occasion to roam. Those inclined to trouble made the most of their opportunities, with offenses ranging from theft and burglary to public intoxication and attempted escape. The county's military obligations simultaneously increased both the demands for prisoners' labor and the dangers for unarmed civilians. The Donegal resident James Work alerted Lancaster's Committee in late summer when a prisoner employed in his neighborhood "got in Drink" and "behav'd ill." "Most of our men is gone to the army," Work reported, and "the poor women and children is afraid to see such . . . men amongst them and going at large." With security concerns on the rise, prospective employers soon encountered resistance from local officials. In mid-September, when the county ironmaster Peter Grubb applied for captive laborers for his Cornwall Furnace, Congress reckoned the "Committee of Lancaster would object to it."[47]

Fifth Series, 2: 1008; "Captain George Musser's Orderly Book, October 1776," Egle, *Notes and Queries* (Annual Vol., Harrisburg, 1900), 128; Sarah Yeates to Jasper Yeates, July 15, 1776, Jasper Yeates Papers, HSP.

46. Council of Safety to President of Congress, Feb. 20, 1776, Force, *AA*, Fourth Series, 4: 1213–14.

47. James Work to William Atlee, Aug. 26, 1776, Peter Force Collection, Series 9, Reel 102, LOC; Robert Treat Paine to Peter Grubb, Sept. 18, 1776, Smith, *Letters of Delegates to Congress*, 5: 197; Sam Boyd to Adam Reigart, Sept. 23, 1776, Peter Force Collection, Series 9, Reel 102, LOC; James Moore to Lancaster Committee, Sept. 23, 1776, Peter Force Collection, Series 9, Reel 102, LOC; Lancaster Committee, Oct. 12, 1776, Force, *AA*, Fifth Series, 2: 1008; "Captain George Musser's Orderly Book," Egle, *Notes and Queries*, 128; Captain Christopher Crawford's Book, Lancaster County, Pennsylvania Papers, 1724–1816, Petitions for Lebanon, 1772–1816, HSP; List of Prisoners in Gaol, Nov. 14, 1776, Peter Force Collection, Series 9, Reel 103, LOC; List of Regulars in Goal, Nov. 15, 1776, Peter Force Collection, Series 9, Reel 103, LOC; Prisoners' Names, Nov. 15, 1776, Peter Force Collection, Series 9, Reel 103, LOC.

Lancaster's newly confined prisoners compounded pressures by harrying residents or attempting to escape. During the construction of the stockade, restless captives routinely eluded their guards to stray from the barracks. On September 11, locals discovered Sergeant Major Wood of the 7th Regiment "in the Stable of Henry Waggoner." Authorities apprehended another prisoner four miles from the borough just weeks later. Two other fugitives ventured as far as Northumberland County, some fifty miles to the north, where they were seized by local authorities after "providing themselves with arms, and making other preparations, which appeared to indicate some ill design." Northumberland officials promptly returned the pair to Lancaster's Committee with a warning that the schemes of such "evil-minded persons, either to instigate the Indians to acts of hostility, or to raise dissensions among the inhabitants, may be attended with the most pernicious consequences."[48]

Determined militants feverishly cracked down on the offenders. At least forty-eight prisoners landed in the county jail between June and December. On August 12, authorities jailed John Allen of the 26th Regiment "for insulting the centereys." Thomas Roparts earned a spell behind bars in late September after fleeing from the barracks. Weeks later, sentries detained two prisoners caught stealing wine from a resident's cellar. James Parker broke jail with a pair of civilian prisoners on the night of October 19. Promising a £10 reward for the fugitives' apprehension, an October 30 advertisement in the *Pennsylvania Gazette* urged "all honest inhabitants" to "intercept such villains, as they are very dangerous to the Commonwealth."[49]

---

48. Captain Christopher Crawford's Book; Northumberland Committee to Paxton Committee, Sept. 5, 1776, Peter Force Collection, Series 9, Reel 102, LOC; "Captain George Musser's Orderly Book," Egle, *Notes and Queries*, 128; Colonel James Burd to William Atlee, Sept. 9, 1776, Peter Force Collection, Series 9, Reel 102, LOC; John Harris to George Fry, Sept. 9, 1776, Peter Force Collection, Series 9, Reel 102, LOC; Lancaster Committee, Sept. 11, 1776, Force, *AA*, Fifth Series, 2: 287.

49. Captain Christopher Crawford's Book; *Pennsylvania Gazette* (Philadelphia), Oct. 30, 1776; "Captain George Musser's Orderly Book," Egle, *Notes and Queries*, 128; Sarah Yeates to Jasper Yeates, July 15, 1776, Jasper Yeates Papers, HSP; List of Prisoners, Aug. 27, 1776, Peter Force Collection, Series 9, Reel 102, LOC; John Harris to George Fry, Sept. 9, 1776, Peter Force Collection, Series 9, Reel 102, LOC; Lancaster Committee, Sept. 11, 1776, Force, *AA*, Fifth Series, 2: 287; James Moore to Lancaster Committee, Sept. 23, 1776, Peter Force Collec-

Even if Whigs exaggerated the dangers posed by their captives, their concerns were genuine. To be sure, many of Lancaster's prisoners refrained from misconduct, passing their captivity in dutiful compliance with local authorities. The borough's captives remained a diverse collection of ethnicities drawn into the King's service and subject to the poor pay and rigorous discipline of the British Army. Some of the prisoners who hired out felt slight affinity for the imperial enterprise and proved eager and reliable laborers. But in a community shaken by the accumulated costs and uncertainties of war, the offending prisoners posed a threat disproportionate to their numbers and the slightest infraction suddenly carried the hint of rebellion. After months of experimentation, the hosting of enemy prisoners had become a thankless and frustrating task for Lancaster's Whigs.[50]

Continental officials now shared locals' exasperation and instituted even stiffer controls. In early October, Congress ordered the appointment of state commissaries to superintend and provide monthly returns of the prisoners. Congress also forbade the prisoners from leaving their designated residences without permission from the newly created Continental Board of War. On November 15, the Board of War reminded Lancaster's Committee of the need to keep their captives under close surveillance. The prisoners "are not only extremely insolent," warned the board, but "guilty of Practices of a very dangerous tendency." "Not satisfied with procuring and conveying intelligence," they circulated "false rumours with the design of damping the spirit of the friends to this country." The board instructed the committee to closely confine "any British prisoner" suspected of "spreading false news, speaking in derogation or otherwise injuring the credit of the Continental currency or conveying any intelligence whatsoever."[51]

---

tion, Series 9, Reel 102, LOC; Sam Boyd to Adam Reigart, Sept. 23, 1776, Peter Force Collection, Series 9, Reel 102, LOC; List of Prisoners in Gaol, Nov.14, 1776, Peter Force Collection, Series 9, Reel 103, LOC; List of Regulars in Gaol, Nov. 15, 1776, Peter Force Collection, Series 9, Reel 103, LOC; Prisoners' Names, Nov. 15, 1776, Peter Force Collection, Series 9, Reel 103, LOC.

50. Houlding, *Fit for Service*; Sylvia Frey, *The British Soldier in America: A Social History of Military Life in the Revolutionary Period* (Austin, TX, 1981); Stephen Brumwell, *Redcoats: The British Soldier and War in the Americas, 1755–1763* (Cambridge, UK, 2001); Spring, *With Zeal and With Bayonets Only*.

51. Board of War to Lancaster Committee, Nov. 15, 1776, Peter Force Collection, Series 9, Reel 103, LOC; Lancaster Committee, Sept. 24, 1776, Force, *AA*, Fifth Series, 2: 491; Continental Congress, Oct. 7, 1776, Force, *AA*, Fifth Series,

Disillusioned officials now approached their captives as sinister conspirators bent on subverting the Revolution. In a province populated by untold numbers of Indians and disaffected, patriots' ability to identify and neutralize their prisoners assumed special urgency. To safeguard their cause and communities, Whigs now sought carefully to contain and demarcate their British captives. On July 3, 1776, Pennsylvania's Council of Safety ordered all paroled British officers to "wear their Uniforms whenever they go abroad." Transgressors would be seized and confined.[52]

The revolutionaries' newly instituted security measures sharpened the boundaries between friend and foe. Now more than ever before, the British redcoat symbolized an enemy of the cause. Thus, while the colonial insurgency had initially blurred the combatants' identities, the contentious encounters between captors and captives sped their estrangement. For Pennsylvania's embattled Whigs, their British captives proved brethren no more. Spurned by their imperial kinsmen, revolutionaries had begun cultivating new identities and allegiances in fierce opposition to their British adversaries.

Among Lancaster's militants, trouble with the prisoners had combined with the climbing costs of war to erase any lingering affection for the British. Local officials echoed the sentiments of Pennsylvania's Council of Safety during spring 1776 by damning the British as "cruel and inveterate foes." Developments on remote battlefields fed fury and frustration at home. Each battle waged and each ounce of blood shed drove another wedge between Whigs and their imperial relations, while drawing the combatants closer to their compatriots in arms. Even the cautious moderates who had long opposed independence soon felt hopelessly alienated from the British. By mid-summer, Edward Shippen, who but a year before had waxed eloquent about the persistent bonds joining Britons and Americans, instead prayed for the "Defeat of our Murdering Enemys."[53]

2: 1389; Continental Congress, Oct. 22, 1776, Peter Force Collection, Series 9, Reel 102, LOC; Council of Safety to Lancaster Committee, Nov. 2, 1776, Peter Force Collection, Series 9, Reel 103, LOC.

52. Council of Safety, July 3, 1776, Force, *AA*, Fourth Series, 6: 1298; Ousterhout, *A State Divided*, 229–78; Knouff, *The Soldiers' Revolution*, 155–231; Silver, *Our Savage Neighbors*, 227–60.

53. Council of Safety to Lancaster Committee, Mar. 19, 1776, Jasper Yeates Papers, HSP; "Edward Shippen to Joseph Shippen July 13, 1776," *PLCHS* 11 (1906–1907), 18. See also James Burd to Edward Shippen, May 18, 1776, Ship-

The war had quickly become an intensely personal affair for both Lancaster's soldiers and civilians. By fall 1776, the county's troops numbered among the thousands of American casualties suffered during the devastating defeats in New York. Embittered survivors wrote home recalling their savage encounters with the enemy. Captain Peter Grubb, Jr., of the State Rifle Regiment reassured relatives following the rebels' mauling at Long Island that "our men behaved with the greatest courage and stood their ground like heroes" against the British "Butchers." Locals felt the losses acutely as spiraling reports told of neighbors, friends, or family killed or captured by the enemy. The Lancaster committeeman William Atlee learned in September 1776 that his brother Samuel, the colonel of Pennsylvania's Musketry Battalion, had been captured on Long Island. Major Edward Burd, grandson of Edward Shippen, likewise numbered among the prisoners seized in New York.[54]

Tales of the mistreatment of American captives resonated locally, conjuring up an increasingly foreign and well-defined enemy. Burd's family received the chilling news in October that he was confined aboard one of the enemies' dreaded prison ships. Former transport vessels anchored off New York, Britain's infamous harbor hulks soon swarmed with thousands of Americans captured during late 1776. Dark, dank, filthy, and overcrowded, fertile breeding grounds for typhus, dysentery, smallpox, and yellow fever, the prison ships quickly became floating coffins. In early January 1777, Shippen mourned a former colleague who "was taken Prisoner . . . used very ill, and is since dead." Moderates like Shippen found British abuses so repugnant because they issued from erstwhile kindred. Enraged militants, meanwhile, identified with their

---

pen Family Papers, 7, HSP; Council of Safety to Colonels, Lancaster County, Nov. 11, 1776, Grubb Family Papers, 1730–1950, Colonel Peter Grubb, Revolutionary War Papers, 1775–1777, HSP; Council of Safety to Colonels, Lancaster County, Dec. 8, 1776, Peter Force Collection, Series 9, Reel 103, LOC; George Ross, Circular to Lancaster County Associators, Dec. 18, 1776, Force, *AA*, Fifth Series, 3: 1273.

54. Peter Grubb, Jr., to Peter Grubb, Sr., Sept. 16, 1776, Grubb Family Papers, Peter Grubb Correspondence, 1765–1779, HSP; Klein, *Fighting the Battles*; *PA*, Second Series, 1: 509–22; *PA*, Second Series, 10: 309–11; Edward Shippen to William Shippen, Sept. 14, 1776, Shippen Papers, BSh62, APS; Sarah Yeates to Jasper Yeates, Oct. 17, 1776, Simon Gratz Manuscripts, Case 2, Box 13, Supreme Court of Pennsylvania; Edward Shippen to Joseph Shippen, Nov. 30, 1776, Shippen Papers, BSh62, APS.

languishing compatriots to the north. One local captured the sentiments of a growing share of the county's patriots when he decried the plight of "our Brave, poor Country-men" who perished in the hands of "English tyrants." Residents of Lancaster began subscribing aid to the families of local volunteers detained by the enemy as early as December 1776.[55]

Patriots vented their frustrations at the enemies who remained most vulnerable and near at hand, the prisoners in their midst. Long smoldering tensions threatened to erupt when locals reeled from losses close to home. After Cumberland County residents received word of their troops killed in Canada, Carlisle's paroled British officers were "pelted and reviled in the streets." Insurgents fumed as British officers exploited liberal paroles, and American captives expired under conversely deplorable conditions. Lieutenant Andre grimly recalled how he and his fellow officers had been "invited to smell a brandished hatchet and reminded of its agreeable effects on the skull." "Several of us have been fired at," he added, "and we have more than once been waylaid by men determined to assassinate us." Incensed by Whigs' hypocrisy, he concluded: "Such is the brotherly love they, in our capitulation, promised us."[56]

For locals, the war with Britain revived an anxiety and animus not felt since the terrifying frontier violence of the 1750s and 1760s, while featuring new villains in their former kinsmen. Locals' resentments found familiar expression in the imagined violence of the American backcountry. Rumors in early August 1776 suggested that a company of Cumberland County militia aimed to retaliate against Lancaster's captives for the alleged atrocities perpetrated against prisoners from Pennsylvania. Only a dozen years after the Paxton Rioters had massacred the defenseless Conestoga Indians in Lancaster's workhouse, the rumors carried a chill-

55. Edward Shippen to Jasper Yeates, Jan. 9, 1777, Jasper Yeates Papers, HSP; Christopher Marshall to Children, Feb. 6, 1778, Christopher Marshall Letterbook, HSP; Christopher Marshall, *Extracts from the Diary of Christopher Marshall, 1774–1781* (1877; repr. New York, 1969), 200–201; Sarah Yeates to Jasper Yeates, Oct. 17, 1776, Simon Gratz Manuscripts, Case 2, Box 13, Supreme Court of Pennsylvania, HSP. For the British prison ships, see Metzger, *The Prisoner in the American Revolution*, 281–91; Bowman, *Captive Americans*, 42–49; Burrows, *Forgotten Patriots*, 12–14, 53–57, 92–93, 197–200. Lancaster Committee, Dec. 17, 1776, Force, *AA*, Fifth Series, 3: 1257.

56. John Andre to Mary Louise Andre, Dec. 17, 1776, as quoted in Hatch, *Major John Andre*, 67.

ing resonance. Fearing for their lives, the prisoners huddled in their barracks, armed with makeshift clubs. The rumors proved unfounded but indicated the depth of hostility backcountry associators now harbored toward their British foes. Militants' enmity sprang from locally oriented grievances—as the British stalked their neighborhoods or bloodied their recruits—but slowly drew them into an expanding revolutionary community.[57]

As views of the British changed, so did the revolutionaries' perceptions of themselves. Locals took pains to distinguish themselves from the British following the declaration of independence, identifying more readily with distant friends of the common cause, the "spirited sons of America," joint members of the revolutionary fold. The conflict's first formal prisoner exchange in late 1776 illuminates locals' supplanting of older attachments for new. In mid-November, the Board of War ordered Lancaster's Committee to forward their British captives under armed escorts to New Jersey's Fort Lee for immediate exchange. General Washington insisted the prisoners remain under close guard during their march lest they stray to gather intelligence.[58]

Local revolutionaries embraced the opportunity to return their captives and reclaim their compatriots. On November 22, Lancaster's Committee exhorted residents to liberate "their distressed fellow-citizens from bondage, and restore them to their country and friends" by helping to forward the British for exchange. The prisoners began their long march to New Jersey a week later accompanied by nearly sixty wagons and an escort of Lancaster militia. The captives' long-awaited departure brought

57. Lancaster Committee, Aug. 5, 1776, Force, *AA*, Fifth Series, 1: 759–60. For the culture of violence in Pennsylvania's backcountry, see Silver, *Our Savage Neighbors*; Kenny, *Peaceable Kingdom Lost*.

58. Lancaster Committee to Colonels, Lancaster County, May 28, 1776, Jasper Yeates Papers, HSP; Edward Shippen to Joseph Shippen, Apr. 1776, Shippen Papers, BSh62, APS; *PA*, Second Series, 13: 531; Council of Safety to Colonels, Lancaster County, Nov. 11, 1776, Grubb Family Papers; William Atlee to Peter Grubb, Nov. 14, 1776, Grubb Family Papers, Colonel Peter Grubb, Revolutionary War Papers, HSP; Board of War to George Washington, Nov. 19, 1776, Force, *AA*, Fifth Series, 3: 762; Board of War to Council of Safety, Nov. 19, 1776, Force, *AA*, Fifth Series, 3: 778; Council of Safety to Lancaster Committee, Nov. 20, 1776, Force, *AA*, Fifth Series, 3: 777–78; Board of War to George Washington, Nov. 23, 1776, Force, *AA*, Fifth Series, 3: 820; George Washington to Board of War, Dec. 4, 1776, Force, *AA*, Fifth Series, 3: 1070.

sighs of relief from anxious residents eager to be rid of their enemies and to return to the familiar rhythms and routines of town life. To locals' mounting consternation, the prisoners' unexpected arrival the year before had placed an increasingly dreaded foe in perilous proximity.[59]

Since early 1776, the prisoners' volatility and the intensifying hostilities had reinforced the budding connections among Lancaster's diverse insurgents. While the community's English and German speakers remained fully conscious of their cultural differences, the new dangers mitigated their ethnic divisions by underscoring their similarities. Prior to the war, many Anglo residents identified more closely with the distant denizens of Britain who shared their language and heritage than with their more inscrutably clannish German neighbors. English speakers' disorienting encounters with their British captives eroded their trans-Atlantic connections while underlining what they shared at stake with their German compatriots. By the summer of 1776, Lancaster's militants identified collectively against the mutual enemies who endangered their cause and community.[60]

The war with Britain thus helped temporarily supersede longstanding cultural divisions in Pennsylvania's hinterland by embroiling English- and German-speaking insurgents in a shared Continental endeavor. Negotiating layers of identity, Lancaster's militants subsumed their familiar cultural attachments within a more broadly encompassing revolutionary identity rooted in common enemies and interests. Just as the insurgents squared off against their enemies in the field, they cooperated in policing their captives and community. The prisoners' guards, with surnames ranging from Lamb and Sullivan to Heiss and Michenfelder, provided a cross-section of the local resistance. Locals' clashes with the British, both at home and abroad, nurtured tentative ties to an emerging revolutionary fold with novel commitments to cause and country. But

59. Lancaster Committee, Nov. 22, 1776, Peter Force Collection, Series 9, Reel 103, LOC; Lancaster Committee, Nov. 27, 1776, Force, *AA*, Fifth Series, 3: 869; Council of Safety to Lancaster Committee, Nov. 30, 1776, Peter Force Collection, Series 9, Reel 103, LOC; Lancaster Committee, Nov. 30, 1776, Force, *AA*, Fifth Series, 3: 918–19; Lancaster Committee to William Atlee, Dec. 16, 1776, Peter Force Collection, Series 9, Reel 103, LOC; "Extracts from Moravian Diaries," *PLCHS*, 92; George Washington to Board of War, Dec. 4, 1776, Force, *AA*, Fifth Series, 3: 1070; *PA*, Second Series, 13: 530–31.

60. For related dynamics, see Silver, *Our Savage Neighbors*.

Lancaster's prisoners also exposed the limits of the insurgents' patriotism by revealing conflicting local and Continental agendas.[61]

The prisoners fueled simmering tensions between residents and Continental authorities. The members of Congress who ordered the British captives to Lancaster asked residents to perform Continental service by deferring to broader military and diplomatic objectives. Locals remained solicitous of their own interests, however, and claimed a more personal stake in the enterprise. Many inhabitants resented the officials who saddled them with their enemies at the risk of their community. Torn between countervailing pressures—the demands of the resistance and their own security—they anxiously awaited the prisoners' departure. Others eagerly capitalized on the prisoners' skills by exploiting their labor. With the captives in private employ, Whig officials worried that locals would resist their exchange. Lancaster's Committee warned in mid-November that residents who refused to return the prisoners would meet with the swift retribution of Continental authorities.[62]

The flagging American resistance gave officials ample reason to doubt local commitments. Patriots had waited in nervous anticipation during the summer of 1776 as a massive expeditionary force consisting of twenty-four thousand British regulars and upwards of eight thousand German auxiliaries assembled on the shores of New York. A series of costly defeats soon sent Washington's battered, exhausted army tumbling in panicked flight through New Jersey and across the Delaware River into Pennsylvania. A despondent George Ross informed a colleague in late November of the "distress of our Soldiers who I have met almost naked and hardly able to walk." Continental officials questioned their capacity to sustain a viable fighting force as staggering losses and expiring enlistments rapidly thinned American ranks.[63]

The British force that pushed toward Pennsylvania now threatened to descend on a deeply divided and dispirited populace. The decision for independence and Pennsylvania's radical constitution had badly fragmented the provincial resistance. Recent military setbacks, meanwhile,

61. "Captain George Musser's Orderly Book," Egle, *Notes and Queries*, 128; Peden, *Revolutionary Patriots of Lancaster County*.

62. Lancaster Committee, Nov. 22, 1776, Peter Force Collection, Series 9, Reel 103, LOC.

63. George Ross to James Wilson, Nov. 26, 1776, Smith, *Letters of Delegates to Congress*, 5: 547.

tested the commitments of the most spirited insurgents. Many of Lancaster County's associators hesitated to march when summoned to impede the British advance on Philadelphia, preferring to remain near their homes and families. Through the closing days of 1776, patriots' zeal gave way to nagging doubts and despair. Only months after boldly declaring their independence, revolutionaries found themselves at the mercy of an uncompromising foe for whom they had lost all affection.[64]

Developments in Lancaster provide a case study of the local production of revolutionary identity. More broadly, Lancaster's story illustrates how the Revolution evolved from a civil conflict grounded within a shared sense of imperial belonging to a contest between disparate British and American nationalities. In the diverse Mid-Atlantic interior, war and revolution disrupted customary modes of identification and association by overriding established bonds of culture and empire. When Congressional officials dispatched their British captives to Lancaster in late 1775, they gambled that close interactions between locals and their prisoners would help mend the breach between combatants. Instead, captors and captives squared off as adversaries, approaching each other with mounting suspicion.

In Lancaster, locals' fledgling patriotism competed with a stubbornly persistent parochialism. The struggle with Britain and the dangers posed by their prisoners reinforced militants' deep-seated preoccupation with internal security while cultivating tenuous attachments to the revolutionary resistance. As the war came home to Lancaster and locals bore the costs of the conflict, militants closed ranks and found support in the company of fellow patriots. Increasingly alienated from the British, the insurgents embraced a peculiar revolutionary identity. While the forging of American identity remained an ongoing and a deeply contested process, Pennsylvania's revolutionaries had begun fashioning themselves anew—into something quite apart from their trans-Atlantic cousins.

64. Ousterhout, *A State Divided*; Ryerson, *The Revolution Is Now Begun*, 207–46; Knouff, *The Soldiers' Revolution*, 195–231; Council of Safety to Lancaster Committee, Dec. 8, 1776, Peter Force Collection, Series 9, Reel 103, LOC; Council of Safety to George Washington, Dec. 13, 1776, Force, *AA*, Fifth Series, 3: 1199; "Extracts from Moravian Diaries," *PLCHS*, 92.

S.C.
P
M.

"From a Nation of Drunkards, We Have Become a Sober People"

The Wyandot Experience in the Ohio Valley during the Early Republic

SHANNON BONTRAGER

In the early nineteenth century at the Upper Sandusky River in the frontier of Ohio, an unnamed Wyandot Christian convert related a story to the Methodist missionary James Finley:

> A few weeks ago, just as I was starting for meeting, a large hawk came and made an attack on my chickens. I took down my gun to shoot him, but remembered that it was the Sabbath, and that if I shot him it would be a bad example. I then took my bow and arrow, and shot him. The next Sabbath, another hawk came in the same way, and I killed him likewise. The third Sabbath the devil sent another one, and I began to think that it might be a temptation to break the Sabbath. So I let that one alone, and there has been none since.

After not shooting the hawk, the Christian Wyandot went into the woods to pray and emerged feeling a sense of calm and relief. Finley considered this an example of Christian evangelical conversion culminating in the act of obedience to the Sabbath. With the aid of this type of early national cultural colonialism, Christian missionaries helped open the

---

Shannon Bontrager is assistant professor of history at Georgia Highlands College. He would like to thank the three blind reviewers and the editors of the *Journal of the Early Republic*, as well as the members of the Trans-Empire Research Cluster organized by Ian Christopher Fletcher at Georgia State University and the members of the Faculty Association for Interdisciplinary Research at Georgia Highlands College, with special thanks to Steve Blankenship, for their critical and constructive comments.

Journal of the Early Republic, 32 (Winter 2012)

door to the Ohio Valley of what historian Eric Hinderaker has described as an "empire of liberty" where "American citizens [liberated] from the constraints of the older European imperial systems" imposed their will on the peoples and the landscape of the Ohio Valley.[1]

American Evangelical Christians employed a strategy against the Wyandot that had been tried before by agents hoping to build European empires out of what historians Jeremy Adeleman and Steven Aron have described as a region of porous borderlands. These borderlands, the historians suggest, were largely void of borders and formed penetrable spaces where Catholicism and French colonialism had existed alongside Huron Indians in the early seventeenth century. The Huron Indians had established a lucrative economic relationship with the French, and the British–Iroquois alliance had counterbalanced the Franco–Huron alliance in North America. Historian Richard White describes these colonial relationships as constituting a middle ground—physical space(s) and also a sociopolitical mentalité where Native Americans retained political and cultural power by playing French and British colonial agents against one another in a landscape where the sovereignty of empires and Native American tribes had remained blurred. Adelman and Aron contend that the French, British, and Native American borderlands facilitated "alliances constructed on trade and diplomacy [that] offered greater security and improved material conditions." These borderlands were dynamic and shifted as the competition between France and Britain had exacerbated the pre-contact rivalry between Iroquois and Huron Indians. When the Iroquois encroached on Huronia, in part, to satisfy their economic and diplomatic alliance with the British, hostilities began that ended with the destruction of Huronia. The Iroquois annihilation of their traditional enemy's homeland had initiated a wide-spread Huronic diaspora. Many Huron Indians migrated to areas around the French trading post at Detroit, where they rebuilt their trading relationship with the French in exchange for greater and closer access to French security.[2]

---

1. James B. Finley, *History of the Wyandot Mission, at Upper Sandusky, Ohio* (Cincinnati, OH, 1840), 195; Eric Hinderaker, *Elusive Empires: Constructing Colonialism in the Ohio Valley, 1673–1800* (Cambridge, UK, 1999), xiii, xiv.

2. Jeremy Adelman and Stephen Aron, "From Borderlands to Borders: Empires, Nation-States, and the Peoples in between in North American History," *American Historical Review* 104 (June 1999), 814–41, quotes on 821, 820; Richard White, *The Middle Ground: Indians, Empires, and Republics in the Great Lakes Region, 1650–1815* (New York, 1991). See also David J. Weber, "Turner,

This region near Fort Detroit was not a "native ground" as historian Kathleen DuVal has described the Arkansas Valley region, where, for example, Osage Indians could "reconstitute *native* concepts of order, geography, and human relations" because they outnumbered significantly the non-Indian population in the region. Here, DuVal contends "the concept of *borderlands* . . . can obscure the fact that Indians constructed and contested their own borders, geographic and metaphoric, long before Europeans arrived." Osage peoples had retained and defined their sovereignty in the Arkansas Valley. This was not the reality in the Great Lakes Region especially as the French and Indian War and the Revolutionary War, according to Hinderaker, had disrupted the socio-economic and geopolitical traditions of cross-cultural interaction in the Ohio Valley. The defeat of the French and the British in these respective wars had culminated with the rise of the American nation, whose leaders quickly turned their attention to the territory west of the Appalachian Mountains. "In the Ohio Valley," remarks Hinderaker, "the United States liberated its citizens to pursue their own interests while it turned the power of empire against the region's Native American population."[3]

These vanishing borderlands, claim Adelman and Aron, after the War of 1812, were replaced with unyielding borders. Native Americans, including the Huron in Michigan and Ohio, who became known to Euro Americans as Wyandot Indians, lost leverage because they were forced to deal with a single American empire. The historians contend that the United States had sought to transform the permeable borderlands into rigid borders. They suggest that Native Americans were caught by these political borders and were powerless to thwart the accompanying social and political transition, which led to indigenous peoples' political and cultural demise. Historians Pekka Hämäläinen and Samuel Truett have criticized this view of borderlands history. They have suggested that historians have overlooked Native American agency because they have largely failed to see borderlands as "interdependent realms." Instead, these authors suggest, scholars have adopted a view of borderlands that encourages unfair and unrealistic binaries: "Europeans have realms,

---

the Boltonians, and the Borderlands," *American Historical Review* 91 (Feb. 1986), 66–81.

3. Kathleen DuVal, *The Native Ground: Indians and Colonists in the Heart of the Continent* (Philadelphia, 2006), 227, 9; Eric Hinderaker, *Elusive Empires*, 269.

Indians have habitats; Europeans mark borders, Native Americans resist them; Europeans strive to dominate, Indians try to survive or coexist; borderlands are born of European failure rather than indigenous initiative." This essay seeks to build on these interpretations and apply them to the period after the War of 1812 when the "middle ground" collapsed.[4]

A case study of the Wyandot Indians at the Upper Sandusky reservation suggests that Native Americans, both traditional and Christian, understood that the disappearance of the middle ground did not make them powerless. Instead they retained the sovereignty of their collective memory of the past and used it to reshape a hybridized national sovereignty that could be used to construct innovative new borders in the face of American capitalism, white encroachment, and government removal policies. They cultivated this sovereignty out of composite collective memories of diaspora and borderlands politics of previous ages. For example, it was no accident that the Sabbath-breaker went into the woods to pray instead of his home or the church. The Wyandot used animals and nature to explain metaphysical phenomena; the hawk, and praying in the woods, was not an example of evangelical Christian conversion. Rather, it exhibited the hybridism that the Wyandot used to understand and assert their social reality in the face of American encroachment. When synchronized with traditional religious ideas, evangelical epistemology proved potentially potent. If remembering the Sabbath could prevent the devil's hawks from killing their chickens, perhaps the metaphor could be extended to prevent the Americans from forcing the Wyandot off their land. Rather than reacting to American borders, they constructed a complex interdependent set of borders that allowed them significant control over their own destiny. This amounted to a complex and dynamic form of sovereignty that included both traditionalists and Christian converts among the Wyandot leadership who deployed refined and sophisticated strategies to respond to the social and political problems brought on by American westward expansion. The first part of this essay will examine the brief history of Wyandot diaspora and hybridity. The second part will investigate the forms of collective memory and agency that the Wyandot leadership employed in

4. Pekka Hämäläinen and Samuel Truett, "On Borderlands," *The Journal of American History* 98 (Sept. 2011), 349.

the face of American expansion. The third part of this essay will explore the successes and limitations of the Wyandot's ability to control their own collective memory and thus control their own destiny.[5]

The destruction of Huronia led to a dispersal of Huron Indians. One group of Huron ventured to Fort Detroit, where they became known as Wyandot, to access French protection and the French trading-post system with its accompanying trans-Atlantic network. This alliance allowed Wyandot traders to access French marketplaces in Old and New France while escaping the Iroquois and British threat to their hunting grounds. In 1738, however, a Wyandot leader named Orontony had made peace with Cherokee and Catawba Indians in the South and led many Huron out of the shadow of Fort Detroit and into the Ohio River Valley near the Upper Sandusky River. Orontony's move was controversial, as Iroquois Indians were simultaneously moving into the Ohio Valley. This move had allowed Orontony's Wyandot to retain their access to the French trans-Atlantic market but also to gain access to the British trans-Atlantic market through their proximity to both the French at Fort Detroit and the British Cuyahoga trading post in the Ohio Valley. As historian Michael McConnel claims, "Orontony's defection led to more than trading advantages for Wyandot and profit-hungry traders. The Wyandot resettlement and the simultaneous arrival of Iroquois at Cuyahoga drew two rival colonial trading systems closer than they had ever been." This was lucrative and risky for Orontony's followers. Orontony had sought the British out, in part, because the British had a more competitive market than the French trading-post system. The French charged too much for goods and could not supply the needs of the Wyandot as well as the

5. Benedict Anderson, *Imagined Communities: Reflections on the Origin and Spread of Nationalism* (New York, 1991); Maurice Halbwachs, *The Collective Memory,* trans. Francis J. Ditter Jr. and Vida Yazdi Ditter (New York, 1980). Sociologist Maurice Halbwachs's 1925 study claimed "collective memory" formed an important social function among groups of people. He understood people to remember things based not on past experiences but on their current political context. People, he claimed, needed to validate their memories by corroborating them with other people; thus collective memory was a social construction that helped people define their present experiences rather than their past ones; collective memory helped build community and identity.

British could. The Wyandot leader could access both markets and thus increase profits from their new home on the Upper Sandusky but he also risked the wrath of the French, who wanted the British military and economic presence out of the Ohio Valley completely. This was devastating for the French, who tried unsuccessfully to bring the Wyandot back into the French fold. The failure to disentangle Orontony's band from the Upper Sandusky River and push British interests out of the Ohio Valley would contribute to the eventual French/Indian War that the French would lose.[6]

Meanwhile, without direct French protection, Orontony could not control the Ohio Valley. Orontony's migration brought competition to the region with the Cherokee and Catawba Indians from the South and with their traditional enemies, the Iroquois, who were also seeking to influence the region. The Wyandot soon lost out economically to the Anglo-Iroquois alliance, and Orontony even had lost the ability to influence his own followers. By 1748 Orontony had left the Ohio Valley, the Wyandot at Upper Sandusky had made amends with the French but remained in Ohio, and the Iroquois had come to dominate the Ohio Valley. The Wyandot at Sandusky, however, continued to employ sophisticated yet malleable political strategies remembered from these years of exodus from Huronia and Detroit. Now led by head chief Tarhe (the Crane) and a new generation of youthful chiefs including one of Tarhe's closest advisors, Between-the-Logs, the Wyandot at Upper Sandusky had sided with the French during the Seven Years' War, the British during the War for American Independence, and the Americans during the War of 1812. Tarhe and the Wyandot leadership knew their sovereignty remain linked to their ability to preserve a landscape that could be as permeable as possible to diverse imperial interests. However the defeat of the British by the Americans in the Revolutionary War brought about drastic change to the landscape and to Tarhe's political strategies. The first government of the United States under the Articles of Confederation had invented the Northwest Territory through the Land Ordinance of 1785, which helped raise revenue, and also had approved the Northwest Ordinance of 1787, which outlined the path to statehood. The Americans refused to negotiate with Native Americans who were

6. Michael N. McConnell, *A Country Between: The Upper Ohio Valley and its Peoples, 1724–1774* (Lincoln, NE, 1992), 63.

already living in the Northwest Territory. This had led to the alliance of Native American tribes who rejected these American policies. Tensions climaxed when Chief Tarhe, influenced by his advisors including Between-the-Logs, convinced his fellow Wyandot to join Shawnee Chief Blue Jacket's confederation of Indian tribes to fight against American forces led by General Anthony Wayne at the Battle of Fallen Timbers. Losing this battle had forced the Indian alliance to sign the Treaty of Greenville, which formally ended the Northwest Indian War and stipulated that Native Americans give up rights to much of what became Ohio.[7]

The politics of the Northwest Territory and the Northwest Indian War, argues Eric Hinderaker, were not the leading edges of American expansion into the West. According to Hinderaker, American individuals, not military or government agents, had defined previously the syntax of American expansion. Under the British Empire, colonists on the Western frontier had violated the attempts by British authorities to control territory gained from the French and Indian War west of the Appalachian Mountains. The Proclamation Line of 1763 and later the Quebec Act had prohibited colonists from settling western lands and had made lawbreakers out of British settlers seeking to move into the Ohio Valley. But the Continental Congress's need to gain soldiers during the Revolutionary War saw Congressmen annex large swaths of the western frontier. This, argues Hinderaker, not only produced more soldiers but also legitimized the men and women squatting on territory that was out of bounds. After the war, the American government could not regain control of this territory or the individuals who were no longer British lawbreakers but had become American citizens and continued to press further inland. The best U.S. officials could do was try to regulate westward expansion.[8]

The American policy toward Native Americans before the War of 1812 sought to limit the scope of expansion by emphasizing Jeffersonian agrarianism, which, as historian Theda Perdue describes, included a civilizing process intended to transform Indians from so-called primitives to republican citizens. This Civilization Policy led to the creation of a factory system, initiated by President George Washington and his Secretary

7. Ibid., 68.
8. Hinderaker, *Elusive Empires*, 186–203, 268–69.

of War Henry Knox and expanded by President Thomas Jefferson, in which the U.S. government tried to discourage frontier Indians from trading with the British and instead encouraged them to access the American marketplace. Thus the U.S. government constructed a series of trading forts in which an American official, called a "factor," would oversee trading practices between Americans and Native Americans. The system was supposed to regulate prices and keep both Indians and white settlers from taking control of the frontier. It also was supposed to help the United States fend off British encroachment on American territory. Native Americans, however, had to cede territory to the government, quit hunting, and adopt an agrarian socioeconomic system. Jefferson and others believed that this factory system would both republicanize and civilize Native Americans while securing and regulating the frontier.[9]

But this policy was not successful. Native Americans resisted it, the British continued to occupy the American frontier resulting in the War of 1812, and individuals such as John Jacob Astor believed the system amounted to the U.S. government competing with his American Fur Trading Company for control of the fur trade. Historian Andrew C. Isenberg claims the peace brought on by the Treaty of Ghent after the War of 1812, "Significantly reduced their [British] support of Indians who resisted the U.S. claims to sovereignty in the West." Thus the factory system failed, and the U.S. government eventually abolished the system in 1822. With the British threat eliminated, the only hindrance to Americans expanding further into the frontier was the presence of Native Americans. Thus the U.S. government began deemphasizing the factory system and emphasizing treaties. In this revised Civilization Policy, government agents attempted to use Native American tribes against each other in order to secure ever more land. Unable to produce alliances such as the one that Tarhe and Chief Blue Jacket had built during the 1780s, one by one Indian tribes, including the Wyandot, gave up their land rights to the American government.

Tarhe, meanwhile, had continued with his attempts to thwart the treaty system by seeking out new opportunities for alliances with other

9. Theda Perdue, "Women, Men and American Indian Policy: The Cherokee Response to 'Civilization,'" in *Negotiators of Change: Historical Perspectives on Native American Women*, ed. Nancy Shoemaker (London, 1995), 91; Francis Paul Prucha, *The Great Father: The United States Government and the American Indians* (Lincoln, NE, 1995), 116–20.

JER RENEWAL FORM

- ☐ Student: $30*
- ☐ K-12 Teachers: $35
- ☐ Community College Teachers: $40
- ☐ Individual, income to $45,000: $40
- ☐ Individual, income above $45,000: $70
- ☐ Institution: $120

Non-U.S. orders, please add $18.00 for shipping.

Provide SHEAR with additional support by becoming a "Friend of SHEAR." Your payment of $500, $300, or $150 will cover your SHEAR membership including your *JER* subscription.

_____ **Sojourner Truth Friend: $500**

_____ **Thomas Skidmore Friend: $300**

_____ **Nicholas Biddle Friend: $150**

PAYMENT METHODS

ONLINE WITH CREDIT CARD at http://www.shear.org

CHECK (made payable to SHEAR and mailed to 3355 Woodland Walk, Philadelphia, PA 19104-4531, Phone: 215-746-5393, Fax: 215-573-3391, Email: info@shear.org)

BILLING ADDRESS

Name ______________________________

Address ______________________________

City ______________ State/Province ______________

Zip/Postal Code ______________ Country ______________

Phone ______________ Email ______________

SHIPPING ADDRESS (if different from mailing address)

Name ______________________________

Address ______________________________

City ______________ State/Province ______________

Zip/Postal Code ______________ Country ______________

*Students: Please submit a copy of your student identification to the SHEAR office.

Native American tribes. The head chief thus sent Chief Between-the-Logs, one of his closest advisors, to build these strategic alliances. Tarhe sent him to the Seneca prophet Handsome Lake and his strong warnings about alcohol, wife beating, and witchcraft but quickly abandoned him when he proved guilty of hypocrisy. Tarhe then sent Between-the-Logs at age 27 to join Tecumseh and Tenskwatawa and live with the Shawnee for an entire year. But he became disillusioned with the Prophet's double standards and returned to Upper Sandusky to report that an alliance with the Shawnee was very unlikely. Upon his return he found Presbyterian missionaries living on the reservation but British traders and Catholic Wyandot eventually pushed them out. Between-the-Logs's search for an effective and sustainable political alliance, and Tarhe's political strategy, had ended frustratingly just as the War of 1812 was beginning.[10]

On the eve of this war, Tarhe and Between-the-Logs changed their political strategy. They traveled to Brownstown, Michigan and rejected the Shawnee proposal of a collective alliance with the British despite the large indigenous support of Tecumseh's plan. The Wyandot leaders instead allied with the Americans, and Between-the-Logs, at Tarhe's recommendation, led the Ohio Wyandot contingent attached to General William Henry Harrison's column that secured Detroit and invaded Canada. Between-the-Logs's objective was to convince Detroit Wyandot who had allied with the British to sever their relationship and join the American and Ohio Wyandot alliance. But the alliance crafted by Tarhe and Between-the-Logs was probably just as much about the Wyandot leadership trying to secure greater leverage in an Indian world where the Wyandot were increasingly becoming politically isolated as it was about helping the Americans defeat the British. This style of leadership marked an innovative understanding of the shifting landscape of middle-ground politics and showcased the creativity with which Tarhe could imagine a middle-ground politic.[11]

---

10. James B. Finley, *Autobiography of Reverend James B. Finley; or, Pioneer Life in the West*, ed. W. P. Strickland (Cincinnati, OH, 1853), 440–41. John Johnston, Agent of Indian Affairs, to Caleb Atwater, June 17, 1819, in Caleb Atwater, *Transactions and Collections of the American Antiquarian Society* (Worcester, MA, 1870), 1: 269–77.

11. James B. Finley, *Life Among the Indians; or, Personal Reminiscences and Historical Incidents Illustrative of Indian Life and Character* (Cincinnati, OH, 1857), 528–29.

Despite the Wyandot alliance with the Americans, the aftermath of the war did not bring much security for them. In 1817, the year Tarhe died, the Wyandot elected Du-en-quot as Tarhe's successor. The new head chief encountered a new political reality as U.S. government officials asked the Wyandot to consider the Fort Meigs Treaty, which guaranteed the Wyandot would receive annual payments of four thousand dollars from the U.S. government in return for living on a reservation at Upper Sandusky. In exchange the Wyandot had to give up most of their land claims in the Ohio Valley and be confined to the Sandusky reservation. Du-en-quot's election signified a political alternative to Tarhe's regime. The new chief inherited a political world where the middle ground was quickly collapsing, and Tarhe and Between-the-Logs had done much to alienate the Ohio Wyandot from other Indian allies. The new head chief turned culturally and politically inward, embracing the old traditions while forsaking the alliance-building that had become the hallmark of Tarhe's leadership. Not only did he offer the Wyandot people an alternative political and cultural vision but also he signified how much the influence of Between-the-Logs's and Tarhe's regime had diminished. Soon after Du-en-quot's election, the head chief persuaded chief Between-the-Logs and Tarhe's other supporters—chief Hicks, chief Mononcue, and others—to sign the Fort Meigs Treaty.[12]

The result of the American invasion of the West was the onset of a new style of empire. This new style, claims Hinderaker, was "one in which individuals exercised a new kind of authority and legitimacy." The author continues, "this was a dramatic inversion of the earlier [French and British] model of imperial development, which was directed from the center and governed by elites. Now government followed in the wake of individual initiative, picking up the pieces of imperial expansion and trying to shape them into something coherent and principled." Individual Americans rushing into the frontier brought to the Ohio Valley a system of empire based on "decentralized, atomized political authority and deeper, sharper lines of racial separation and hatred" as they rede-

12. Andrew C. Isenberg, "The Market Revolution in the Borderlands: George Champlin Sibley in Missouri and New Mexico, 1808–1826," *Journal of the Early Republic* 21 (Autumn 2001), 445–65; Richard White, "The Fictions of Patriarchy: Indians and Whites in the Early Republic," in *Native Americans and the Early Republic*, ed. Frederick E. Hoxie, Ronald Hoofman and Peter J. Albert (Charlottesville, VA, 1999), 73.

fined the Ohio Valley landscape. American settlers, not government or military agents, had created a marketplace in Ohio in which not only commercial interests but religious interests including Moravians, Methodists, Lutherans, Baptists, Quakers, Anglicans, and Presbyterians all invaded the area. The result was that racial borders, economic borders, and religious borders hardened as Americans constructed their identities out of the shared memories from the Ohio Valley. So too did these memories and older memories of diaspora affect Ohio Indians, particularly the Wyandot. Gone were the borderlands politics cultivated by Indians such as Orontony and Tarhe and the British and the French of the past. Now a new landscape took shape; one in which centralized empires no longer existed. Rather, decentralized regimes and individuals pursuing economic prosperity and racial subordination had produced a landscape of borders in the Ohio Valley.[13]

The Wyandot were more than capable of confronting this new political landscape, employing lessons remembered from a long tradition of hybridity in groundbreaking and original ways to reconceptualize sovereignty and assert new Wyandot borders after the War of 1812. The collapse of Huronia, their leaving the security of the French at Fort Detroit to venture into a riskier and potentially more advantageous environment in the Ohio Valley, and their complex alliances among other Native American tribes as well as European and American empires all helped produce a collective memory of the past and a mentalité of hybridity. This was represented even in miscegenation of the tribes throughout the region. One of the consequences of disbandment and hybridity was intermarriage; as Hinderaker points out "by 1750 nearly every community of any size in the valley contained a complex mixture of peoples who retained their tribal labels as a source of ethnic identity, but whose politics were more often driven by local concerns that cut across tribal identities." The geopolitics, as well as the ethnic makeup of the Wyandot was that of a long history based on the ideals of hybridity and shared memories of exodus, of which they retained control.[14]

---

13. Hinderaker, *Elusive Empires*, 168.

14. Ibid., 52.

Adelman and Aron acknowledge that their use of the terms "borderlands" and "borders" came out of the theoretical discussions of Herbert E. Bolton and Frederick Jackson Turner about the European and American frontiers. Critics claim that by using categories constructed by English-speaking theorists who privilege Euro American hegemony and sovereignty, historians risk losing Native American practices of resistance but also innovation and agency. Hämäläinen and Truett suggest that instead of examining spaces of European creativity, scholars should focus on "indigenous cores" in which "Indians created the conditions for borderlands history rather than simply looking at how they acted within it."[15]

Chicana feminist scholar and activist Gloria Anzaldúa provides some insight on how Native Americans could have been creative and inventive in reimagining a dynamic and constantly shifting political and cultural landscape. She unapologetically used the term "borderlands" in *Borderlands/La Frontera* to describe her experiences of living in between the borders of the English and Spanish language; Mexican, English, and Indian ethnicity; and as a Lesbian in a heterosexual world. For her the borderlands make up a landscape where multiple borders proliferate, and it is this idea that may help explain Wyandot agency in reconstructing borders and re-envisioning sovereignty. She is referring to a physical location and a psychological condition where "two or more cultures edge each other, where people of different races occupy the same territory, where lower, middle and upper classes touch, where the space between two individuals shrinks with intimacy." Her definition of the borderlands comes from poetry and cultural criticism, not history, and it is here that this essay shifts its use of the term borderlands away from Adelman's and Aron's definition and toward Anzaldúa's definition. Anzaldúa's description of the borderlands allows for an analysis of individuals on the ground struggling with the effects of Native American cultural and political legacies overlaid onto Euro American imperial legacies. She suggests that "borders are set up to define the places that are safe and unsafe, to distinguish *us* from *them*" and are established by Native American as much as by Euro Americans. She claims "a border is a dividing line, a narrow strip along a steep edge" and contends "a borderland is a vague and undetermined place created by the emotional residue of an unnatural

15. Hämäläinen and Truett, "On Borderlands," 352.

boundary. It is in a constant state of transition." Those who reside in this type of borderlands are faced with a choice.[16]

This essay claims that the condition of the borderlands forces individuals to remain rigid and to die or embrace flexibility proactively. It takes the term "hybridity" to include this sort of flexibility that is dynamic, ever-changing, transcendent, and inclusive of many different and even contradictory ideas. It is also a flexibility or hybridity that is embedded in an individual's experience of negotiating the borderlands which constitutes a struggle over internal as well as external factors. Anzaldúa writes, "In the Borderlands/you are the battleground/where enemies are kin to each other;/you are at home, a stranger." The solution, she contends, "to survive the Borderlands" is that individuals "must live *sin fronteras*/be a crossroads."[17]

It is this condition of crossroads, flexibility, and hybridity that the Wyandot used to destabilize American settlers where borders were proliferating as Americans had expanded into the Ohio Valley. Individually, not all Wyandot were willing to experiment with living in between the contradictions of a hybrid experience. Some remained rigid. Yet the conscious experience of transcending borders posed a formidable remaking

16. Gloria Anzaldúa, *Borderlands/La Frontera: The New Mestiza* (San Francisco, CA, 1987), 102; John R. Wunder and Pekka Hämäläinen, "Of Lethal Places and Lethal Essays," *American Historical Review* 104 (Oct. 1999), 1229–34. Adelman and Aron concede that their essay did not address Native American agency adequately but retained that their model could, if appropriately applied, be useful for Native American scholars as well as historians of European and American empires. Their critics include among others Christopher Ebert Schmidt-Nowara, "Borders and Borderlands of Interpretation," *American Historical Review* 104 (Oct. 1999), 1226–28; Evan Haefeli, "A Note on the Use of North American Borderlands," *American Historical Review* 104 (Oct. 1999), 1222–25; see also Hämäläinen and Truett, "On Borderlands," 359. Stephen Aron has recently revised his understanding of borderlands in "Frontiers, Borderlands, Wests" in *American History Now*, ed. Eric Foner and Lisa McGirr (Philadelphia, 2011), 261–83.

17. Adelman and Aron describe the Great Lakes region as moving from borderlands (where vague porous borders overlap) to borders (where borders are distinct and rigid). Despite Anzaldúa's conception of borderlands originating in the region along the Rio Grande River Valley, she is describing the borderlands as the place between these rigid distinct borders, where individual bodies and individual personalities must exist and negotiate often against their will. Anzaldúa, *Borderlands/La Frontera*, 25; Ibid., 216, 17.

of the Ohio River Valley as a new space that stabilized Wyandot control of the region and destabilized American settlers' influence in the region. This experience was based on the collective memory cultivated through the Huronic diaspora, the experience of moving to the Upper Sandusky River, and the violence of the Indian wars. These experiences allowed Wyandot Indians to develop new strategies for reasserting their sovereignty; strategies that were as decentralized, as individualistic, and as effective at producing hybridity as the Americans were at producing decentralized and atomized patterns of settlement.

In the new decentralized marketplace of Ohio, Methodist missionary James Finley set up an evangelical mission at the Upper Sandusky reservation in 1816. The next year, Wyandot chiefs signed reluctantly the Fort Meigs Treaty, which articulated rigid geographic borders that eroded Wyandot territorial sovereignty. Many of the signers, not all, came to regret the treaty. Wyandot chiefs Between-the-Logs, Hicks, and Mononcue—supporters of Tarhe's alliance strategy—went to Washington, DC, with the leaders of the Seneca and Delaware to lobby, largely unsuccessfully, the Secretary of War and Congress to give back some land and increase some annuities. Finley, meanwhile, had made some headway in raising some converts on the reservation. He documented his work with the Wyandot in his 432-page book *History of the Wyandot Mission*, published in 1840. Finley and his text had many overlapping and often contradictory meanings. One historian has attempted to reclaim Finley as a "Lion of the Forest," whose writings significantly aided in the civilizing process of America's frontier. Historian Martin Walsh used discursive theory to deconstruct Finley's imperialistic text to discover its "underground meaning" and the Wyandot voice that Finley consciously tried to obfuscate but actually unconsciously exposed. His *History* represented the work of an evangelical missionary and an amateur early ethnohistorian. It is in many cases the only primary-source evidence documenting the Wyandot experience. But his mission to the Wyandot was equally a mission to Americans back east, and his inductive reasoning and sacred methodology underscored his patriarchal content and moral lessons based on stereotypical depictions. The book was a critique of Jeffersonian agrarianism as the major economic and cultural force. This system was supposed to produce a social body of moral citizens, but it also contributed to what historian Charles Sellers has called an emerging "market revolution" that helped the United States consolidate land and reorganize labor through emerging practices of capitalism. Thus, for Finley and many other missionaries, Jeffersonian Agrarianism and its aftereffects—although important—were inherently flawed as a civilizing process. Instead of a secular force, missionaries such as Finley believed the civilizing process actually resided in an evangelical Christian theology. This represented an American Christian evangelical cultural border in the Ohio Valley that accompanied the geographic borders created from the Fort Meigs Treaty. Finley's statements thus have sociological and historical content but also hyperbole and drama, and his book takes a peculiar form as a history, a socio-religious experiment, a novel, and a gospel. Whereas the tenets of Jeffersonian agrarianism suggested that individuals must above all things be civilized first, Finley's thesis was that Native Americans, and by implication easterners involved in the market revolution, must be Christianized before they could be civilized. When juxtaposed with Finley's other works, including his *Autobiography of Reverend James B. Finley*; *or, Pioneer Life in the West*, *Life Among the Indians; or, Personal Reminiscences and Historical Incidents Illustrative of Indian Life and Character*, and *Memorials of Prison Life*, the Methodist's moral fiber seems rigid if not authentic, paternalistic if not earnest, and flawless if not sympathetic. Despite these limitations, the Methodist's narrative provides interesting, even if unintended, examples of Wyandot agency.[18]

18. Frederick Hoxie, "Introduction," in *Native Americans and the Early Republic,* ed. Frederick E. Hoxie, Ronald Hoffman, and Peter J. Albert (Charlottesville, VA, 1999) ix; Finley, *Autobiography*, 442. Although there is a problem of memory—Finley published his *History* in 1840, twelve years after he left the mission—he kept a journal while living on the reservation and based his history on his journal. Martin W. Walsh, "The 'Heathen Party': Methodist Observation of the Ohio Wyandot," *American Indian Quarterly* 16 (Spring 1992), 189–211. Walsh points out that Finley never learned to speak Wyandot; in fact, Finley communicated through a translator the entire duration of his stay in Upper Sandusky. Joel W. Martin, "Cultural Contact and Crises in the Early Republic: Native American Religious Renewal, Resistance, and Accommodation," in *Native Americans and the Early Republic*, 226–60. "Underground Meaning" describes the deconstruction/demythologization of a hegemonic text to uncover alternative and hidden meaning(s). Charles Sellers, *The Market Revolution: Jacksonian America, 1815–1846* (New York, 1991); David H. Unser, Jr., "Iroquois Livelihood and Jeffersonian Agrarianism: Reaching Behind the Models and Metaphors," in *Native Americans and the Early Republic*, 200–13; Robert Abzug, *Cosmos Crumbling: American Reform and the Religious Imagination* (New York, 1994); R. Laurence Moore, *Selling God: American Religion in the Marketplace of Culture* (New York,

Contrary to Finley's claims, there was never a majority of Christians among the Wyandot community, but three of Finley's prized converts were the three influential chiefs who went to Washington in hopes of amending the Fort Meigs Treaty. He was able to convert them, in part, because Finley's evangelicalism brought with its religious energy a political critique of the head Wyandot chief Du-en-quot. These "Christian" chiefs were innovative leaders who believed they understood better the new borderlands reality. This became evident one Sunday morning when Du-en-quot and several non-Christians, including his formidable military ally War-Pole, attended one of Finley's Christian meetings. The head chief sought to prevent a Christian/non-Christian political split on the reservation and hoped to transcend the border represented by evangelical Christianity. But Du-en-quot was not quite equipped to realize what his Cherokee counterparts were able to achieve further south in Georgia. Historian Claudio Saunt has suggested that Cherokee leaders were capable of mixing traditional Indian myths with "European-style history" of the nineteenth century that accentuated "authentic" national origins by linking national histories to national sovereignty. When confronting white Americans they abandoned traditional narrative devices that incorporated "dreams, imaginary animals, and other elements unwelcome in history" and instead used "linear narratives and source citation" in order to authenticate and legitimize their sovereignty in the minds of nineteenth-century Europeans. These narratives "shrewdly revised Christian stories to give Indians a divine right to America." De-un-quot possessed similar intellectual skill and employed a similar hybrid strategy, but had to rely on an older narrative tradition where, as Saunt suggests Native Americans "sought common ground with colonists by recounting stories about the past that freely mixed elements from Indian and European traditions."[19]

1994); Mark Noll, ed., *God and Mammon: Protestants, Money, and the Market, 1790–1860* (New York, 2002); James B. Finley, *Memorials of Prison Life* (Cincinnati, OH, 1850). Finley served as a chaplain to prison inmates in the Ohio penitentiary. Charles C. Cole, Jr., *Lion of the Forest: James B. Finley, Frontier Reformer* (Lexington, KY, 1994).

19. Historian John Bowes numbers the Christian Wyandot in 1843 (the year of removal) at 200 out of 700 total inhabitants at the Upper Sandusky reservation. See John P. Bowes, *Exiles and Pioneers: Eastern Indians in the Trans-Mississippi West* (New York, 2007), 161. Claudio Saunt, "Telling Stories: The Political Uses

Du-en-quot had "dressed up and painted" his body, and his allies likewise had "their head bands filled with silver bobs." As well they wore "nose-jewels and ear-ings, [sic] and many bands of silver" were on Du-en-quot's arms and legs. De-un-quot painted animals on his body and painted his face because he believed it would protect him from bad spirits. Finley decided to make an example of the chief and his entourage and began to preach on the pride of men's hearts. He concluded his sermon by referencing the head chief's dress saying, "therefore, all our hearts must be evil, and that continually; that we are proud, and of this we have an example before us, in our grandfather, the head chief." Finley continued "that my friend has a proud heart, is evident from his dress, and painting himself" and added "my friend does not think the Great Spirit has made him pretty enough—he must put on paint to make himself look better. This is plain proof that he is a proud man, and has an evil heart." After the Methodist's sermon, De-un-quot rose and peacefully contested Finley sermon and suggested that the Bible had little relevance for the Wyandot.[20]

De-un-quot tapped into the collective memory in the room. He told the story of the Wyandot god Tijuskà'a's confrontation with the white man's god at the base of a mountain over who would control North America. The two deities decided that whoever could move the mountain would have control of the land. The white man's god knelt, opened a book, and began to pray but nothing happened. Tijuskà'a, however, communicated with the Big Turtle who, according to Wyandot mythology, held the North American continent on her back. The Wyandot deity waved a magic wand and "began to pow-wow, and beat the turtle shell, and the mountain trembled, shook, and stood by him." Only then did the Big Turtle shift her weight and cause the mountain to move. To the Wyandot, this myth was the product of collective memory that helped them explain where the Native American and European borders

of Myth and History in the Cherokee and Creek Nations," *Journal of American History* 93 (Dec. 2006), 674–75.

20. Finley, *History*, 164–65. To Finley, painting one's body was a rejection of God's creation. He argued, instead, that humans should be content with their bodies and avoid the desire to paint them. Wyandot knowledge, however, claimed that face and body painting could protect one from evil spirits including disease. Finley, *Autobiography*, 437.

existed. It was a hybridized collective memory of the past used to explain the present geopolitical reality of an encroaching American empire.[21]

Unlike the Cherokee, however, Wyandot intellectuals had not yet crafted a "legitimate" linear history of the Wyandot, which made it more difficult for Du-en-quot to transcend the cultural border that evangelical Christianity represented. To Finley, this religiohistorical explanation was inauthentic, nonsensical, and childish, and he sought to delegitimize De-un-quote's narrative by attacking the chief with slander. Finley announced that in ways of war and hunting he was De-un-quot's "son":

> But when it came to matters of religion, he is my son, and I am his father. He has told us a long and queer story. I wonder where he obtained it? He may have dreamed it, or has he heard some drunken Indian tell it; for you know that drunkards always see great sights, and have many revelations, which sober men never have.

It was an unfair and disrespectful response because everyone in the room (except Finley?) knew the story came from a Wyandot tradition, not a drunk. But for some in the audience who were unhappy with De-un-quot's governance, particularly Between-the-Logs—who himself only recently had reluctantly given up face and body painting—Finley's slander effectively critiqued De-un-quot's headship. Chief Between-the-Logs seized the moment to challenge De-un-quot's political leadership. Between-the-Logs stood up and declared that he would take the Christians of the tribe under his control while De-un-quot would lead the non-Christians; the two groups would form their own separate policies. This was not just a religious divide but it could also be seen as a political divide between those who supported Du-en-quot and those who had supported Tarhe's policies and Between-the-Logs's role in Tarhe's regime. But De-un-quot quickly diffused the challenge, saying "No—I am the head of the nation, and the head ought to be believed. With these two arms I can take hold of both parties, and try to keep you both steady." His insistence on leading both Christian and traditional adherents marked the mentalité of hybridity.[22]

---

21. Finley, *History*, 165.

22. Finley, *History*, 166; Finley, *Autobiography*, 440–41. Indeed Du-en-quot had signed the treaty of Fort Meigs, but Between-the-logs and Mononcue also signed this treaty and must share some responsibility for agreeing to terms they did not want. There were few alternatives, and the treaty was probably the best choice among bad ones.

Borders in the Ohio borderlands could be transcended with strategies based on hybridity. Chief De-un-quot suggested that Wyandot politics had the power to transcend these borders. He articulated a composite view of dealing with religious and political borders, and it worked in authenticating his leadership among the Christian Wyandot. This must have also impressed Between-the-Logs, who instead of following through with a political movement against the chief accepted his authority and collaborated with Du-en-quot to run the reservation government, build a school, thwart squatters, and keep access to the mill on the river. This did not mean that Between-the-Logs ceased to criticize the methods of the head chief, but he cooperated with Du-en-quot when it came to furthering the agenda of the reservation and embraced the head chief's leadership style where Christians and non-Christians worked together. The head chief successfully stabilized the community, and Christian evangelical and Wyandot traditions coexisted. Like Du-en-quot, chief Between-the-Logs was concerned with social stability on the reservation, and it was here that he was the most skeptical of the head chief's leadership and most embracing of Finley's evangelicalism.

Tarhe's successor was attempting to reinvigorate the traditional feasts of their ancestors. The old myths, the old prophecies, and the old memories that accompanied them had become obsolete to Between-the-Logs because they now involved alcohol. As historian Peter Mancall notes, "liquor continued to be extremely important to Indians throughout the Great Lakes region. Whether used by traders in transactions for food or peltry or as gifts to maintain good relations with Indians and to entice them to particular posts, liquor quite literally lubricated the fur trade." An individual struggle for Between-the-Logs, the use of alcohol had become a significant border in Ohio that had caused many people to overindulge and become vulnerable to the exploitations of white traders. That alcohol as an economic and cultural border had been reintroduced under Du-en-quot's leadership was a second plank in Between-the-Logs's political critique of the head chief. For Between-the-Logs, Finley's evangelical revivalism had posed an innovative opportunity to cultivate an alternative composite methodology precisely because it forbade the use of alcohol.[23]

23. Peter C. Mancall, "Men, Women, and Alcohol in Indian Villages in the Great Lakes Region in the Early Republic," *Journal of the Early Republic* 15 (Autumn 1995), 425–48, quote on 436.

It is important here to differentiate between evangelicalism as an interpretation of Christianity and evangelicalism as a form of epistemology. Evangelicalism as an expression of Christianity transformed the Protestant world by critiquing the Calvinist doctrine of predestination. This led to the First Great Awakening. The Second Great Awakening used this evangelical approach to produce revivalism in the early nineteenth century. Revivalism, with which Finley identified, became an epistemology for which evangelicals could detect the true working of the Holy Spirit in man. Once hearing the word of God, an individual might experience a significant physical reaction. If the physical reaction was deemed "authentic" by trained observers of the clergy, the reaction became evidence, or proof, of conversion. If the believer continued on his "new life," the evidence became more convincing over time.[24]

Evangelicalism as an epistemology stripped of its theological tenets, however, could reinvigorate the indigenous individual. Consider the following account from Finley at a Methodist quarterly meeting in which Wyandot chief Seuteash addressed the white audience:

> I have been a great sinner and drunkard, which made me commit many great crimes, and the Great Spirit was very angry with me, so that in here (pointing to his breast,) I always sick. No sleep—no eat—no walk—drink whisky heap; but I pray the Great Spirit to help me quit getting drunk, and forgive all my sins, and he did do something for me. I do not know whence it comes, or whither it goes. (Here he cried out, "waugh! Waugh!" as if shocked by electricity.) Now me no more sick—no more drink whisky—no more get drunk—me sleep—me eat; no more bad man—me cry—me meet you all in our great Father's house above.

Finley's paternalistic transcription aside, the story suggested revivalism posed a powerful opportunity; just as the Holy Spirit, manifested through electricity, could transcend Seuteash's internal struggle with

24. For a discussion of evangelicalism and its definitions see Craig James Hazen, *The Village Enlightenment in America: Popular Religion and Science in the Nineteenth Century* (Urbana, IL, 2000); Nathan O. Hatch, *The Democratization of American Christianity* (New Haven, CT, 1989); Richard J. Carwardine, *Evangelicals and Politics in Antebellum America* (Knoxville, TN, 1997); Mark A. Noll, George A. Rawlyk, and David W. Bebbington, eds., *Evangelicalism: Comparative Studies of Popular Protestantism in North America, the British Isles and Beyond, 1700–1990* (New York, 1994).

alcohol, so too could evangelical revival intersect an individual's internal struggle with the decentralized marketplace. This epistemology was precisely what Between-the-Logs was seeking. He too had succumbed to the power of alcohol. After the War of 1812, he returned to Sandusky and began drinking heavily. He reportedly killed his wife in a drunken stupor after accusing her of being a witch. He had also gone into debt with white traders who exploited him. The solution to these troubles, for Between-the-Logs, was not an external political struggle based on treaties between the Wyandot and the American government. He thought the Fort Meigs Treaty gave up too much territorial sovereignty and threatened the social stability of the Wyandot. He believed rather that the solution should be based on the individual's struggle to confront white imperialist borders, and the epistemology of revivalism seemed to have the power to invert external borders just as it had the power to reshape internal struggles. Thus he was encumbered by new American borders and Wyandot traditions. Between-the-Logs had become convinced that evangelicalism as an epistemology, not traditional feasts or treaties, could efficaciously reconcile his internal struggle with external American borders and Wyandot traditions. And it gave Between-the-Logs, and other Wyandot, a new epistemology from which to remember and reinterpret Tarhe's political strategies in a new landscape of multiplying indigenous and Euro American borders.[25]

This sort of amalgamation was nothing new. Wyandot thinkers had been incorporating different ideas into their religious practices for centuries. Wyandot religious beliefs were dynamic and complex, and their leaders were influenced heavily by the experiences of diaspora and hybridity. This gave the Christian Wyandot the experience and skill to incorporate aspects of Christianity without assimilating into Western

25. Finley, *History*, 99–100. Seuteash's sounds "as if shocked by electricity" were important signs for Finley. He interpreted them to mean that the Holy Spirit was present in Seuteash's conversion, which is important evidence for a revivalist who believed that the Holy Spirit became manifest in energy sources described by converts to feel like electricity. Finley spoke on behalf of Seuteash, so the true meaning of the chief's words is not exact when one considers the process described by Edward Said as "Orientalism." We might call this "Indianism" as it applies to the relationship between Finley and the Wyandot. Nevertheless, Finley believed Seuteash's conversion was authentic because he believed evidence of electricity "proved" it. See Said, *Orientalism* (New York, 1978).

culture. It is important to note that the Wyandot Christians saw the worthiness of evangelicalism not for its Christian understanding of time, space, or theology but for its epistemological value in recollecting the past and making it useable in the present. It was effective because Christian Wyandot took evangelicalism as a structure of American decentralized imperialism, inverted it into a type of Wyandot agency, and then used it to assert control over their political and cultural destinies. One example occurred when Chief Mononcue accompanied Finley on a preaching trip to a white settlement. After the sermon, Mononcue appealed to the settlers, saying that "the scalping knife and tomahawk are buried, not only in practice, but God has taken away the disposition out of my heart, and I hope out of yours also." He referred to the collective memory of past wars and the power of Christianity to transform the boundaries of the Ohio Valley between Wyandots and white Americans. It was an assertive appeal in which Mononcue stressed that they could live in peace as neighbors, "but one thing must be done, if this is the case. You, my friends, must leave off bringing your water of death, (meaning whiskey) and selling to my people, or we never can live in peace." The next year, Mononcue accompanied Finley on a trip to Michigan and stayed at a white man's house. Mononcue noticed the man had alcohol and asked Finley if the man was a Christian. Finley replied that the man was. Mononcue in disbelief asked, "How can that be . . . all such ought to be kept out of the Church, or turned out if they were in and would not quit it." Evangelicalism as an epistemology only worked, in the mind of Mononcue, if it insulated the Wyandot from alcohol. If this border could not be inverted, neighborly coexistence would be impossible despite the Christian belief of white people.[26]

It was highly unlikely that the Christian Wyandot viewed their new experiences as exclusively Christian. It was more probable that Christian Wyandot had a different understanding of the Christian God than Finley. The Methodist missionary, who did not speak the Wyandot language, used the language of "great spirit," "Homendezue," and "God" interchangeably when trying to discuss the Christian God with the Wyandot. Christian Wyandot used the same terms. In the late nineteenth century, anthropologist C. M. Barbeau contended that Hamendiju was translated as "His-voice-is big or powerful" and that the name was "unknown in

26. Finley, *History*, 131, 222.

the narrations of earliest missionaries and explorers." The main Wyandot word denoting an "almighty" was a product of cultural exchange and likely came into usage only after European missionaries took Christianity to them. The Wyandot of Barbeau's time used "Hamendiju" to refer to the "'Great Man above'" who "'has all the powers, and he rules over many spirits who obey his commands.'" Rather than understanding God as Finley did, Wyandot believers translated God into their mother tongue.[27]

This theological flexibility became an important aspect in the Christian Wyandot ability to embrace aspects of Christianity without assimilating into American culture. In fact, chief Mononcue seemed never to let go of his traditional view of time and space. While in New York, Mononcue saw a statue of a great sea turtle and claimed it was his grandmother; a clear reference to the traditionalist cosmological ethos. The Wyandot translated God into their mother tongue and amalgamated traditional and evangelical epistemologies primarily by ignoring evangelical theology. This constituted an evolution in Christianity—what religious studies scholar Lamin Sanneh describes as world Christianity—a Christian expression that de-centers the European understanding of religion and congeals around the mother tongue and experiences of native people(s). Separating evangelical theology from European history made Christian revivalism—as an epistemology—relevant to Native Americans' efforts to transcend external borders. It became a new experience in the Ohio Valley and remade the borderlands in which the Wyandot and American settlers had to navigate. In doing this the Wyandot had invented a completely new interpretation of evangelical Christianity one based on a composite of Wyandot and Christian beliefs. Indeed the competing epistemologies of experiencing the borderlands—Du-en-quot's approach versus Between-the-Logs's and Mononcue's evangelical epistemology—demonstrated how dynamic and fluid the borderlands could be. This dual Wyandot experience of the borderlands should be seen as a multivalent strategy of agency that, on the one hand, allowed Christian Indians to confront white Americans face to face as individuals on their own theological turf and, on the other hand, permitted non-Christian Indians to assert their ideas about transcending and remaking borders in spaces

27. C. M. Barbeau, "Supernatural Beings of the Huron and Wyandot," *American Anthropologist* 16 (Apr.-June 1914), 288–313, quote on 301, 302.

where few, if any, whites could go. This hybridized strategy was conceived from the experiences of diaspora as remembered by a new generation of Wyandot leadership who sought to rebuild sovereignty in the post-Revolutionary reality of borderlands.[28]

From Between-the-Logs's perspective, evangelicalism, as an epistemology, seemed to help bring stability to the reservation. The Christian Wyandot chiefs found in Finley a formidable ally in chastising white traders. For example, white traders often attended Finley's church meetings on the reservation, and Finley rebuked them. "I made this my opportunity of telling the Indians how wicked these traders were, in selling them whiskey and in making them drunk: then robbing their children and wives of what they ought to have to clothe and feed them." The missionary also assumed a powerful office that the Wyandot exploited, when Finley took on the duties of government sub-agent in 1824. After a dispute with sub-agent Charles Shaw, the government replaced him with Finley, mainly because Finley agreed to do the job without pay. The Methodist now held the religious and secular offices in the region. The Wyandot exploited this arrangement because the previous sub-agent had allowed many whites to squat on their land; Finley

28. Finley, *History*, 347. Walsh, "The 'Heathen Party,'" 200; Lamin Sanneh, *Whose Religion is Christianity?: The Gospel Beyond the West* (Grand Rapids, MI, 2003), 10. Sanneh focuses on postcolonial Africa for his description of world Christianity defined as the moment that the Christian God is translated into the indigenous mother tongue. The Wyandot, much like many African communities, were also negotiating a decolonizing space, and thus Sanneh's description of world Christianity aptly describes the hybridity of Wyandot traditions and evangelical Christianity. See also David Lindenfeld, "The Varieties of Sioux Christianity, 1860-1980, in International Perspective," *Journal of Global History* 2 (Nov. 2007), 281–302; Jean Comaroff and John L. Comaroff, *Of Revelation and Revolution* (Chicago, 1991); Anthony P. Cohen, *The Symbolic Construction of Community* (London, 1985), 55–56. Cohen, an anthropologist, claims that members of a community usually take different meaning(s) from the symbols while maintaining their membership in the community. In fact, the symbols further cement the boundaries between different groups interacting with the same symbols. This characterizes the relationship between traditional and Christian Wyandot who, although they interpreted the symbols differently, retained a Wyandot identity because of their shared colonized relationship to the colonizer.

prosecuted the squatters and got much of the land back. This was probably less the work of Finley and more the imaginative leadership of the Wyandot Christian chiefs who effectively manipulated his office to protect their territory. Between-the-Logs's past political proficiency at negotiating and evaluating political alliances for Tarhe's regime before the middle ground collapsed gave him plenty of experiences from which to remember when fashioning an alliance with the Methodist missionary and even with the U.S. government to assert Wyandot control of the land.[29]

Finley's dual position also formed a conduit through which Wyandot chiefs could criticize U.S. government removal policy. When the Secretary of Indian Affairs Thomas McKenney, himself an evangelical and a devotee to the idea that only Christian Indians could become civilized, wrote to Finley in 1824 warning him to prepare the Indians for removal, the Wyandot responded to the War Department. They "reminded the Secretary that at the last treaty (the treaty at Fort Meigs) they were told, and most sacredly promised, that if they would cede all their lands, except the present reservations, they would never be spoken to again on this subject." They also reminded the Secretary that, "Governor Cass promised, in the most solemn manner, that the President would make a strong fence around them, and maintain them in the peaceable and quiet possession of that spot for ever." As evidence of their ability to stay on the land, the chiefs claimed that they "were making progress in religion, and in the cultivation of their lands; their children were at school, and promised to make good citizens; that they were now happy, and well satisfied." The Wyandot had demanded explicitly that the United States acknowledge Wyandot sovereignty. These sorts of strategies were imagined by Wyandot leaders in the era before the middle ground collapsed but crafted now in effective and innovative ways.[30]

They persuaded Finley to recommend against removal. He wrote, "Their prospect for civilization is very promising," and he "used [his]

---

29. Finley, *History*, 121. See Robert E. Smith, "The Clash of Leadership at the Grand Reserve: The Wyandot Subagency and the Methodist Mission, 1820–1824," *Ohio History* 89 (Spring 1980), 181–205 http://publications.ohiohistory.org/ohstemplate.cfm?action=detail&Page=0089181.html&StartPage=181&EndPage=205&volume=89¬es=&newtitle=Volume%2089%20Page%20181, accessed Aug. 15, 2011; Finley, *History*, 326.

30. Francis Paul Prucha, *The Great Father*, 141, 294.

influence to persuade the Indians not to sell, but remain where they were." McKenney then sent Judge Leib to inspect the Upper Sandusky reservation, and the Wyandot did everything they could to make sure the judge issued a favorable report. Judge Leib's report to the War Department supported Wyandot claims, noting "in short, they are the only Indians within the circle of my visits, whom I consider as entirely reclaimed, and whom I should consider it *a cruelty to attempt to remove.*" He added "they are so far advanced, in my opinion, as to be beyond the reach of deterioration." Where Du-en-quot would most certainly have had difficulties, the Christian Wyandot used Finley to provide them with insulation from encroachment and removal.[31]

The Christian Wyandot also used Finley as a fundraising source from church congregations in the East. The Missionary Society of the Methodist Episcopal Church and the Philadelphia Missionary Society gave the Wyandot $2,160.47 for clothing and feeding of 50 to 60 children. This was over half of the annual government allotment received from the Fort Meigs Treaty. But the most powerful way the Christians influenced their destiny was not through Finley's paltry but helpful fundraising, but through evangelicalism. Although Finley brought this epistemology to the Wyandot, the Christian contingent hybridized it and used it to control the geography of emerging borders. For example, one year Between-the-Logs needed to spend the summer hunting to raise enough money to pay off his debts. A few weeks after his hunting party left the village, Finley began hearing reports of Indians holding church services in the woods. Out of curiosity, some whites started attending but also tried to trade with the Wyandot. Between-the-Logs confronted them. Although he could not read, he had Finley mark the passage of the Ten Commandments in his Bible. He opened the Bible to this place and asked a white man to read the passage after which Between-the-Logs chastised him. "Here you are trying not only to break this law of God but to get us poor Indians to do so too. Of this you ought to be ashamed; and never do so again. My white brothers, go home, and never go to trade again on the Sabbath." As Sanneh notes, "Bible translation [into the mother tongue] enabled Christianity to break the cultural filibuster of its Western domestication to create movements of resurgence and renewal." Between-the-Logs used the experience of borderlands and the epistemol-

31. Finley, *History*, 300–301, 366.

ogy of evangelicalism to translate the Bible and transcend unofficial but effective borders in the forest.[32]

Despite all of this, evangelicalism held significant weaknesses. Primarily it could not overcome the process of "Indianism." No matter how Christian, how civilized, how sophisticated the Wyandot were, they could never overcome the stereotypes Americans leveled against them. For example, Finley took Between-the-Logs and Mononcue on a three-month tour to New York City, Philadelphia, and Baltimore to raise funds and awareness of the mission at Upper Sandusky. Several missionary societies had heard of what transpired among the Wyandot and were anxious to see first-hand the effects of evangelicalism in the minds of "the heathen." This was a lucrative journey, as they collected seven hundred dollars in New York, yet they paid a high price in the face of exploitation. Bishop Soule had forwarded a letter to Finley in New York asking the missionary to dress the chiefs in a particular fashion. "We wish to see them in Baltimore, in a plain, decent, and comfortable English habit in full." Between-the-Logs did not disappoint; he entertained the congregation beyond all expectation. While he was preaching, his interpreter fell sick. Undaunted, the chief proceeded to act out a dramatic interpretation of the crucifixion. Finley exclaimed,

> To close his description of the scene, this eloquent chief then leaned his head on his left shoulder, signifying that Christ had dismissed his spirit. Then he turned his right side to the congregation, and with this left hand pulled up his vest; and with his right hand, representing a spear, he struck his side as though he had pierced to his heart, and drew it back quick with a whizzing [sic] noise, as if you had heard the blood streaming, and held his hand out, as though the blood was dripping from it as from the point of the spear. This was a scene beyond description. The whole congregation was in a flood of tear, and expressed their feelings by shouts of joy . . . for no man could speak and act as he did, without supernatural aid.

This was a classic translation of the Crucifixion story into Between-the-Log's mother tongue. But the Americans were unwilling to transcribe the hybrid translation. Thus they only witnessed what they wanted to witness—a heathen turned Christian. Instead Bishop Soule got more than he had wished; Between-the-Logs had entertained the people and

32. Ibid., 247–50; Sanneh, *Whose Religion is Christianity?*, 130.

the people wondered at the power of the Holy Spirit and the bodily performance of a "converted heathen." Finley retranslated Between-the-Logs into a "converted heathen" for his book, and the Wyandot received nothing in return from this congregation, not even money. In fact, Between-the-Logs's performance seemed only to empower the stereotype; he had become the metonym of "Christianize, then civilize."[33]

A second problem with this mixed traditional–evangelical epistemology was that the overly rigid moral code of evangelicalism often did not resolve the internal struggles with borderlands but, sometimes, magnified them. Chief Seuteash did not succeed at remaining a Christian and eventually returned to drinking. Chief of the Big Turtle Tribe, Seuteash began drinking whiskey within a few years after he converted. Finley went to him and accused the chief. "You must have slackened your hold of the Saviour, or you could not have fallen in this way." The chief agreed and claimed he had become discouraged and stopped praying—soon after white traders had convinced him that prayer was pointless. Seuteash promised to re-reform and gave up whiskey for a period. When he started drinking a second time, Finley returned; this time the missionary challenged the chief's masculinity. Finley said,

> I am disposed to believe that you are not half the great man or chief that the people say you are . . . I think Molly . . . is a much stouter *man* than you are, and has much more courage to resist than you have. You must be a perfect *squaw*, and worse, if you cannot quit getting drunk, and prevent whiskey from overcoming you.

According to Finley, only weak men and women could fail. Seuteash, now challenged, promised to repent but eventually gave up the epistemological exercise; it was too difficult and exacerbated his internal struggle with borderlands. For Seuteash, evangelicalism had produced uncomfortable spaces and became something to forget.[34]

Despite experiences like Seuteash's, new interdependent relationships between non-Christian and Christian Wyandots and Christian mission-

---

33. The term "Indianism" is similar to the process Edward Said describes, except it pertains specifically to American's treatment of Native Americans. Finley, *History*, 354–55, 359–60.

34. Ibid., 334.

aries could reconstruct the Ohio River Valley. Although Finley believed he was bringing Christianity to the Wyandot at Upper Sandusky, it seems that the Wyandot were much more in control than Finley could understand. The Wyandot constructed a new interpretation of Christianity—one that separated the religion from the American national narrative—based on the memories of Wyandot traditions and political strategies of hybridism developed in a previous era when the middle ground was more stable. Nevertheless, at the very moment that Pequot Indian and Christian convert William Apess's "An Indian's Looking-Glass for the White Man" criticized white America for erasing Native American culture, Finley's text likewise erased Wyandot culture; white America would not find out about the innovative hybrid Wyandot Christian critique of American expansion in part because Finley's book effectively destroyed this heterogeneity in the minds of Eastern readers. He retold the Christian story not as a Wyandot story but as an American story where James Finley became a type of Christ and Wyandot chiefs became a type of twelve disciples all working together to bring salvation to the Wyandot, just as Jesus brought salvation to sinners. Despite his claims that Wyandot removal was immoral because he had "civilized" them, his *History* was imperialistic because it had tied American history to Christianity and failed to acknowledge how the Wyandot translated god into their own language, constructed their own identity, and built their own notions of sovereignty. American imperialism was not so much enacted in the American periphery, but in the case of Finley's *History,* it had affected the imagination of people in the American core. As Sanneh reminds, "No human being deserves to have his or her mother tongue denied whatever the appeal of a lingua franca." From this perspective, Finley's text helped construct a type of interlanguage by mixing Christianity and American history together into a single myth. This in turn helped legitimize the lingua franca of expansion as invented by the American core in order to imagine the imperial periphery.[35]

In deconstructing Finley's text, it becomes evident that the Wyandot had dismantled successfully this fiction at Upper Sandusky. Finley exaggerated the claim that over half the Wyandot population had converted

35. William Apess was the first Native American author accepted into the canon of American literature. Sanneh, *Whose Religion is Christianity?*, 73; Prucha, *The Great Father*, 247–48.

when he left. This ultimately blinded him from giving credit to the Wyandot for what they had achieved. The Christian Wyandot had developed an entirely new expression of evangelical Christianity based on hybridity, while both Christian and traditionalist Wyandot had reshaped the Wyandot core and reshaped the landscape of the Ohio Valley. They had made borders that confronted the atomized expansion of American settlers successfully. Despite overlapping memories and internal disagreements, the Wyandot had succeeded in creating an infrastructure that first stymied U.S. efforts to remove them and proved later removal would be remembered forever as an immoral action. Indeed the Wyandot were first officially asked to remove their nation in 1824 but successfully delayed the process for years and finally left Ohio in 1843. One chief claimed, "From a nation of drunkards, we have become a sober people." It was neither the drunkenness nor sobriety that was important as much as how this statement represented the sovereignty of collective memory and a hybridized method of agency.[36]

36. Finley, *History*, 376.

Women and Property in Early Louisiana

Legal Systems at Odds

SARA BROOKS SUNDBERG

On the night of October 6, 1834, Ursule Trahan, a middle-aged French-speaking farm woman from West Baton Rouge Parish, Louisiana, filled the cart sitting outside her home with most of the furniture, bedding, kitchen utensils and cash from the house. She then drove away into the night leaving her house, her husband, and the rest of her moveable property behind. Two weeks later Ursule Trahan filed a petition in the Fourth District Court in West Baton Rouge Parish that claimed her actions were necessary because of her husband's "mismanagement" of the couple's property, and her fears that he would squander her dowry along with the property the couple held in common. She asked that the Court "enjoin" her husband, Rosémond Bourg, from any further "administration or alienation of her property." She also requested a legal separation of property from her husband, a complete inventory of their mutual property, and the right to exclusive administration of her own

Sara Brooks Sundberg teaches in the Department of History and Anthropology at the University of Central Missouri. This project received financial support from a Franklin Research Grant, American Philosophical Society; Michael Kraus Research Grant in Colonial American History, American Historical Association; and Creative Assistance Grant, University of Central Missouri. Portions of this research were originally presented as papers at the Tenth Annual Conference of the Omohundro Institute of Early American History and Culture, Smith College; the Ninety-ninth Annual Meeting of the Organization of American Historians, Washington, DC; and the 121st Annual Meeting of the American Historical Association, Atlanta, Georgia. The author would like to thank the panelists, commentators and audiences from these conferences, along with the anonymous reviewers from the *JER* for their critical comments and suggestions.

Journal of the Early Republic, 32 (Winter 2012)

property. Ailing and illiterate, Ursule Trahan approved her petition with the mark of an X.[1]

For his part, Rosémond Bourg denied his wife's allegations and claimed not only that he had managed the couple's property with "great care," but also had dutifully cared for her during her recent illness. In fact, her "malicious" petition prevented him from harvesting the couple's cotton and corn crop for that year—a better crop, he claimed, than Ursule Trahan had ever produced independently on the farm. Rosémond Bourg claimed his wife's behavior left him "entirely destitute of all these necessities." The Court placed an injunction against Bourg, preventing him from selling or changing the property in question in any way until it reconvened to consider his wife's petition. The final decision of the Court in response to Ursule Trahan's petition is not extant.[2]

Ursule Trahan's story is significant because it contradicts commonly accepted ideas about early American women's "enforced dependence" and legal disability under American law. Two things are apparent from her story: One is that she understood her legal rights and believed that the equity guaranteed her under the civil law legal system in Louisiana allowed for redress of her grievances against her husband. The other is that she owned property that provided her both the motivation and security to challenge a marriage she believed detrimental to her own interests. Ursule Trahan acquired the wealth that underwrote her separation from her husband because of rights guaranteed to her under Louisiana civil law. These included the right to inherit equally, with her brothers and sisters, from her parents' estate, the right to half of the community property from each of her marriages, and the right to own separate property. None of these privileges were fully available to women under the common-law system that prevailed in most early American colonies and states. After each of her first two husbands' deaths, Trahan received the marital portion legal under Louisiana civil law or half of the community property of the marriage. As a result, between 1829 when her first husband died and 1834 when Trahan died, she increased the value of her property by half. Each time she remarried Trahan protected

1. Case #480, *Ursule Trahan, wife of Rosémond Bourg* v. *Rosémond Bourg, her husband*, Fourth District Court, West Baton Rouge Parish, West Baton Rouge Courthouse, Port Allen, Louisiana (hereafter cited as WBR).

2. Ibid.

the inheritance she had received from her parents and her marital portions from the previous marriages as separate property, thereby preserving it for her own use and for eventual division among her children. By the time she died Trahan owned a modest estate made up of two tracts of land totaling about 48 acres, seven slaves, a few livestock, farming equipment, and household furnishings. Altogether her estate appraised at nearly $7,000. It was this estate that she accused her third husband of wasting through poor management.[3]

What does Ursule Trahan's case against her husband tell us about women, law, and property in the early republic? Law was a critical factor in determining women's rights to property and, as a result, it played a crucial role in shaping women's power and independence in early America. Ursule Trahan's story echoes these themes, reminding us that it mattered deeply to individual women whether they owned and controlled property. In Trahan's case her rights to the property she owned provided her power over her marriage, even if that power was only the ability to leave her husband and still maintain economic security. How she acquired her property is also an important facet of her story. Trahan acquired her wealth because there were elements of civil law that enabled women to maintain a measure of control over property. Equally important is the fact that Trahan and her family were ethnic French. Unlike her Anglo neighbors, she possessed a familiarity with civil law rooted in her family history and a long tradition of French and Spanish civil law in Louisiana. Her actions indicate that she not only understood the law but also suffered no hesitation in applying it. Finally, when viewed in the broader context of women's property rights in the early republic, Trahan appears to be a fortunate woman, despite her personal troubles. The year she filed her court case in Louisiana, Trahan lived in the only place

---

3. Marylynn Salmon, *Women and the Law of Property in Early America* (Chapel Hill, NC, 1986), xv; despite their overall legal disability scholars have demonstrated that some women found ways to manipulate the law to their advantage. See, for example, Vivian Bruce Conger, *The Widows' Might: Widowhood and Gender in Early British America* (New York, 2009); and Linda L. Sturtz, *Within Her Power: Propertied Women in Colonial Virginia* (New York, 2002); Succession Records, #'s 174, 213 and 250, WBR; Marriage Bonds Book I, WBR. The American law system referred to here is the system of laws that governed in England and that England exported to its colonies. The civil law refers to legal systems, based on Roman laws, that were transported to America from continental Europe.

in the United States that fully provided married women the kind of legal rights to property that were possible under civil law. To appreciate what that means for women's property-holding in the early republic, it is important to know how typical her experience is among all women in early Louisiana and how her story compares with those of women under common law, the predominant legal system in the early republic.[4]

Certainly some nineteenth-century observers, like English women's-rights activist Harriet Martineau, believed that women benefited economically from the civil law tradition and that they were better off in

---

4. Economists disagree over the relative weight of money in shaping the distribution of power in modern households in comparison to other factors such as patriarchy. This study addresses that question in a historical context. See Joyce P. Jacobsen, *The Economics of Gender* (Malden, MA, 1998), 83–84. The role of custom in shaping legal practice in Louisiana is discussed in Hans W. Baade, "Marriage Contracts in French and Spanish Louisiana: A Study in Notarial Jurisprudence," *Tulane Law Review* 53, no. 1 (1978), 1–92; in 1835, a year after Trahan sued in court, twenty-three states and four territories were part of the United States. Many southern and upper Midwest states and territories in this group were at one time governed by civil law but, through various repealing mechanisms when they were annexed to the United States, removed the civilian legal system and replaced it with common law, though not always all at once. Some states, like Michigan, expressly repealed civil law and others, like Florida, adopted common law but retained married women's property rights, but only for women who married prior to 1818. In 1835 Louisiana's next-door neighbor, Texas, was soon to become an independent republic. The provisional government of Texas mandated common law in criminal matters and the Louisiana Civil Code in civil matters, replacing the Code with their own legislation in 1836. See Judith T. Younger, "Marital Regimes: A Story of Compromise and Demoralization, Together with Criticism and Suggestions for Reform," *Cornell Law Review* 67, no. 1 (1981), 53; Laurel A. Clark, "The Rights of a Florida Wife: Slavery, U.S. Expansion and Married Women's Property Law," *Journal of Women's History* 22, no. 4 (2010), 43; and Jean A. Stuntz, *Hers, His, & Theirs: Community Property Law in Spain & Early Texas* (Lubbock, TX, 2005), 136–37. Louisiana's legal system, like Texas, is a mixed legal system because it incorporated some elements of common law, particularly in regard to court procedures and jury trials. For a discussion of how this occurred in Louisiana and the role of the judiciary in that process, see Mark Fernandez, *From Chaos to Continuity: The Evolution of Louisiana's Judicial System, 1712–1862* (Baton Rouge, LA, 2001). The Americanization of English common law also required adaptations in law to local conditions and customs, as in the example of discontinuing primogeniture. Women's property rights and legal status were not areas where legal scholars argued for any accommodation or change in common law. See Ellen Holmes Pearson, *Remaking Custom: Law and Identity in the Early American Republic* (Charlottesville, VA, 2011), 105–111.

places like Louisiana in terms of property-holding and personal freedom than women in common law jurisdictions.

> If this condition of the marriage law would strike any English persons as a peculiarity it is well that they should know that it is the English alone who vary from the old Saxon law, that a wife shall possess half. . . . I never met any lawyer, or other citizen with whom I conversed on the subject, who was not ashamed of the barbarism of the law under which a woman's property goes into her husband's hands along with herself.

There is no quantitative study of the practical effects of civil law on Louisiana women's property holding to support Martineau's observation. When historians have examined law in relation to women and property the focus has generally been on a single legal system or a comparison of provisions between civil and common legal systems, as Martineau does. One article has focused on a comparison of colonial New Mexico and New York and found that that women under civil law in New Mexico enjoyed "tangible benefits" and "income producing property" when compared with women under common law in New York. But, colonial New Mexico and New York were vastly different in terms of physical environment, economy, and culture, introducing the possibility that regional differences, as well as law, influenced women's property ownership. Thus, we still need to compare common and civil law jurisdictions from similar environs. We also need to know more about what happened to women's property rights and property when the colonial period ended, especially in places like Louisiana where civil law, or elements of civil law, was retained.[5]

---

5. Harriet Martineau, *Society in America* (London, 1837), 3: 121–22; for other examples of nineteenth-century observations that comment favorably on civil law and its effects on women's property holding and influence see Susan C. Boyle, "'Did She Generally Decide?' Women in Ste. Genevieve, 1750–1805," *William and Mary Quarterly* 44 (Oct. 1987), 775–89; Donna C. Schuele, "Community Property Law and the Politics of Married Women's Rights in Nineteenth-Century California," *Western Legal History* 7, no. 2 (1994), 255; historical studies about women and the law in early Louisiana have mostly outlined Louisiana's marital laws as they pertained to women during the French and Spanish colonial periods. See Vaughan Baker, Amos Simpson, and Mathé Allain, "*Le Mari Est Seigneur*: Marital Law Governing Women in French Louisiana," in *Louisiana's Legal Heritage*, ed. Robert R. Macdonald and Edward Haas (Pensacola, FL, 1983), 1–6; Jack D. L. Holmes, "'Do It, Don't Do It!' Spanish Laws on Sex and Marriage,"

This study addresses these questions by analyzing Louisiana women's property-holding with a comparable region during the early years of the republic. Specifically, this study compares female wealth-holding in four Louisiana parishes under Louisiana civil law with female wealth-holding in two neighboring counties in southern Mississippi under common law between 1811and 1835. Together, the Mississippi and Louisiana jurisdictions provide a baseline of information about the effects of civil and common law on women's wealth-holding along a contiguous transect of counties and parishes with highly similar plantation economies. Viewed in this perspective, the comparison of women's property-holding under civil and common law demonstrates the positive influence of civil law on women's property-holding, and it exposes issues pertaining to the adherence to civil law. Louisiana women benefited economically from civil law in comparison with Mississippi women under common law, but not all women in Louisiana benefited equally. Ethnic French women, like Ursule Trahan, received more economic benefits from civil law than their Anglo counterparts because they and their families adhered to Louisiana law. Ethnicity and legal custom were not only key factors in explaining why Louisiana retained civil law; they were key factors in determining whether women benefited from the law.[6]

---

in *Louisiana's Legal Heritage,* 19–42; Nina Nichols Pugh, "The Spanish Community of Gains in 1803: *Sociedad de Gananciales,*" *Louisiana Law Review* 30, no. 1 (1969), 1–17. Carole Shammas's quantitative study of women's wealth is an example of an investigation of the economic effects of law in multiple common law regions. See "Early American Women and Control Over Capital," in *Women in the Age of the American Revolution*, ed. Ronald Hoffman and Peter J. Albert (Charlottesville, VA, 1989), 134–54; Deborah A. Rosen, "Women and Property Across Colonial America: A Comparison of Legal Systems in New Mexico and New York," *William and Mary Quarterly* 60 (Apr. 2003), 355–81. Historian Jack P. Greene argues that the cultural remnants from political transfers in early America, like civil law, are "relatively understudied." This essay speaks to the need for more study on this topic. See Jack P. Greene, "The Cultural Dimensions of Political Transfers: An Aspect of the European Occupation of the Americas," *Early American Studies* 6 (Spring 2008), 1, 13–14.

6. There are numerous studies that demonstrate the positive economic effects of civil law on women, especially for Spanish colonial and Hispanic America. Among these studies the closest in comparison to this study are those about upper Louisiana (the Illinois Country) under French and Spanish colonial legal systems, both of which informed Louisiana law. See Boyle, "Did She Generally Decide?" and Judith A. Gilbert, "Esther and Her Sisters: Free Women of Color as Property

The respective legal systems of both Louisiana and Mississippi have a long history. Louisiana began as a French colony and followed French civil law principles until 1763, when the region became part of Spanish colonial America governed by Spanish civil law. After the Louisiana Purchase in 1803, the region encompassed in present-day Louisiana became an American territory known as the Territory of Orleans, with the exception of a section of the northern Gulf coast east of the Mississippi River, known as West Florida, which was occupied alternately by Great Britain and then Spain. Two of the Louisiana parishes in this study, East Baton Rouge and West Feliciana Parishes, were located in the westernmost part of West Florida. Adams and Wilkinson County, Mississippi, also part of this study, were initially settled by the French and later became part of Spanish West Florida, until 1795 when the northern boundary of West Florida was reconfirmed at the 31st parallel. The counties became part of the Mississippi Territory in 1798 and quickly adopted common law. The other two Louisiana parishes in this study, Point Coupee and West Baton Rouge Parishes lying west of the Mississippi river, were originally part of the Louisiana Purchase and later part of the American Territory of Orleans. West Florida declared its independence from Spain in 1810 and joined with the rest of Louisiana to become a state in 1812. The area that encompasses Louisiana today, with the exception of West Florida between 1763 and 1783 while it was governed by Great Britain, has a continuous history of civil law. This happened, in part, because longtime Spanish- and French-speaking inhabitants resisted the wholesale imposition of common law in the Territory of Orleans. The new state constitution in 1812 even included a provision that effectively prevented the adoption of common law. (See Figure 1.)[7]

Owners in Colonial St. Louis, 1765–1803," *Gateway Heritage* 17, no. 1 (1996), 14–23. Because I am concerned with property laws as they pertain to women I do not examine the experiences of black women, most of whom, in this region, were typically considered to be property themselves. The small number of free women of color in the parishes and counties I investigated precluded discussing them as a group.

7. For an overview of Louisiana's colonial and early statehood history, see Bennett H. Wall, Light Townsend Cummins, Judith Kelleher Schafer, Edward F. Haas, and Michael L. Kurtz, *Louisiana: A History* (Wheeling, IL, 2002), 3–86; and Rose Meyers, *A History of Baton Rouge, 1699–1812* (Baton Rouge, LA,

Much of Louisiana's French-speaking population lived, and still lives, in a distinct region of the state south of the 31st parallel along the boundary between Louisiana and Mississippi. From the state boundary, the eastern terminus of the French-speaking sector extends along a line that runs in a southeasterly direction along the Mississippi River to the Gulf. The western boundary of French settlement falls along a line that extends from the 31st parallel in a southwesterly direction to the far southwest corner of the state. All of the Louisiana parishes in this study lie within or along this wide triangle of ethnic French settlement.[8]

Anglo settlement in Louisiana is located mostly north of the 31st parallel, but Anglo settlers began migrating in significant numbers into British West Florida, including West Feliciana and East Baton Rouge Parishes, in the late 1700s. Enticed by rich soils and generous land grants from the British and later by the refuge the region offered Loyalists from the American Revolution, this region comprised a largely Anglo population intent on establishing large-scale plantation agriculture. West Feliciana Parish formed part of the southern boundary of the Natchez District, a prosperous, cotton-growing region that encompassed Adams and Wilkinson counties and extended northward all the way to Vicksburg,

---

1976). The Anglo-American treaty of 1783 set the boundary at the 31st parallel even though Spanish control extended to the 32nd parallel. Pinckney's Treaty reconfirmed the 31st parallel as the northern boundary. See D. Clayton James, *Antebellum Natchez* (Baton Rouge, LA, 1968), 28–29 and Thomas Perkins Abernethy, *The South in the New Nation, 1789–1819: A History of the South,* Vol. 4 (Baton Rouge, LA, 1961), 242–43; French inhabitants in upper and lower Louisiana were among those who resisted the wholesale imposition of common law but only lower Louisiana retained a civilian legal system. See George Dargo, *Jefferson's Louisiana: Politics and the Clash of Legal Traditions* (Cambridge, MA, 1975); Morris S. Arnold, *Unequal Laws Unto a Savage Race: European Legal Traditions in Arkansas, 1686–1836* (Fayetteville, AR, 1985); Stuart Banner, *Legal Systems in Conflict: Property and Sovereignty in Missouri, 1750–1860* (Norman, OK, 2000); Edward F. Haass, "Louisiana's Legal Heritage: An Introduction," in *Louisiana's Legal Heritage*, 4. I would like to thank Marshall D. Sundberg for assistance with the maps.

8. Ethnic French are those French-speaking immigrants to Louisiana from France or Canada and their descendants; a nuanced explanation of the French-speaking population in Louisiana is found in Carl A. Brasseaux, *French, Cajun, Creole, Houma: A Primer on Francophone Louisiana* (Baton Rouge, LA, 2005); the overall pattern of ethnic settlement is drawn from Fred B. Kniffen, *Louisiana, Its Land and People* (Baton Rouge, LA, 1968), 5–9.

Figure 1: Map of Study Area, Adams and Wilkinson County, Mississippi, and West Feliciana, East Baton Rouge Parish, West Baton Rouge Parish, and Pointe Coupee Parish, Louisiana.

Mississippi. The ethnic composition of a sample of the counties and parishes in this study, drawn from the 1820 census, confirms this pattern. Beginning with Wilkinson County, Mississippi, in the north, the large percentages of Anglo inhabitants gradually decreased, replaced by ethnic French inhabitants further south and west of the Mississippi River. (See Figure 2.)[9]

---

9. Anglo is used here to denote white, English-speaking immigrants to Louisiana and their descendants. The percentages for each ethnicity in Figure 2 are based upon identification and analysis of names from the 1820 census; consequently, the percentages are only estimations. Ethnic settlement patterns are corroborated by J. L. Dillard, "Languages and Linguistic Research in Louisiana," in *Louisiana Folklife: A Guide to the State*, ed. Nicholas R. Spitzer (Baton Rouge, LA, 1985), 35–47; two studies that discuss the development of Anglo settlement in

Regardless of the region's ethnic diversity, the overall similarity in occupations and wealth distribution within the region make it a comparable economic unit. Ninety-five percent, or more, of those in this study who identified their occupation for the 1820 U.S. census claimed agriculture as their means of making a living. Cotton and sugar plantations predominated throughout the region, with cotton mostly east of the Mississippi River and sugar west of it. Slaveholding predominated throughout the region. Slaves made up anywhere between 40 percent and 75 percent of the total population in each of the parishes and counties. Parishes on the west side of the river exhibited smaller total populations than those on the east side of the river. But, the overall wealth distribution among the counties and parishes was roughly the same. Approximately 50 percent of those inventoried in each county and parish owned less than $2,500 in wealth. Another 25 percent, like Trahan, owned wealth somewhere between $2,500 and $10,000. Only about 25 percent owned property worth more than $10,000, but this category included planters of extraordinary wealth like Julien Poydras of Point Coupee Parish. Poydras owned multiple plantations and more than a $1,000,000 in property at his death. In practical terms the region's wealth distribution meant that a planter like Trahan with only 48 acres and several slaves stood about in the middle of the wealth distribution but that one could find a wide range of plantation sizes in all of the parishes and counties. (See Figures 3 and 4.)[10]

West Florida are Light Townsend Cummins, "An Enduring Community: Anglo-American Settlers at Colonial Natchez and in the Felicianas, 1774–1810," *Journal of Mississippi History* 55, no. 2 (1993), 133–55; and Andrew McMichael, *Atlantic Loyalties: Americans in Spanish West Florida, 1785–1810* (Athens, GA, 2008); for the location and character of the Natchez District in the nineteenth century see Michael Wayne, *The Reshaping of Plantation Society: The Natchez District, 1860–1880* (Chicago, 1983), 6–8.

10. I selected census data for 1820 because it represents a midpoint in the time frame of the study. The percentages for those engaged in agriculture are East Baton Rouge 95 percent, West Feliciana 100 percent, West Baton Rouge 99 percent, Point Coupee 99 percent, Adams 97 percent, and Wilkinson 100 percent. East Baton Rouge Parish and Adams County reported the largest numbers engaged in commerce with 4 percent and 3 percent, respectively. This is not surprising as jurisdictions are the locations for the towns of Baton Rouge and Natchez. The percentages of slaves are East Baton Rouge 40 percent, West Feliciana 56 percent, West Baton Rouge 56 percent, Point Coupee 75 percent, Adams 66 percent, and Wilkinson 59 percent. This information is compiled from census

The time frame for this study begins in 1811, when West Florida joined with Orleans Territory as an American-held territory. This occurred just three years after the first set of laws promulgated under American rule took effect in Orleans Territory. The new code of laws, *A Digest of the Civil Laws Now in Force in the Territory of Orleans 1808 with Alterations and Amendments Adapted to Its Present System of Government,* drew upon French and Spanish colonial laws and conformed, in style, to the Napoleonic Code. Scholars debate whether the *Digest of 1808* derived more from French or Spanish legal sources, but the *Digest of 1808* clearly reflected Louisiana inhabitants' preferences for civil law. The *Digest of 1808* made legal customs a critical source for legal rules when it defined custom as a "long series of actions constantly repeated, which have by such repetition, and by uninterrupted acquiescence acquire the force of a common and tacit consent." When the Territorial Legislature approved the *Digest of 1808* Spanish colonial law still governed Spanish West Florida, including West Feliciana and East Baton Rouge parishes. Whether Louisiana families lived on the east side of the Mississippi River under Spanish colonial law or the west side in American territory under the *Digest of 1808*, they shared similar civil law principles and customs. By 1811 both sides of the river officially shared the same legal code. *The Louisiana Civil Code* of 1825 superseded the *Digest of 1808* but made no substantive change to the general rules that facilitated women's acquisition of property. Thus, women in Louisiana benefited from a long history of civil law and were familiar with and accustomed to the property rights it afforded them.[11]

---

data found at the University of Virginia Library's Historical Census Browser (http://fisher.lib.virginia.edu/census). See Kniffen, *Louisiana*, 136–40, for a discussion of early nineteenth-century agriculture in Louisiana. Wealth information here and throughout the paper was compiled from 1,368 probate inventories from Louisiana and 1,555 inventories from Mississippi. These probate records are housed in Mississippi at the Chancery Clerk Office, Adams County, Natchez; and Chancery Clerk Office, Wilkinson County, Woodville; and in Louisiana at the Clerk of Court Office, West Feliciana Parish, St. Francisville; Clerk of Court Office, East Baton Rouge Parish, Baton Rouge; Clerk of Court Office, West Baton Rouge Parish, Port Allen; and Clerk of Court Office, Point Coupee Parish, New Roads.

11. The legal code of Paris or *Coutume de Paris* provided the framework for governance of French colonial Louisiana after 1712. *Nueva Recopilación de Castilla*, *Recopilación de las Indias*, *Las Sietas Partidas,* the laws of *Toro, Ordenamento de Alcalá* and *Fuero Juzgo* were sources for governance for Spanish colonial

The Mississippi law that governed Adams and Wilkinson counties relied on English common-law rules generally described by William Blackstone in *Commentaries on the Laws of England*. Mississippi did not create its own legal code until 1854. This study ends in 1835 to avoid possible effects from the Mississippi Married Women's Property Act passed by the state legislature in 1839. This act, and others like it throughout the country, granted married women under common-law systems limited privileges to own separate property. Although some historians doubt whether Married Women's Property acts actually enhanced

---

Louisiana after 1769 until the Louisiana Purchase in 1803, and in Spanish West Florida until 1810; see Haas, "Louisiana's Legal Heritage," 3; and Ferdinand Stone, "The Law With a Difference and How It Came About," in *The Past as Prelude: New Orleans, 1718–1968*, ed. Hodding Carter (New Orleans, LA, 1968); reprinted in Judith Kelleher Schafer and Warren M. Billings, *An Uncommon Experience: Law and Judicial Institutions in Louisiana, 1803–2003* (Lafayette, LA, 1997), 30; for a summary of arguments in the debate over the weight of French and Spanish sources in the *Digest of 1808*, see A. N. Yiannopoulous, "The Early Sources of Louisiana Law: Critical Appraisal of a Controversy," in *Louisiana's Legal Heritage*, 87–106; Haas, "Louisiana's Legal Heritage," 3. In this article I make reference to the *Digest of the Civil Laws Now in Force in the Territory of Orleans, with Alterations and Amendments Adapted to its Present System of Government* (New Orleans, LA, 1808) as it appears in the LSU Law Center Digest of 1808 Online at http://www.law.lsu.edu/index.cfm?geaux=digestof1808.home accessed June 18, 2011 (hereafter cited as Digest of 1808 online) and to the *Civil Code of the State of Louisiana of 1825* (New Orleans, LA, 1854 (hereafter cited as *Civil Code*); the *Code of Practice,* 1825, accompanied the issue of the *Civil Code.* It clarified procedures for civil and criminal procedures; see Digest of 1808 online, Preliminary Title, art. 3 for the definition of laws and customs; in this article I focus on rules that facilitated women's acquisition and accumulation of property. There was an important change in the interpretation of rules governing women's ownership of property, though it is not clear how much it affected the application of the law. The redactors of the *Digest of 1808* did not accurately interpret Spanish law in force before the *Digest of 1808* concerning women's ownership of community property during marriage. As a result, the *Digest of 1808* ruled that "she (the wife) had no sort of right in them (marital property) until her husband be dead" (Digest of 1808 online, bk. 3, tit. 5, art. 66). Spanish law preserved wives' ownership rights, husbands "held" a wife's portion of the marital property, administering it on behalf of the marriage. The State Supreme Court upheld the Spanish interpretation of wives ownership rights, and the *Civil Code* in 1825 removed the wording that required a husband's death before a wife's ownership rights began (*Civil Code*, bk. 3, tit. 6, art. 2373); see also William Q. DeFuniak and Michael J. Vaughan, *Principles of Community Property* (Chicago, 1943; repr. Tucson, AZ, 1971), 263–64.

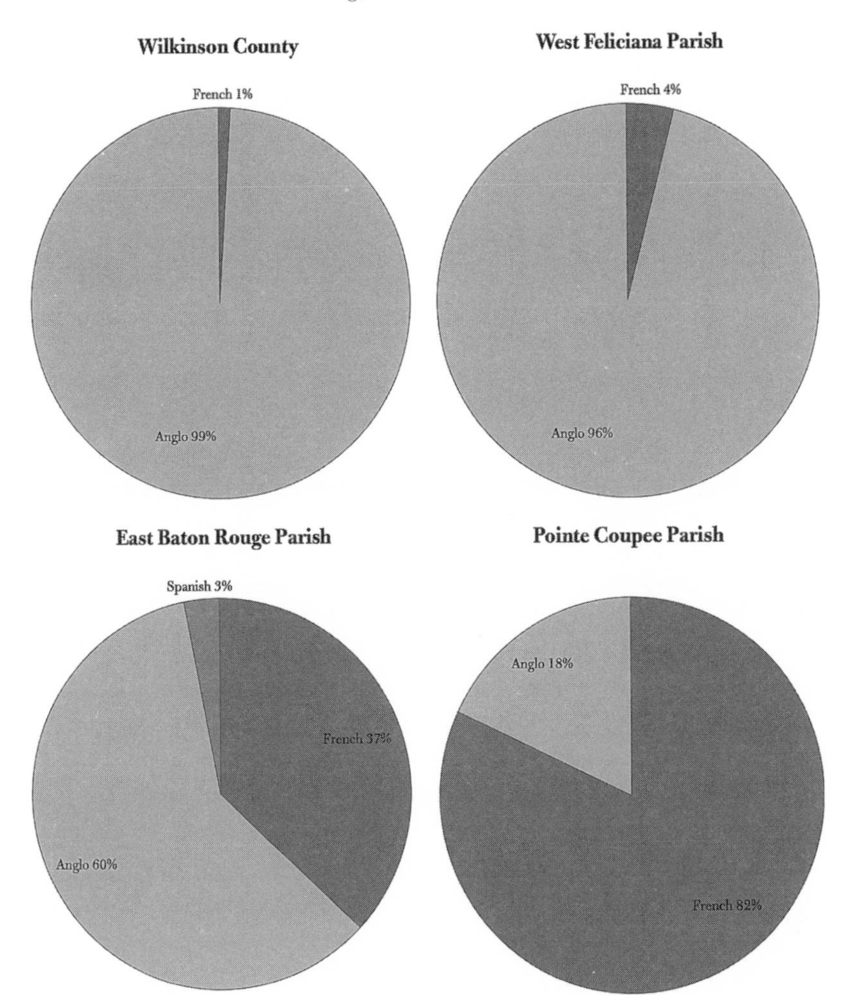

Figure 2: Ethnicity of selected parishes compiled from surnames in the 1820 U.S. Census.
Source: http://ftp.us-census.org/pub/usgenweb/census/ms/wilkinson/1820/pg0361.txt http://www.us-census.org/pub-ftp/la/pointecoupee/1820/index.txt ; http://ftp.us-census.org/pub/usgenweb/census/la/e-batonrouge/1820/pg00004.txt ; http://www.rootsweb.ancestry.come/~lawestfe/census1820A.htm. (accessed December 2, 2009).

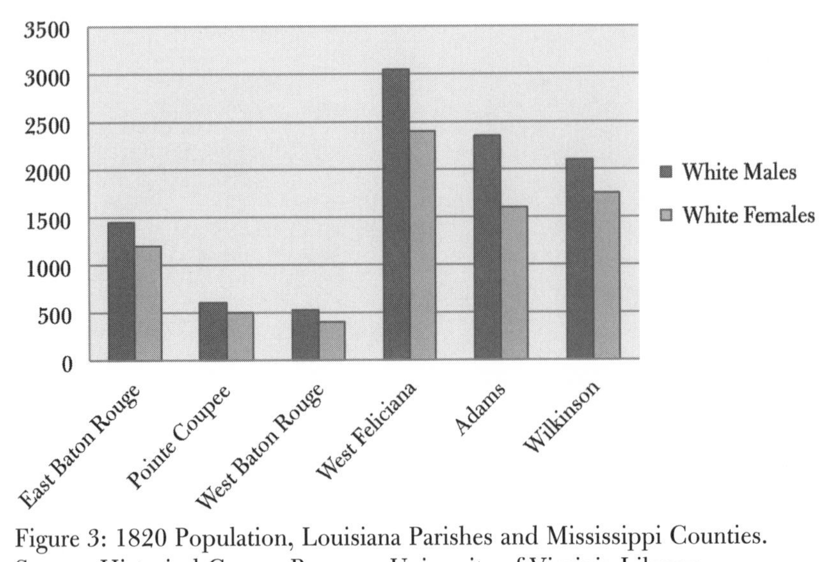

Figure 3: 1820 Population, Louisiana Parishes and Mississippi Counties. Source: Historical Census Browser, University of Virginia Library, fisher.lib.virginia.edu/collections/stats/histcensus.

women's property-holding, the 1839 Act in Mississippi did alter the rules for women's property-holding, changing the grounds for comparison.[12]

The *Digest of 1808* is an appropriate place to begin a comparison of Louisiana civil law with Mississippi common law because it established the basic framework for Louisiana's civilian system of private law. First, when a couple married under the *Digest of 1808*, all property accrued during the course of the marriage became part of the *Community of Acquests and Gains*, unless it was declared one of several types of separate property, in which case the spouse owned the property individually. The *Digest of 1808* defined community as all the "profits of all the effects

12. Sir William Blackstone, *Commentaries on the Laws of England,* 4 vols. (Chicago, 1979); possibly the earliest Married Woman's Property Act passed in 1835 in Arkansas. For a discussion of this Act and the Mississippi Married Woman's Property Act in 1839, see Amanda Sims, "Patriarchy and Property: The Nineteenth-Century Mississippi Married Women's Property Acts" (master's thesis, Brigham Young University, 2007), 18, 39–45. Carole Shammas, "Re-Assessing the Married Women's Property Acts," *Journal of Women's History* 6, no. 1 (1994), 9–30; for a more positive conclusion about the effects of such acts, particularly in the southwest, see Clark, "The Rights of a Florida Wife."

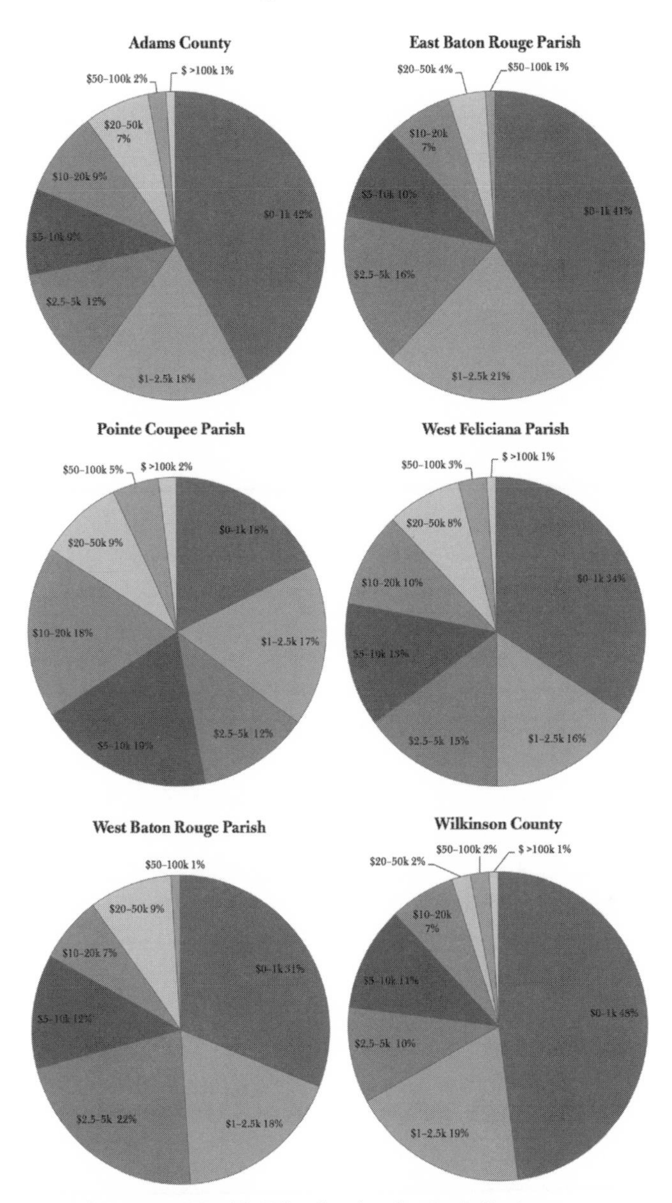

Figure 4: Total Percent Wealth Distribution by Jurisdiction
Source: Inventories and Succession Records, Clerk of Court Offices: Adams County, Natchez, Mississippi; Wilkinson County, Woodville, Mississippi; West Feliciana Parish, St. Francisville, Louisiana; East Baton Rouge Parish, Baton Rouge, Louisiana; West Baton Rouge Parish, West Baton Rouge, Louisiana; and Point Coupee Parish, New Roads, Louisiana.

. . . the produce of the reciprocal labor and industry of both husband and wife; and of the estates they may acquire during the marriage." The wording of the provision acknowledged a partnership model of marriage but, in reality, a husband became "head and master" of the community. A husband's decisions as "head and master" of the couple's community property could be challenged, if the wife proved that he sold her property or defrauded in her some way. In practice, the full economic benefits from the *Community of Acquests and Gains* came for women at the end of the marriage. When husbands died widows received half of the community property of the marriage as their marital portion, and they owned and managed it as they saw fit.[13]

Community property was only one type of marital property that provided economic benefits for Louisiana women. Under Louisiana civil law a wife's separate property consisted of her dowry "that which she brings to the husband to assist him in bearing the expenses of the marriage" and *paraphernal* property "that which formed no part of the dowry." *Paraphernal* property might include property that a wife owned prior to marriage or that she received by gift or inheritance after marriage. In a fairly typical manner for West Baton Rouge Parish, Ursule Trahan and Rosémond Bourg's 1834 marriage contract enumerated her separate property, exempted her from any debts he may have incurred prior to their marriage, and acknowledged that the couple would share community property. Husbands possessed the exclusive right to manage their wives' dowries, but wives held tacit mortgages on their estates for the value of their dowries so that when marriages ended wives expected to see the full value of the dowries returned to themselves or their heirs. Husbands could not sell property that was immoveable, from their wives' dowries, unless expressly stipulated in the marriage contract or ordered by a judge on account of extreme circumstances. That was especially important in Louisiana because the law classified both realty and slaves as immoveable property. This provision likely improved the chances that wives possessed land, and the labor to work the land, at the end of a marriage.[14]

---

13. Rudolfo Batiza, "The Louisiana Civil Code of 1808: Its Actual Sources and Present Relevance," *Tulane Law Review* 46, no. 1 (1971), reprinted in Schafer and Billings, *An Uncommon Experience*, 54; Digest of 1808 online, bk. 3, tit. 5, arts. 64, 66, 67 & 68.

14. Digest of 1808 online bk, 3, tit.5, art. 12; Marriage Contract between Ursule Trahan and Rosémond Bourg, Notarial Book I, #288, 516, WBR. Trahan's contract did not specify any of her property as *dotal,* even though in the

Louisiana law provided various other protections for women's property. Wives could sue for separation of property to protect their separate property if they believed, as Ursule Trahan did, that their dowry was in jeopardy because of their husband's mismanagement or debts. Separation of property protected Trahan's dowry but did not end her marriage. To leave him permanently, Louisiana law required that she petition for separation of bed and board or divorce. It is not clear that the conditions of Trahan's marriage met the legal standards for either one. Marie Prosper's marriage did meet those standards. In 1836 Prosper filed for separation of property, and she filed for separation of bed and board and "absolute" divorce. Separation of bed and board provided for a division of goods and effects but only divorce dissolved the marriage, and divorces were hard to get. Prosper accused her husband, Emile Escourt, of "daily intoxication and ebriety" that resulted in "total neglect" of their affairs and the sale of portions of her separate property, including immoveable property. She also accused him of verbal abuse and with threats to kill her, both grounds for separation of bed and board and divorce. The Fourth District Court in West Baton Rouge Parish found for Prosper as plaintiff and returned her separate property, and then ordered her to restore the four hundred dollars her husband had brought to the marriage plus an additional six hundred dollars. Beyond separation of property and divorce, wives and widows could also renounce community property if they feared that debts from their marriages

court case against her husband legal documents refer to her dowry. Out of forty-seven marriage contracts from West Baton Rouge Parish between 1816 and1835, only seven of the contracts contained *dotal* provisions. Under Spanish colonial law a groom could also bring property in the support of the marriage, called *arras*. The *Digest of 1808* did not contain provisions specifically for *arras*. A few of the marriage contracts from West Baton Rouge Parish that enumerated *dotal* provisions also included gifts from the groom to the marriage, though the term *arras* is not used. Historian Joseph W. McKnight found these patterns common in marriage contracts. See McKnight, "Spanish Law for the Protection of Surviving Spouses in North America," *Annuario de Historia del Derecho Español* 57 (1987), 368–69. Wives could not sell *dotal* property either. Extreme measures that could justify a decree for the sale of *dotal* property include providing bail for a spouse, purchasing food for a family, satisfying debts owed from the dowry, and making repairs to *dotal* immoveables. For provisions pertaining to dotal property, see Digest of 1808 online, bk. 3, tit. 5, arts. 29, 53, 39 & 40; slaves are designated as immoveable, bk. 2, tit. 1, art. 19.

exceeded their property. That is what East Baton Rouge resident Constance Duplantier did when she renounced the community between herself and her deceased husband, well-known Revolutionary War veteran Armand Duplantier. Renunciation implied that wives exhibited little or no influence over their husband's management of their community property and that they were victims of poor or wasteful management. Duplantier petitioned for separation of property from her husband fifteen years earlier. Renunciation provided her another way to protect the property she had left after her marriage.[15]

Wives owned and could administer their *extra dotal* or *paraphernal property*, although the law prohibited them from selling, granting, or mortgaging it without their husbands' consent, or in the absence of his consent, the consent of the court. But women's control of their separate property was not entirely constrained by their husbands. In 1830 Charlotte Swayze and Anthony Doherty of West Feliciana Parish signed and notarized a marriage contract that stipulated there would be no Community of Acquests and Gains between them and that all of Charlotte's property, at the time of their marriage or in the future, be *paraphernal.* The couple agreed that Swayze retain sole possession and management of all her property. Even without such an agreement some women man-

15. For Separation of Property, see Digest of 1808 online, bk. 3, tit. 5, art. 86; for causes of separation of bed and board, see Digest of 1808 online, bk. 1, tit. 5, arts. 1–4; Fourth District Court, Case # 499, Marie Prosper wife of Emile Lescourt vs. Emile Lescourt, 35–36, WBR; The Digest of 1808 bk. 1, tit. 5, art. 17 called for a "separation of goods and effects" with separation of bed and board. Between 1805 and 1827 the Louisiana State Legislature granted only 46 divorces. In 1827 the State Legislature granted parish courts the authority to divorce couples by judicial decree. See George Elliot Howard, *A History of Matrimonial Institutions, Chiefly in England and the United States*, Vol. 3 (Chicago, 1904), 41. See Digest of 1808 online, bk. 1, tit. 4, arts. 13–18. Among the grounds for divorce described in the 1827 statute were defamation, abandonment, cruelty and adultery; see also *Civil Code*, bk. 1, tit. 4, art. 133, 18–21 and bk. 3, tit. 5, art. 2410. I am indebted to Brenda K. Perkins for directing me to information about Constance Duplantier's suits against Armand Duplantier, later published in Brenda K. Perkins, *Armand Duplantier en Amérique: A Biographical Time Line* (Baton Rouge, LA, 2003) 48–50. For these suits, see Constance Duplantier v Armand Duplantier, 1814–1815, Parish Court #313, microform #767, Orleans Parish Louisiana, New Orleans Public Library, New Orleans, Louisiana; East Baton Rouge Parish Judges Book, Vol. 2, 1825–1832, Feb. 2, 1831, microform L87, roll #37, Louisiana State Library, Baton Rouge, Louisiana.

aged their separate property and shaped it to meet their own needs. When Mary Nowlin's husband died she immediately stepped forward to claim the plantation where the couple resided. She explained that earlier, with her husband's consent, she had purchased the plantation where they resided with her own money and "in her name" and improved the plantation with money from her separate property. Like Ursule Trahan, Nowlin's property composed almost all of the couple's estate. Thus, both women wielded economic power within their marriages, and they used their legal rights to assert control over their property during marriage. Given her husband's limited resources, it is hard to imagine Nowlin's husband denying his wife's request to administer her separate property and purchase their home. Like Rosémond Bourg he would have been destitute without his wife's property.[16]

Forced heirship under Louisiana law also worked to the advantage of female property ownership because it required that legitimate children, male and female, inherit equally from their deceased parent's community property. Under the *Digest of 1808*, testators with one or more children could devise only about one-fifth of their estate through their wills, the other fourth-fifths devolved to their children. That percentage increased to one-half with the *Civil Code* of 1825. Still, daughters, as well as sons, enjoyed the opportunity to inherit a significant portion of their parent's estate both in the form of real and personal property. The economic autonomy Charlotte Swayze negotiated for herself in her marriage contract with Anthony Doherty stemmed, at least in part, from the equitable inheritance she had received from her father, Stephen Swayze. Stephen Swayze's will conformed to Louisiana law stipulating that Charlotte and her four brothers and sisters "share equally and alike out of my real and personal estate." The division was to take place only after the property

16. Digest of 1808 online, bk. 3, tit. 5, art. 58 and bk. 1, tit. 4, art. 22; couples could "regulate their matrimonial agreements as they please." See Digest of 1808 online, bk. 3, tit. 5, art. 1; Marriage Contract, 12/27/1830, Notarial Record D, West Feliciana Parish Courthouse, St. Francisville, Louisiana, 83 (hereafter cited as WF); Inventory Record Book 1819–1825, Samuel Johnson, 5/9/1882, 290. Louisiana law permitted married women who acted as public merchants to manage property related to their "trade" without obtaining their husbands' consent. I found no examples of married women declared public merchants in the rural, predominately agricultural region of this study. See Digest of 1808 online, bk. 1, tit. 4, art. 25.

of Stephen Swayze's first wife, Charlotte's mother, had been determined and divided between Charlotte and the children from his first marriage. Thus, Charlotte received her share of her mother's half of the community property of his first marriage and then, when her father died, she received her share of her father's estate, including property in the form of land and slaves. Similarly, Ursule Trahan's legal agency built upon property, partially accumulated through inheritance from her father, in her case from a cash settlement. At least one-third of women from West Baton Rouge Parish owned land and slaves, "income-producing property," at their deaths. It is likely many of these women originally inherited some of this property or the means to buy it from their parents.[17]

Ursule Trahan and the other women considered here demonstrate that certain features of Louisiana law facilitated women acquiring property of their own, especially provisions pertaining to community property, forced heirs, and separate property. A survey of common law in Mississippi reveals the disadvantages Mississippi women faced in accumulating property compared with women in Louisiana. Mississippi common law conformed to the principle of coverture which, in the words of English legal commentator William Blackstone, "the very being or legal existence of the woman is suspended in marriage." A husband's powers over marital property translated into "virtual ownership" of a couple's marital property with no legal incentive for the husband to acknowledge a wife's equal contribution to marital property or acknowledge the cooperative nature of marriage. In Mississippi when a husband died a widow was entitled to dower, a minimum one-third interest in the real or immoveable property of the marriage, or she could claim the property her husband left her in his will. She could not do both. Widows did not obtain outright ownership of property through dower interest; rather they

17. See provisions for forced heirs in the Digest of 1808 online, bk. 3, tit. 5, art. 68 and bk. 3, tit. 1, art. 17; the legal portion by will is described in bk. 3, tit. 2, art. 19 and in *Civil Code* bk. 3, tit. 2, art. 1480; Probate Record 1811–1819, Will, Stephen Swayze, 11/16/1818, 415, WF. Stephen Swayze's estate, before debts, was estimated at $34,000. Swayze's children, including Charlotte, intended to sell the land and keep the slaves they inherited. See Inventory Record Book 1819–1825, Stephen Swayze, 5/15/1820, 72–74, WF; and Allie Bayne Windham Webb, ed., *Mistress of Evergreen Plantation: Rachel O'Connor's Legacy of Letters, 1823–1845* (Albany, NY, 1983), 31; Succession Papers, Inventory and Partition, Jean Baptiste Trahan, Conveyance Book F, 425, WBR.

acquired it as a life estate that meant they could use the property during their lifetime but could not sell or devise it. In Mississippi, as in most common-law states, the law also entitled widows to a minimum of one-third of their husband's personal or moveable property, after all the debts of the estate were settled. Slaves were designated moveable property in Mississippi. A widow could claim personal goods such as clothing or jewelry, and she was entitled to any property she brought to the marriage, at least that part of her property the couple still owned. Women sometimes protected the property they inherited during marriage by claiming dower rights in it, thereby ensuring it would not be sold during the life of the marriage. Because coverture applied to all marital property under common law, including any property or wages women owned prior to their marriages, married women in Mississippi did not own separate property unless they created separate estates. Separate estates required court action and were not commonly available to all women. When separate estates were devised, they were usually placed under the authority of a trustee or other representative, making them difficult for women to access. Finally, under common law in Mississippi, daughters inherited equally with sons only if their fathers died intestate. They might not if he wrote a will. In theory, a man could devise all of his estate, and Mississippi law did not require that he leave anything to his children.[18]

---

18. Other studies have found one or all of these three features of civil law economically beneficial to women, especially in the colonial Americas. In French colonial America, Susan C. Boyle found women's *dotal* or separate property and equitable rules for forced heirs important factors in women's control over property. Deborah A Rosen found in Spanish colonial New Mexico rules for community property, forced heirs, and separate property enhanced women's economic well-being. For a later period see Deena Gonzalez, *Refusing the Favor: The Spanish-Mexican Women of Santa Fe, 1820–1880* (New York, 1999); and Janet LeCompte, "The Independent Women of Hispanic New Mexico, 1821–1846," *Western Historical Quarterly* 12 (Jan. 1981), 17–35. Outside of colonial North America, see Edith Couturier and Asunción Lavrin, "Dowries and Wills: A View of Women's Socioeconomic Role in Colonial Guadalajara and Puebla, 1640–1790," *Hispanic American Historical Review* 59 (May 1979), 280–304; Kimberly Gauderman, *Women's Lives in Colonial Quito: Gender, Law, and Economy in Spanish America* (Austin, TX, 2003). For less positive assessments of the influence of civil law on women's legal status and wealth, see Andy Daitsman, "Unpacking the First Person Singular: Marriage, Power and Negotiation in Nineteenth-Century Chile," *Radical History Review* 70 (Winter 1998), 26–47,

Probate inventories provide useful information about whether women benefited from civil law in Louisiana in comparison with common law in Mississippi because they list the type and amount of property women owned at their decease, as well as frequently indicating what a woman received at the decease of a parent. Quantitative analysis of women's and men's inventories also indicates how wealth was distributed. In general, probate information is biased toward the wealthy but the relatively high percentages of probates in this study allows for a confident estimation of the wealth of all decedents. This is evident when the annual predicted decedents for each county and parish for both males and females is compared to the number of actual probates. In Point Coupee Parish, for example, as many as 87 percent of men and 30 percent of women who would be expected to go through probate were probated. There are indications that ethnicity played a role in whether an estate was probated. Decedents, both male and female, in the civil-law parishes of East and West Baton Rouge and Point Coupee parishes, all with significant percentages of French-speaking inhabitants, were the most likely to be probated. West Feliciana, with its predominately Anglo population, is nearer in its percent of probated decedents to the largely Anglo common-law counties of Adams and Wilkinson counties in Mississippi. (See Table 1.)[19]

---

and Alida C. Metcalf, "Women and Means: Women and Family Property in Colonial Brazil," *Journal of Social History* 24 (Winter 1990), 277–98; William Blackstone, *Commentaries on the Laws of England*, Book I, 430. For the general rules that govern Mississippi property law I have relied primarily on Amanda Sims's informative master's thesis, "Patriarchy and Property: The Nineteenth-Century Mississippi Married Women's Property Acts," 33–39.

19. Probate inventories are not a precise measure of a decedent's wealth because they frequently do not include all the debts owed to or by an estate. My calculations pertaining to the inventories include debts whenever possible. Carole Shammas's quantitative study, "Early American Women and Control over Capital," served as a model for this study. In order to determine the number of probated estates one might expect in the Louisiana and Mississippi jurisdictions, I calculated the number of expected decedents using census figures from 1820 and the average number of probates for 3–5-year periods that were comparable in the records from each jurisdiction. These data were compared against published data from the "west" model life table, level 1. This calculation indicated the expected

It is expected that fewer women than men would be probated overall but, among all the women probated, women from Louisiana were far more likely to be probated than their common-law counterparts in Mississippi. In the Mississippi counties the percentages of females who were probated was approximately half that of those who were probated in the Louisiana parishes. For example, 30 percent of women who could be expected to go through probate in Point Coupee Parish were probated, compared with only 13 percent of women in both Adams and Wilkinson Counties. These figures suggest that the likelihood a woman was probated was much greater if she was an inhabitant of a Louisiana parish governed by civil law and she was ethnic French. The actual percentages for women's probates among all probates, male and female, corroborate these findings. First, the percentage of female probates rises immediately as across the border between the legal systems of Mississippi and Louisiana and then rises even more deeper into French-speaking portions of Louisiana. A striking 37 percent of probates in West Baton Rouge Parish, where Ursule Trahan resided, were women compared with only 6 percent in Wilkinson County, Mississippi. (See Tables 1 and 2 and Figure 5.)

Louisiana women's favorable economic position relative to women in Mississippi is also demonstrated by their percentage of wealth among all probated decedents. The percentages of women's wealth among all probated decedents (testate and intestate), including both real and personal property, reveals that Adams County, the wealthiest county in the region, had by far the lowest percentage of wealth owned by women. Although this percentage was doubled in neighboring Wilkinson County, it was still only half that of any of the civil law parishes in Louisiana. (See Table 3.)

Probate information for William and Mary Cobb illustrates the kind of wealth women could accumulate over time in a fertile, plantation region like West Feliciana Parish. William Cobb died intestate around 1814, leaving his wife, Mary, with two young sons and an estate worth approximately $5,442.00, all of which appeared to be community

---

mortality that can be compared against the actual number of probates. See Ansley J. Coale, Paul George Demeny, and Barbara Vaughan, *Regional Model Life Tables and Stable Populations*, 2nd ed. (New York, 1983), 3-36, 37, 42, 55, 63. The table is modeled after Carole Shammas, Marylynn Salmon, and Michel Dahlin, *Inheritance in America: From Colonial Times to the Present* (Galveston, TX, 1997), 16.

Table 1: Average Percentage of Adult Decedents with Probated Estates

	Female			*Male*		
County/Parish	*Avg. Probates*	*Expected Deaths*	*Percent Probates/Deaths*	*Avg. Probates*	*Expected Deaths*	*Percent Probates/Deaths*
Adams, MS (1819–1823)	3.6	28	13	32.4	67	48
Wilkinson, MS (1819–1823)	1.0	27	13	9.2	50	18
West Feliciana, LA (1819–1823)	5.4	34	16	14.0	66	21
East Baton Rouge, LA (1818–1822)	6.0	23	26	29.3	38	77
West Baton Rouge, LA (1818–1822)	2.5	8	31	6.0	14	43
Point Coupee, LA (1820–1823)	3.0	10	30	13	15	87

Source: Ansley J. Coale and Paul George Demeny, *Regional Model Life Tables and Stable Populations*, 2nd ed. (New York, 1983), 3-36, 37, 42, 55 & 63; Inventories and Succession Records, Clerk of Court Offices: Adams County, Natchez, Mississippi; Wilkinson County, Woodville, Mississippi; West Feliciana Parish, St. Francisville, Louisiana; East Baton Rouge Parish, Baton Rouge, Louisiana; West Baton Rouge Parish, West Baton Rouge, Louisiana; and Point Coupee Parish, New Roads, Louisiana. Census data for 1820 at UVA Historical Census Browser: http://fisher.lib.virginia.edu/census. The table is modeled after Carole Shammas, Marylynn Salmon, and Michel Dahlin, *Inheritance in America: From Colonial Times to the Present* (Galveston, TX, 1997), 16.

Table 2: Women's Percentages of Probated Decedents, 1811-1835

Parish/County	*Men*	*Women*	*Total*	*Percent Women*
Adams, MS	895	89	984	9
Wilkinson, MS	530	36	566	6
West Feliciana, LA	597	109	706	15
East Baton Rouge, LA	174	32	206	16
West Baton Rouge, LA	159	94	253	37
Point Coupee, LA	152	69	221	31

Source: Inventories and Succession Records, Clerk of Court Offices: Adams County, Natchez, Mississippi; Wilkinson County, Woodville, Mississippi; West Feliciana Parish, St. Francisville, Louisiana; East Baton Rouge Parish, Baton Rouge, Louisiana; West Baton Rouge Parish, West Baton Rouge, Louisiana and Point Coupee Parish, New Roads, Louisiana.

property. Mary petitioned for administration or curatorship of the children's property and to serve as guardian or tutrix of the children. No outstanding debts were identified, so Mary's petition gave her authority over considerable income-producing property. The inventory of the Cobbs' estate included five hundred acres, five slaves, and a crop of corn and cotton "standing in the field." Cobb also possessed numerous livestock, including one-hundred thirty-eight hogs and fifty-one cattle and six horses. There were two spinning wheels and a loom, along with four plows and a harrow and sundry household furniture. Evidently Mary and her family managed the property well. At her death in 1853 Mary Cobb's inventory listed twelve hundred acres of land and slaves worth $71,250.00 and a total estate worth $92.532.00, a seventeen-fold increase in wealth during her lifetime.[20]

Another sign that Louisiana women fared relatively well in terms of property holding is that they owned their legal share of family wealth according to community property laws. If families in Louisiana adhered to the law the percent of women decedents should be proportional to the percent of total wealth. This is apparent in Figure 4, where women's percent of probate wealth for each jurisdiction is compared to the percent of women probated. In the Louisiana parishes the probated wealth owned by women is nearly proportional to the overall number of probated decedents in each parish. Although Adams County, Mississippi, was by far the wealthiest jurisdiction in this study, only 5 percent of the wealth belonged to women. Not only is this the lowest proportion of

20. Probate Records, Inventory of William Cobb, 9/2/1814, Drawer 22; Inventory of Mary Cobb, 9/11/1853 Drawer 9, WF.

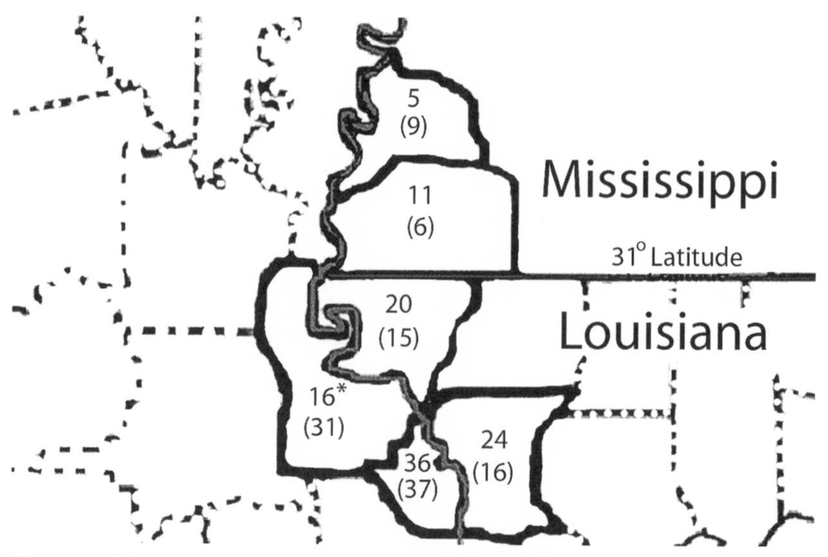

Figure 5: Women's percentage of wealth in the counties and parishes studied; in parentheses, women's percent of probates in the same jurisdictions. Source: Inventories and Succession Records, Clerk of Court Offices: Adams County, Natchez, Mississippi; Wilkinson County, Woodville, Mississippi; West Feliciana Parish, St. Francisville, Louisiana; East Baton Rouge Parish, Baton Rouge, Louisiana; West Baton Rouge Parish, West Baton Rouge, Louisiana; and Point Coupee Parish, New Roads, Louisiana.

wealth owned by women, the actual total is less than that for women in any of the Louisiana parishes, including West Baton Rouge Parish, the poorest, and least populated, of the Louisiana parishes. In West Baton Rouge, where the inhabitants were predominately French-speaking, the figures are most striking. Women made up more than one third of probated estates, and they owned more than a third of all probated wealth in the parish. In Point Coupee Parish, the properties owned by a single planter, Julien Poydras, comprised nearly half of all the probated wealth. This unusual circumstance skews women's percent of wealth, to only 16 percent. If the Poydras estate is excluded, women owned 28 percent of the total probated wealth in the parish, a number comparable to that of East Baton Rouge and West Feliciana parishes across the river, and in line with the number of probated women decedents.[21]

21. Julien Poydras owned several plantations. His wealth totaled over a million dollars. See Probate Inventories, Julien Poydras, 7/22/1824, Clerk of Court Office, Point Coupee Parish, New Roads, Louisiana.

Table 3: Probated Wealth, 1811-1835

Parish/County	*Men*	*Women*	*Total*	*Percent Women*
Adams, MS	6,484,020	500,392	9,908,975	5
Wilkinson, MS	2,610,121	314,442	2,924,563	11
West Feliciana, LA	4,688,065	1,185,076	5,873,141	20
East Baton Rouge, LA	1,717,832	556,279	2,274,111	24
West Baton Rouge, LA	935,393	525,520	1,460,913	36
Point Coupee, LA	2,985709	556,029	3,541,738	16

Source: Inventories and Succession Records, Clerk of Court Offices: Adams County, Natchez, Mississippi; Wilkinson County, Woodville, Mississippi; West Feliciana Parish, St. Francisville, Louisiana; East Baton Rouge Parish, Baton Rouge, Louisiana; West Baton Rouge Parish, West Baton Rouge, Louisiana and Point Coupee Parish, New Roads, Louisiana.

Why did women's wealth in the Mississippi counties compare so unfavorably to that of women in Louisiana, especially when they were as similar in geography, culture, and economy as Wilkinson County and West Feliciana Parish and when some families even owned property in both jurisdictions? Only one out of twenty probated estates in Wilkinson County belonged to women, compared with one out of seven in West Feliciana. Also, women in Wilkinson County owned only 11 percent of probated wealth, compared with 20 percent in West Feliciana Parish. The primary difference between the two regions in terms of women's property-holding is the common law that governed Mississippi and the civil law that governed Louisiana. Women in Louisiana fared significantly better in terms of wealth-holding than women under common law in Mississippi.[22]

The comparison between women's wealth in mostly Anglo West Feliciana Parish and mostly French-speaking West Baton Rouge and Point Coupee parishes is as striking as that between the Louisiana parishes and Adams and Wilkinson Counties in Mississippi. West Baton Rouge is especially noteworthy. There were many fewer women in West Baton Rouge Parish, but proportionately nearly twice as many of them owned wealth at their deaths. Why were women in West Baton Rouge so much

22. The stark differences in female wealth-holding between the Louisiana parishes and Mississippi counties is not an anomaly. A common-law county that mirrors the information from Mississippi is Bucks County, Pennsylvania, in the 1790s. Women in Bucks County owned only 7 percent of the probated wealth, less than half of their proportion of the probate sample. Female ownership of wealth in Bucks County did not reach the levels of the Louisiana parishes until the 1890s. See Shammas et al., *Inheritance in America*.

better off in terms of ownership of property than women in West Feliciana Parish? All of these parishes were governed by civil law. In this comparison the answer likely lies in custom. Anglos in West Feliciana Parish and French-speaking men and women in West Baton Rouge Parish were more likely to adhere to the form of law they understood from long experience. Ethnic French in West Baton Rouge Parish were more likely to follow civil law. That was not the case in predominately Anglo West Feliciana Parish, where provisions in men's wills mirrored patterns typical in common-law jurisdictions, such as bequeathing wives only a life interest in family property, denying her the unrestricted ownership of half of the community property provided under Louisiana law. Altogether 42 percent of the wills of married men from West Feliciana Parish gave their wives less than they would have received had they not written any will. All of the wills identified from West Feliciana Parish that gave women less than Louisiana law stipulated came from Anglo households.[23]

This was not, strictly speaking, illegal. According to the *Digest of 1808*, Louisiana couples who desired to follow "laws, statutes, customs and usages" of another state or territory could do so as long as they made their intentions clear in a marriage contract. Those who married and then moved to Louisiana had one year to draw up such a contract. Marriage contracts were not typical in West Feliciana Parish and none were identified that expressed such legal preferences. But, the common-law legal tradition lingered on among English-speaking inhabitants sustained as much by the deeply rooted common-law customs of the "homogenous," English-speaking population in the parish as it was by any legal provision. This also helps to explain why there is no evidence of protest from wives whose marital portion was reduced on account of common-law practices.[24]

---

23. Wills drawn from Probate Record Books, Vol. 1–6, 1811–1835, WF.

24. Stuart Banner argues that unwritten norms provided a legal framework for colonial St. Louis and that they were commonly understood and perpetuated by the relatively homogenous French-speaking population there, much to the frustration of American authorities who sought order through formal, written laws. In this study common-law principles become the unwritten norms, perpetuated by the relatively homogenous Anglo population in West Feliciana Parish. See Stuart Banner, "Written Law and Unwritten Norms in Colonial St. Louis," *Law and History Review* 14 (Spring 1996), 33–80, especially 73; Dargo, *Jefferson's Louisiana*, 11–13; and the discussion concerning legal adherence in William M. Offutt,

Even though women benefited from civil law economically, critics of women's property rights under civil law point to the fact that married women under Louisiana civil law were no more legally empowered to manage their property than women under common law in places like Mississippi. Wealthy Margaret Johnson Erwin, who bought her own Mississippi delta plantation, complained bitterly that,

> Women have such small say . . . men are not really appealing when one witnesses the insane muddle they have led us into—relegating us to the parlor, the vapors, childbearing, and even (for our own good, they say) from the problems of our own properties.

Erwin referred to her husband's management of her property under common law in Mississippi. Civil law, too, failed to produce a true economic partnership between spouses, in part, because the Louisiana civil law assigned control over a couple's community property exclusively to husbands during the life of the a marriage. The reality of women's ownership and power of administration over community assets through marriage did not materialize until their husbands were deceased.[25]

Jr., "The Limits of Authority: Courts, Ethnicity, and Gender in the Middle Colonies, 1670–1710," in *The Many Legalities of Early America*, ed. Christopher L. Tomlins and Bruce H. Mann (Chapel Hill, NC, 2001), 357–87. What evidence there is of Anglo men from West Feliciana Parish acknowledging that their wills did not conform to civil law comes from the late Spanish colonial period. Several wills from West Feliciana Parish, while it was still part of Spanish West Florida, concluded with a reference to a King's Decree that allowed property from an estate to be divided by executors designated by the testator, rather than by government or military authorities. See Probate Record Book 1811–1819, Will, Adville Atkins, 4/18/1808; Will, John O'Connor, 10/28/1807; Will, Roger Smyth, 1809, WF. I would like to thank Amandine-Marie Cagnioncle for translation of the decree. See Wills Envelope, King's Ordinance, 9/27/1793, Missouri History Museum, Library and Research Center, St. Louis, Missouri. Three cases that came before authorities in Spanish West Florida protested wills devised by Anglo men that reduced wives' marital portion. Two of those cases were brought by wives themselves and the third case by the second husband of the woman concerned in the will. See Archives of Spanish West Florida, Vol. 10: 93–97, 283–84; Vol. 3: 381, Louisiana and Lower Mississippi Valley Collection, LSU Libraries, Baton Rouge, Louisiana.

25. See, for example, Younger, "Marital Regimes," 59, and DeFuniak and Vaughan, 10–107; John Seymour Erwin, ed., *Like Some Green Laurel: Letters of Margaret Johnson Erwin, 1821–1863* (Baton Rouge, LA, 1981), 107.

The limited sphere of Louisiana wives' property management may not have been always rigidly followed. Historian Joseph McKnight finds that throughout regions, like Louisiana, where Spanish civil law still influenced legal practices, women joined with their husbands in economic activities, even though the law did not require their participation. The experiences of women like Mary Nowlin and Mary Cobb demonstrate that women's wealth was far from static. Approximately one out of every five transactions that conveyed land, slaves, or other goods in West Feliciana and West Baton Rouge parishes involved a woman as either the seller or purchaser. The women most likely to be represented in the transactions were female heads of households. But the names of women in East Baton Rouge Parish who were identified as heads of households in the 1820 and 1830 censuses account for only about 7 percent of the total transactions involving women. Some female heads of household appeared multiple times, suggesting that out of the total number of conveyances involving women the number of female heads of households was small. Married women, not just widows and single women, were represented in the records.[26]

Women, like Ursule Trahan, also took advantage of the protections civil law afforded their property. Legal petitions asking for separation of property imply women's awareness of property management and they suggest that some women thought they could do a better job of managing their separate property than their husbands. Between 1821 and 1830 approximately 7 percent of all the cases brought to the Third District Court in West Feliciana Parish involved cases about separation of bed and board or separation of property, and about half of these cases asked for both.[27]

This study demonstrates that women benefited economically from the civilian legal system in comparison with women from similar regional

26. McKnight, "Spanish Law for the Protection of Surviving Spouses in North America," 379; Vendee Records, Clerk of Court, East Baton Rouge Parish, Baton Rouge, Louisiana; U.S. Census Bureau, 1820 and 1830 Census Schedules for the State Of Louisiana, East Baton Rouge Parish, microform, Roll 32, Middleton Library, LSU Libraries, Baton Rouge, Louisiana.

27. These percentages are based on 242 cases from the Record of Judicial Proceedings, Third District Court, 1821–1829, WF.

and economic backgrounds under common law. The marital property regime and inheritance provisions under Louisiana law provided women the opportunity to accumulate economic resources. Possession of wealth in land and slaves and farm implements facilitated economic security at the same time as it allowed them opportunities to participate in the economic life of their families and communities. Women bought and sold property, acted as administrators of estates, and managed farms and households. They exhibited authority in their economic transactions, even if the law did not always allow them to act autonomously. Behind the raw numbers of women's wealth there is also evidence to suggest that women's wealth and the economic security it brought provided women some "bargaining power" within marriage. Women negotiated marriage contracts that enabled them to protect, and in some cases, manage their own property during marriage. In other cases they made difficult decisions about their marriages in an effort to preserve their economic security. For most women the wealth they accumulated under civil law probably allowed them to work with their husbands and families in what the law, and they, viewed as an economic partnership.[28]

The other significant finding of this study is the role of ethnicity and custom in shaping the benefits women received from civil law. In the transect of counties and parishes surveyed for this study, women's percentages of probated wealth gradually increased south and west across the Mississippi River from common-law Anglo counties in Mississippi into civil-law, increasingly ethnic French parishes in Louisiana. Women in early Louisiana, like those of French ancestry in West Baton Rouge Parish and Point Coupee whose families, by heritage and custom, were more familiar with the civil legal tradition, endured fewer challenges to their legal rights and reaped more economic benefits from the law. The information from predominately Anglo West Feliciana Parish illustrates the encroachment of common-law practices into the civil-law system and the negative effect it had on married women's economic partnership with their husbands. That said, white women in West Feliciana Parish were still better far off in terms of personal wealth than their neighbors in

28. For the separation of authority and autonomy in women's public actions see Jean R. Soderlund, "Women's Authority in Pennsylvania and New Jersey Quaker Meetings, 1680–1760," *William and Mary Quarterly* 44 (Oct. 1987), 722–49; Jacobsein, *Economics*.

Adams or Wilkinson County, where common law prevailed both in custom and practice.

It is well understood that in the early years of the nineteenth century Louisiana was a place where the imposition of common-law legal traditions, especially in matters pertaining to family law, faced strong resistance from French and Spanish inhabitants with a long cultural tradition of civil law. What is less understood is how much these two legal systems were at odds in terms of their economic consequences for women. Because Louisiana retained much of the civil legal tradition, women in Louisiana continued to benefit economically from the law, essentially inverting patterns of legal disenfranchisement and loss of authority over property that often happened when political transfers to Anglo or American government resulted in Anglicization of the law. Anglicization of Dutch civil law in New York, for example, changed inheritance practices, gradually diminishing ethnic Dutch women's control over property. In Louisiana it was Anglo women, like those in West Feliciana Parish whose husbands adhered to the customs of common law, who were the ones most likely to suffer economically, not ethnic French women whose families were already accustomed to civil law. The fact that married women's legal rights and property-holding were at the center of this legal admixture is not surprising given the key roles that marriage, family, and property play in the formation of society. A legislative manifesto published 1806 in Orleans Territory in favor of maintaining civil law highlights this point in its acknowledgment of the disruption a change from civil law to common law would cause in Louisiana:

> Everyone knows today and from a long experience how successions are transferred, what is the power of parents over their children and the amount of property of which they can dispose to their prejudice, what are the rights which result from marriages affected with or without contract, the manner of which one can dispose by will. . . . Each of the inhabitants dispersed over the vast expanse of this Territory, however, little educated he may be, has a tincture of this general familiar jurisprudence, necessary to the conduct of the smallest affairs, which assures the tranquility of families; he has sucked this knowledge at his mother's breast, he has received it by the tradition of his forefathers. . . . Overthrow this system all at once. Substitute new laws for the old laws; what a tremendous upset you cause!

The differences in household government and inheritance between civil and common law must have seemed just as disconcerting to Anglo inhabitants steeped in the customs of common law as the prospect of wholesale adoption of common law customs was to Louisiana inhabitants accustomed to civil law.[29]

Women did not collectively promote the legal system in Louisiana, but neither were they invisible. In making use of their rights, as Harriet Martineau rightfully observed, Louisiana women provided a visible, alternative model for the relationship between law, women, and property in early America. Much of early American women's legal history documents women's legal disability or their efforts to manipulate the law in order to find a measure of control over their property and their lives. Ursule Trahan, and other women in Louisiana like her, acquired property and exerted authority over it using legal provisions that were readily available to all white women in early Louisiana.

29. David E. Narrett, *Inheritance and Family Life in Colonial New York City* (Ithaca, NY, 1992); Linda Briggs Biemer, *Women and Property in Colonial New York: The Transition from Dutch to English Law, 1643–1727* (Ann Arbor, MI, 1983); Dargo, *Jefferson's Louisiana*, 139. Two studies argue women retained some property rights from civil law in the American period, in part, because these laws were related to westward expansion. I find no evidence for that in Louisiana or Mississippi. For arguments pertaining to Florida see Clark, "The Rights of a Florida Wife," 56–57, and for Texas see McKnight, "Spanish Law for the Protection of Surviving Spouses in North America," 406.

S.C.
P
M.
N.J.
N.Y.
Unite and Conquer

"From the New World to the Old, and Back Again"

Whig University Leaders and Trans-Atlantic Nationalism in the Era of 1848

BRIAN M. INGRASSIA

When Alexis de Tocqueville and Gustave de Beaumont toured the United States in 1831–1832, they did not visit any colleges, and in *Democracy in America*, Tocqueville merely commented on the sparse availability of higher education in the states. This virtual silence, though, was not reciprocated when Americans interested in university education traveled to Europe. The "Old World" offered intriguing insights to sojourners such as Henry Tappan, a native of upstate New York who had served as a professor of moral and mental philosophy at the University of the City of New York in the 1830s before initiating the University of Michigan's transformation into a research-oriented institution in the 1850s (see Figure 1). Tappan met with Tocqueville during an 1851 European tour and recorded his impressions and thoughts in a lengthy (yet obscure) travel narrative titled *A Step from the New World to the Old, and Back Again, With Thoughts on the Good and Evil in Both.* According to Tappan's account, he and Tocqueville discussed intellectual and political life over breakfast at Versailles, lamenting that few

---

Brian M. Ingrassia teaches in the Department of History at Middle Tennessee State University, Murfreesboro, Tennessee. He would like to thank the Bentley Historical Library at the University of Michigan, as well as the following individuals who commented on earlier drafts of this article: Rob Baker, Larry Grubbs, and David Sehat at Georgia State University; Jason Tebbe of the Calhoun School; Junius Rodriguez, Kathy Whitson, and Scott Hemmenway at Eureka College; Paul Murphy of Grand Valley State University; William W. Cutler III of Temple University; and two anonymous readers.

Journal of the Early Republic, 32 (Winter 2012)

Figure 1: Henry Philip Tappan (1805–1881) is best known as the president of the University of Michigan from 1852 to 1863, but before his tenure in Ann Arbor he taught at the University of the City of New York (present-day NYU) and traveled to Europe. In 1851 he examined universities in England, Scotland, and the German states. Credit: BL000938, Bentley Historical Library, University of Michigan.

"literary men" entered American politics. Recalling the conversation, Tappan observed that Americans could elevate intellect and negate the influence of demagogues "only by the creation of those great institutions of learning, which, like the University of Paris and the French Institute, both multiply the number of scholars and collect them in associations where they can co-work together, sustain each other, and make their legitimate power and influence to be felt."[1]

In 1852, shortly after his return from Europe, Henry Tappan became president of the University of Michigan. During his tenure in Ann Arbor, which lasted until 1863, Tappan built research facilities like the Detroit Observatory, assembled a strong faculty, and bought hundreds of books in Berlin for the university library. When historians discuss Tappan, however, they do not recall his conversation with Tocqueville about the cultural impact of French institutions. Some, such as Thomas Bender, note the irony that a proponent of urban higher education ultimately became famous as the president of a then-provincial university. Others, including George Marsden, invoke Tappan's seemingly romantic or mystical fascination with Prussian higher education, and begin their analyses with the presumption that he wanted to import German-style education to America. Indeed, it is tempting simply to say that Tappan and other midcentury academic leaders borrowed ideas from Germany—then a collection of states, not yet a unified nation—and thus paved the way for late nineteenth-century developments in higher education such as the founding of the Johns Hopkins University (upon a German university model) in 1876. Yet Germany's influence upon America's nineteenth-century universities, as Marsden concedes, is difficult to define precisely. In fact, the German origin story of American higher education has become such a well-worn chestnut that historian James Turner even argues that it is largely mythical. Reformers were selective in their appropriations, insofar as they "discarded the *educational* program of German universities" yet "took the German invention of highly specialized *professorial* research . . . and built on it the advanced segment of American university education." Americans did not replicate German universities:

1. Henry Philip Tappan, *A Step from the New World to the Old, and Back Again, With Thoughts on the Good and Evil in Both* (2 vols., New York, 1852), 2, 281–82; Leopold Damrosch, *Tocqueville's Discovery of America* (New York, 2010), 103–104; Alexis de Tocqueville, *Democracy in America*, ed. J. P. Mayer, trans. George Lawrence (1835; repr. New York, 1988), 55.

They merely appropriated one aspect of German higher education and then built institutions unlike those in the German states.[2]

It is difficult to determine the extent and meaning of German influences upon mid nineteenth-century American universities because historians have focused too narrowly upon curriculum and upon Germany itself. Rather than trying to unearth German antecedents to America's late nineteenth-century research institutions, we should seek to understand what Europe—and its universities—meant to midcentury thinkers like Tappan. Though they were certainly influenced by German thought, Americans were not just seeking curricular inspiration from a single country or region. Rather, they were using European institutions as a touchstone upon which to test their own ideas about the social roles of knowledge and education in an era dominated by Europe's 1848 revolutions and conflicts over America's western frontier. By refocusing our analysis of midcentury universities within a historiographical lens that takes nationalism and political ideology into account, we begin to see how higher education was a symbol that conveyed a particular vision of America's future. For Tappan and other Whig educators, such as Francis Wayland—a noted moral philosopher and pioneer political economist who served as the president of Brown University from 1827 to 1855, implemented Brown's innovative yet unsuccessful "New System" in 1850, and influenced the ideology of Whigs and early Republicans such as Abraham Lincoln—comprehensive universities could strengthen the United States in a time of expansion, polarization, and international com-

---

2. James Turner and with Paul Bernard, "The 'German Model' and the Graduate School: The University of Michigan and the Origin Myth of the American University" in James Turner, *Language, Religion, Knowledge: Past and Present* (Notre Dame, IN, 2003), 69–94; Thomas Bender, *New York Intellect: A History of Intellectual Life in New York City, from 1750 to the Beginnings of Our Own Time* (New York, 1987), 110–114; George M. Marsden, *The Soul of the American University: From Protestant Establishment to Established Nonbelief* (New York, 1994), 101–112; Laurence R. Veysey, *The Emergence of the American University* (Chicago, 1965), 10. On Tappan's work at Michigan, see Frederick Rudolph, *The American College and University: A History* (1962; repr. Athens, GA, 1990), 99–100, 233–234; Charles Perry, *Henry Philip Tappan: Philosopher and University President* (Ann Arbor, MI, 1933), 191–195, 212–248; Tappan to Cha[rle]s Palmer, Nov. 5, 1853, transcript in Henry Philip Tappan Papers, 1840–1936 (hereafter HPT), Bentley Historical Library, University of Michigan, Ann Arbor (hereafter BHL).

petition. These educators wanted a nation that could grow temporally, not just spatially; such a nation would not have to renew itself perpetually, either through political revolution or territorial expansion.[3]

Tappan and Wayland argued, like other thinkers and politicians since the founding of the United States, that a carefully planned and strategically placed university could create national culture. As a repository of knowledge, such a university could foster the diversified growth that would unify the country and help it grow culturally and economically. This notion found particular traction with Whigs, who saw higher education as an important *internal improvement* that could build the country's cultural infrastructure the same way Henry Clay's proposed American System would have expanded its physical infrastructure. Although the Whig program faltered in the early 1840s, it gained new urgency at the end of that decade, a time of social instability and political fragmentation. It also shifted. By 1850, thinkers like Tappan and Wayland no longer called for a *national university*; rather, they proposed a multitude of universities that might fulfill *national purposes*. Besides building infrastructure, these universities could also serve as cultivators of traditional discipline, thus strengthening students' mental and moral faculties and providing a moderating cultural influence for the nation. This type of training, so valued by Whigs, was particularly important at a time when American expansionists—like democratic revolutionaries in Germany, France, Italy, and Hungary—challenged the political and social order. Although Tappan and Wayland, like many of their compatriots, cheered 1848 revolutionaries like Lajos (Louis) Kossuth, they embraced a more cautious nationalism. Disdaining the tyranny of

3. On midcentury American nationalism and political ideology, see Daniel Walker Howe, *The Political Culture of the American Whigs* (Chicago, 1979); Eric Foner, *Free Soil, Free Labor, Free Men: The Ideology of the Republican Party before the Civil War* (1970; repr. New York, 1995); Edward Widmer, *Young America: The Flowering of Democracy in New York City* (New York, 1999). On American nationalism in relation to western expansion, see Adam Arenson, *The Great Heart of the Republic: St. Louis and the Cultural Civil War* (Cambridge, MA, 2011). On expressions of early1800s American nationalism in relation to Britain, see Sam W. Haynes, *Unfinished Revolution: The Early American Republic in a British World* (Charlottesville, VA, 2010). On nationalism more generally, see Benedict Anderson, *Imagined Communities: Reflections on the Origin and Spread of Nationalism*, rev. ed. (1983; London, 1991).

monarchs as well as of the masses, American intellectuals sought stable institutions that would assert and preserve what they saw as the nation's unique democratic character. Academic leaders wanted universities to build national culture so the United States could compete in a world of nations while still maintaining a morally superior position in that world. In short, they wanted to have the cultural institutions that characterized European powers—yet avoid both the monarchies and revolutions of 1848.[4]

Connections between education and nationalism went back to America's founding era, when some thinkers and statesmen contended that the United States should create a national university. At the 1787 Philadelphia Convention, both Charles Pinckney and James Madison submitted proposals for such an institution. Philadelphia physician Benjamin Rush also advocated a Federal University where citizens could study both scholarly and practical disciplines, and thus form an intellectual identity independent from Britain. Rush's university, though never created, would have gathered scientific data from the diverse states and employed four researchers to glean Europe's newest ideas for the institution's professors. This push for a national university resembled Madison's 1783 proposal for a relatively wide-ranging Congressional library intended to serve as a repository of national knowledge.[5]

4. On 1848's influence upon America, see Widmer, *Young America*, 15–16, 58–59, 193–194; Timothy Mason Roberts, *Distant Revolutions: 1848 and the Challenge to American Exceptionalism* (Charlottesville, VA, 2009); Paola Gemme, *Domesticating Foreign Struggles: The Italian Risorgimento and Antebellum American Identity* (Athens, GA, 2005), 3–4, 72–82; Bruce C. Levine, *The Spirit of 1848: German Immigrants, Labor Conflict, and the Coming of the Civil War* (Urbana, IL, 1992). On the American System and education, see Howe, *Political Culture of the American Whigs*, 3, 16, 136–138, 157, 188; Marsden, *Soul of the American University*, 84–86. On 1800s ties between America and Europe, see Ian Tyrrell, *Transnational Nation: United States History in Global Perspective since 1789* (New York, 2007), 39–51; Thomas Bender, *A Nation among Nations: America's Place in World History* (New York, 2006), 122–33.

5. David Madsen, *The National University: Enduring Dream of the USA* (Detroit, 1966); James Madison, *Journal of the Federal Convention*, ed. E. H. Scott (Chicago, 1898), 64–72, 549–550; Benjamin Rush, "To Friends of the Federal Government: A Plan for a Federal University" in *American Higher Education:*

Throughout the 1790s and early 1800s (when the Library of Congress was created), politicians continued to stress the need for a national university. George Washington and John Adams did so in 1796. Ten years later, well before the Whig Party emerged and advocated a similar course of action, Thomas Jefferson suggested that the nation use a federal surplus for domestic projects, including roads, canals, and public education. He saw these projects as internal improvements that would permanently tie the nation together. In 1810, likewise, James Madison explained that a national university would expand the "features of national character" and augment "social harmony." But by 1817, Madison's successor, James Monroe, articulated a stance that would later characterize the Jacksonian Democrats. He reminded Congress that since the Constitution did not grant the federal government power to fund internal improvements, a constitutional amendment would be necessary to allow appropriations for infrastructure development. Were such an amendment ratified, Monroe suggested, Congress should also fund "seminaries of learning" throughout the states (rather than a single national university). Nearly a decade later, in 1825, John Quincy Adams revived the call for a federal university. While roads and canals were essential for unifying the nation's disparate regions, "moral, political, [and] intellectual improvement[s]" were necessary for both individuals and society as a whole. The United States, said Adams, should establish a national university so it could make contributions to learning and science equal to those made by European nations.[6]

No national university was founded, but the need for higher education did not abate. By the 1820s, hundreds of small colleges, typically affili-

---

A Documentary History, ed. Richard Hofstadter and Wilson Smith (Chicago, 1961), 1: 153–55. On Madison's proposal for a congressional library, see Carl Ostrowski, *Books, Maps, and Politics: A Cultural History of the Library of Congress, 1783–1861* (Amherst, MA, 2004), 8–14.

6. James Madison, "Second Annual Message," *A Compilation of the Messages and Papers of the Presidents*, ed. James D. Richardson (New York, 1897), 2: 470; James Monroe, "First Annual Message," *Messages and Papers*, 2: 587; John Quincy Adams, "First Annual Message," *Messages and Papers*, 2: 877–878; George Washington, "Eighth Annual Address," *Messages and Papers*, 1: 194; Thomas Jefferson, "Sixth Annual Message," *Messages and Papers*, 1: 396–97; John Adams, "Address of the Senate to George Washington, President of the United States," *Messages and Papers*, 1: 197.

ated with Protestant denominations, sprouted throughout the United States, especially in newly settled frontier areas and towns touched by the revivals of the Second Great Awakening. Although most of these colleges were small and taught Christian morality and ethics to undergraduates, some college leaders saw their institutions as having national importance. In 1826, for example, Philip Lindsley of Cumberland College (later the University of Nashville), proclaimed, "Let us make ample provision for every species of instruction—scientific, literary, professional—which our country demands." Such instruction, he declared in 1832, served an important purpose: "We have a national literature to create." The quest for a "national literature" (or *national character* or *national culture*) was not unique to collegians. Early republic poets and writers like Philip Freneau and Joel Barlow had eagerly sought to create a distinctly American literature; Noah Webster's spelling books and dictionaries attempted to create a distinct American language and literary style. Their thirst for a national print culture echoed those early nineteenth-century Americans whose celebrations or festivals expressed nationalist spirit. Still, by 1820, British critic Sydney Smith asked in the *Edinburgh Review*: Who reads an American book? This jab irritated Americans who were only then—with publications by writers such as James Fenimore Cooper—starting to create a unique literature. By the 1830s, Ralph Waldo Emerson spoke on the promise of the "The American Scholar" at Harvard, while younger thinkers like his pupil, Henry David Thoreau, began heeding the call.[7]

Despite this budding literary nationalism, some antebellum Americans still desired a large university that would serve as a central institution to

7. Philip Lindsley, *The Works of Philip Lindsley, D.D., Late President of the University of Nashville*, ed. LeRoy J. Halsey (Philadelphia, 1866), 1: 154; Lindsley, "Baccalaureate Address, October 3, 1832," *Works*, 1: 354–55; see also Rudolph, *American College*, 116–18. On national culture, see Russel Blaine Nye, *The Cultural Life of the New Nation, 1776–1830* (New York, 1960), 235–67; David Waldstreicher, *In the Midst of Perpetual Fetes: The Making of American Nationalism, 1776–1820* (Chapel Hill, NC, 1997). On Emerson and Thoreau, see Philip F. Gura, *American Transcendentalism: A History* (New York, 2007), 101–102, 199–201. On the hundreds of antebellum colleges, see Donald G. Tewksbury, *The Founding of American Colleges and Universities before the Civil War, with Particular Reference to the Religious Influences Bearing upon the College Movement* (New York, 1932).

tie the nation together and build up its culture. Such an institution would be a storehouse and factory of knowledge, not a cultivator of individual souls. In 1829, Jared Sparks, then the editor of the *North American Review*, opined in a letter to George Bancroft that America's colleges were not universities. He urged, "let us have an establishment where we can teach young men something about the operations of their own mind[s], the doings of the world, and the business of life. Europe is full of such institutions; it is time for one at least in America." Advocates of this university of national importance argued that it should be located in America's primary metropolis, New York. In October 1830, a number of prominent thinkers convened in that city to create a comprehensive university that would draw upon European precedents to unite and strengthen the young nation. These men included Sparks, James Marsh, Francis Lieber, and Benjamin Silliman. Although George Bancroft did not attend the convention, he did send a letter contending that a university (not a college) should be a place where scholars pursued "all valuable truth." Such an institution, in turn, would provide national cohesion. Bancroft wrote that a university's aim was "to furnish a concentration of all useful knowledge; to collect, to digest, to diffuse all the learning, which can in any manner be made the fit subject of public instruction and promote the honor and advantage of the nation." New York, like Berlin, was a metropolis that needed highly trained professionals, so it could easily support an institution of multiple disciplines. Like the rest of American society, said Bancroft, the nation's educational institutions had "yet to receive the impress which they are to bear forever"; a university in New York, therefore, might leave an indelible mark upon American character.[8]

The founders of the University of the City of New York (later New York University) tended to be both nationalistic and cosmopolitan in outlook. Some, like Benjamin Silliman and Jared Sparks, had founded or edited scientific or literary publications intended to imbue the nation

8. Sparks to Bancroft, June 10, 1829, quoted in *Correspondence of George Bancroft and Jared Sparks, 1823–1832, Illustrating the Relationship between Editor and Reviewer in the Early Nineteenth Century*, ed. John Spencer Bassett (Northampton, MA, 1917, 136–37; Bancroft quoted in *Journal of the Proceedings of a Convention of Literary and Scientific Gentlemen, Held in the Common Council Chamber of the City of New York, October, 1830* (New York, 1830), 45–46, 50. On NYU's founding and early years, see Bender, *New York Intellect*, 91–104.

with its own cultural identity. Others had significant ties to Germany or admired the nationalist movements that had arisen there and elsewhere in Europe in response to the Napoleonic Wars. For example, Francis Lieber, a veteran of the Napoleonic Wars, studied at Berlin before fighting in the army of Alexander Ypsilanti during the Greek Revolution and then moving to Boston in 1827, where he headed a public gymnasium founded on the principles of the Prussian *Turner* (gymnastics) movement. George Bancroft, whose letter was read at the 1830 New York convention, was one of the first Americans to pursue graduate studies at Göttingen shortly after 1815. Germany, for some antebellum Americans, signified cultural unity as well as erudition. George Ticknor, who also studied at Göttingen, noted that even though Germany was a collection of politically disunited states, the "republic of letters" was more cohesive there than anywhere else. When speaking with a German thinker, said Ticknor, one could immediately understand that Germans saw their country as comprising all areas with a common approach to philosophy, education, and religion. When antebellum American thinkers looked to Germany, in other words, they often saw a place that seemed to be the reverse of the United States: It possessed the infrastructure of cultural nationalism, if not a coherent national political structure.[9]

Once established, the University of the City of New York was a place of innovation that embraced a wide range of academic subjects that could have provided a solid foundation for the metropolis and the nation. Besides a liberal arts course, the university offered scientific study and by

---

9. George Ticknor to Edward Channing, June 16, 1816, quoted in *Life, Letters, and Journals of George Ticknor*, ed. George Stillman Hillard and Anna Elior Ticknor, 6th edition (Boston, 1877), 1: 98; George Ticknor to Elisha Ticknor, June 20, 1816, quoted in *Life, Letters, and Journals*, 1: 101. For information on Lieber, Bancroft, Silliman, and Sparks, see Frank B. Freidel, *Francis Lieber: Nineteenth-Century Liberal* (Baton Rouge, LA, 1947), 8–23, 29–33, 50–61; John Spencer Bassett, *The Middle Group of American Historians* (New York, 1917), 64–90; Chandos Michael Brown, *Benjamin Silliman: A Life in the Young Republic* (Princeton, NJ, 1989), 302–309, 322; Damrosch, *Tocqueville's Discovery of America*, 100, 105–106. On American reactions to the French Revolution, see Rachel Hope Cleves, *The Reign of Terror in America: Visions of Violence from Anti-Jacobinism to Antislavery* (Cambridge, UK, 2009). On Napoleonic-era German culture and education, see Eric Dorn Brose, *German History, 1789–1871: From the Holy Roman Empire to the Bismarckian Reich* (Providence, RI, 1997), 66–72.

1835 initiated coursework leading to master's degrees. The first faculty included Henry Tappan; it also included Samuel Morse and Leonard Gale, who collaborated on the electric telegraph, an invention that facilitated communication between the nation's disparate regions. Yet this promising university, like other institutions, was dramatically affected by the Panic of 1837, which sent it into debt. Seven of the eight professors in the science and letters faculty blamed the institution's financial crisis on the alleged mismanagement of Chancellor James H. Mathews. Subsequently, in 1838, the administration removed the faculty members, including Tappan, who had protested Mathews's policies. The fired professors (sounding like the urban artisans who were at that time beginning to comprehend and challenge the market economy's threat to labor autonomy) wrote that the president had acted as an autocrat and insulted higher learning by treating the professors as employees, rather than as intellectuals. If such a tragedy could befall a group of honest and learned men, they caustically observed, Americans might as well "invite the return of the dark ages." The 1837-1843 depression may not have sent the United States into historical oblivion. It did, however, disrupt an emerging Whig narrative of social progress by reducing funding for internal improvements, including education.[10]

At roughly the same time the Panic of 1837 disrupted educational progress—and the University of the City of New York showed signs that it could not fulfill America's need for a national university—Congress was deciding how to use Englishman James Smithson's bequest for an institution to increase and disseminate knowledge. Some Americans, after President Andrew Jackson deferred to Congress on the matter, suggested using the money to found a national university. In July 1838, John Forsyth, President Martin Van Buren's secretary of state, even

10. Professors of the Faculty of Science and Letters, *History of the Controversy in the University of the City of New-York with Original Documents and an Appendix* (New York, 1838), 50, 3-8, 41-42, 49; Perry, *Henry Philip Tappan*, 83. On artisan labor, see Sean Wilentz, *Chants Democratic: New York City and the Rise of the American Working Class, 1788-1850* (1984; repr. New York, 2004). On the 1830s depression and the electric telegraph, see Daniel Walker Howe, *What Hath God Wrought: The Transformation of America, 1815-1848* (New York, 2007), 505, 692. On Tappan's upstate New York background, see Perry, *Henry Philip Tappan*, 21-23, 34-42; John Quincy Adams, *A History of Auburn Theological Seminary, 1818-1918* (Auburn, NY, 1918), 58, 76-77.

solicited advice from prominent thinkers, including Brown's Francis Wayland. In his works on moral philosophy, Wayland promulgated a type of education that would discipline young men's bodies, minds, and morals. His political economy also promoted the social benefits of the division of labor and echoed Henry Clay by arguing that education, like roads or ports, should be publicly managed. In his 1838 response to Forsyth, Wayland asserted that Smithson's bequest should fund an educational institution. The nation already had enough small colleges that taught discipline, he opined, and theological seminaries or professional schools could be founded on private or regional bases. Smithson's gift should fund a philosophical school for college graduates. This "National University," he said, "would raise up and send abroad in the several professions a new grade of scholars, and thus greatly add to the intellectual power of the nation." Wayland contended that the institution could only be established after a careful survey of Europe's best universities.[11]

Congress ignored Wayland's suggestion. Some, like Senator John C. Calhoun, opposed accepting Smithson's donation altogether. Representative John Quincy Adams, chair of a House committee charged with creating a plan for the Smithson money, stated that he did not favor using it to found a university. The former president would rather create an astronomical observatory than "avail ourselves of a stranger's munificence to rear our children." Others suggested founding a museum or lecture series, or publishing tracts for widespread distribution. Vermont Whig George Perkins Marsh even argued that a comprehensive national library equal to that of Göttingen—the German university where many

11. Wayland to Forsyth, Oct. 2, 1838, quoted in Francis Wayland and H. L. Wayland, *A Memoir of the Life and Labors of Francis Wayland, D.D., LL.D., Late President of Brown University, Including Selections from his Personal Reminiscences and Correspondence* (New York, 1867), 1: 330, 328–332. On the founding of the Smithsonian, see Jackson, *Messages and Papers*, 3: 1406; Paul H. Oehser, *The Smithsonian Institution*, 2nd ed. (1970; Boulder, CO, 1983), 1-11; Howe, *What Hath God Wrought*, 468–69. On Wayland and antebellum moral philosophy, see Howe, *Political Culture of the American Whigs*, 37, 269–270; Stewart Davenport, *Friends of the Unrighteous Mammon: Northern Christians and Market Capitalism, 1815–1860* (Chicago, 2008), 36–38, 56–57, 76–77; D. H. Meyer, *The Instructed Conscience: The Shaping of the American National Ethic* (Philadelphia, 1972), 103–104. For Wayland's views on public education (expressed in the mid-1840s), see Wayland, *University Sermons: Sermons Delivered in the Chapel of Brown University*, 2nd ed. (Boston, 1849), 261.

Americans had studied—might be more useful and appropriate than a scientific institution. This would have been a sensible suggestion for nineteenth-century American thinkers who wanted library resources equal to those in Europe: Some criticized the United States for not elevating the Library of Congress into a true national library with hundreds of thousands of volumes, while others simply argued that better library resources would advance classical scholarship and provide the foundation for a unified literary culture. Despite proposals such as Marsh's, in August 1846, Congress established the Smithsonian as an institution devoted to scientific collection and investigation. Such an establishment lent itself to a more cosmopolitan outlook than a national university. As Smithsonian secretary Joseph Henry explained, the institution was supranational in nature and could not be used—like tax-funded internal improvements—for nation-building. The United States of America would have been irresponsible, Henry said, "to accept the administration of a bequest intended for the good of mankind, and to apply it exclusively to its own use."[12]

Although Smithson's bequest did not fund a university devoted to education and knowledge production, the resulting debate may have inspired some Americans to seek alternate ways to create educational institutions that would build the nation and help it compete with Europe. In 1840, just two years after the federal government ignored his Smithsonian suggestion, Francis Wayland conducted the European tour that he had envisioned as essential to the planning of a national university.

---

12. Adams quoted in Smithsonian Institution, *Eighth Annual Report of the Board of Regents of the Smithsonian Institution, Showing the Operations, Expenditures, and Condition of the Institution up to January 1, 1854, and the Proceedings of the Board up to July 8, 1854* (Washington, DC, 1854), 117; Henry, "Report of the Secretary," *Eighth Annual Report*, 7; George Perkins Marsh, "Smithsonian Institution—Speech of Mr. G.P. Marsh, of Vermont, in the House of Representatives, April 22, 1846," *Appendix to the Congressional Globe for the First Session, Twenty-ninth Congress* (Washington, DC, 1846), 850–54. See also Oehser, *Smithsonian Institution*, 16–17; Howe, *What Hath God Wrought*, 468. On libraries, see Ostrowski, *Books, Maps, and Politics*, 129–30; Caroline Winterer, *The Culture of Classicism: Ancient Greece and Rome in American Intellectual Life, 1780–1910* (Baltimore, 2002), 54–56, 97–98.

Isaac Davis, a Brown University trustee who joined Wayland's tour of Great Britain, recalled that Wayland spent over a week eagerly inspecting Oxford's "chapels, libraries, and printing establishments" and "examin[-ing] the discipline, courses of study, and educational advantages" the university offered. Although Wayland was impressed by the British universities, he was also ambivalent. Wayland admired Europe's great palaces and gardens, like those at Versailles, as well as the continent's cultural institutions. Yet such opulence offended his republican sensibilities. He favored America's cities, politics, and morality, as well as its opportunities for "universal education." Although America did not possess the "books, libraries, [and] lectures" of Europe, said Wayland, it did have institutions designed to cultivate disciplined minds. In the best of all possible worlds, the United States could have strong national culture *as well as* disciplined lives and democratic institutions.[13]

Two years after his European sojourn, Wayland published *Thoughts on the Present Collegiate System in the United States* (1842). Although this little book could be seen as Wayland's manifesto on university reform, we might also read it as an artifact of a Whig nationalism crafted in opposition to European politics. Wayland stressed that although Europe's monarchies had great universities, he still believed in widespread, democratic education. He argued, employing a typical Whig concept, that educational improvements were necessary for national progress. Echoing Bancroft's 1830 letter to the New York convention, Wayland noted that it was an opportune time to perfect American higher education. The nation's institutions were still being formed, and they were "not yet hedged about by precedents which can never be abolished, nor bound up by statutes which can never be amended." American colleges, rooted in Oxford and Cambridge, did not necessarily complement America's emerging social structure; nor did they play a strong role in the formation of the national character. But Wayland stressed that the United States, unlike England, was young and could still change. Invoking a process that Benjamin Rush had articulated more than half a century earlier, Wayland observed that Americans had cut the intellectual umbilical cord that once tied them to Britain.[14]

---

13. Davis quoted in Wayland, *Memoir*, 2: 3–44; Wayland, *Memoir*, 2: 22, 23–24.

14. Francis Wayland, *Thoughts on the Present Collegiate System in the United States* (Boston, 1842), 9, 1–8, 20–21, 78; *Memoir*, 2: 10.

Ever the political economist, Wayland saw that universities could serve important social and economic roles. They could even provide a centrifugal force that might hold the expanding nation together. He lamented, "We have no centre to which talent of all kinds tends. A class, as soon as it leaves the walls of College, is scattered in a few days to every State and Territory in the Union. The College or University forms no integral and necessary part of the social system." To remedy this problem, he envisioned universities like those in Britain or the German states, which prepared young men for national service via focused and thorough scholarly training. Each American college, said Wayland, could improve by making itself "more nearly to resemble a real University; that is, to make it a place of education in all the most important branches of human learning." After all, he noted, the purpose of a university was "to foster and cultivate the highest talent of the nation, and raise the intellectual character" of the people.[15]

Wayland wanted universities to unify the nation both socially and geographically. As Daniel Walker Howe has observed, Whigs usually saw the nation as growing in *time* (economic and cultural development), rather than *space* (geographical expansion). But by the 1840s, the Whigs were not winning this battle. After William Henry Harrison died in 1841, the Whigs were unable to implement Clay's American System or reestablish a national bank; moreover, the push for territorial expansion gained steam after James K. Polk defeated Clay in the 1844 presidential election. In the next two years, Congress annexed Texas while Polk's administration negotiated the Oregon Treaty with Britain and initiated war with Mexico over disputed land in Texas. For Democrats, western lands provided a safety valve for rising social tensions, a place where those displaced by capitalism could start over. Land ownership conveyed independence and limited social upheaval. But Whigs saw things differently. Wayland, for one, hoped that education would provide unity and cultural cohesion, and thus help the nation build upward (not just outward) by harnessing the power of capitalism. Yet even if there were no national university, perhaps an array of colleges such as Brown could build themselves into universities of national scope: institutions of higher education that were internal improvements able to bring about more internal improvements. As stewards of the public good, wrote Wayland,

15. Wayland, *Thoughts on the Present Collegiate System*, 41, 48, 108–110.

universities could "furnish means for the most perfect development of the intellectual treasures of the country."[16]

Even though Wayland admired European universities and complained that America had wasted its resources by building too many small colleges, he still thought that his nation's democratic institutions made it exceptional. In an 1849 collection of chapel sermons delivered at Brown, Wayland proclaimed, "[L]et any man cast his eyes over our beloved country. . . . Let him enter our schools, academies, and colleges, and take notice that the door is thrown wide open to intellectual improvement, and that facilities in abundance are every where [*sic*] afforded for the cultivation of meritorious talent." This progress was the result of history, and it had been brought about by the cumulative actions of America's forebears. Education was necessary to perpetuate such advances and maintain republican government, especially in the turbulent era of 1848. In a sermon on "The Recent Revolutions in Europe," Wayland admired the spirit of liberty that Europe seemed to be embracing, but he noted that freedom could only be enjoyed properly if it were accompanied by the cultivation of intellect and morality. He even argued that widespread funding of education might make Europeans able to govern themselves—once they had thrown off monarchy's shackles. Europe, its morality properly cultivated, could avoid perpetual revolution and the resulting cycle of freedom, anarchy, and despotism. Whig-style education, bred in the New World, could teach the Old World's citizens the discipline necessary to enjoy and respect their newfound freedom, without always having to begin society all over again.[17]

As part of a committee charged with improving Brown, Wayland soon developed a plan intended to help the university build the nation's culture and economy, as well as train students in the ways of moral and mental discipline. The committee submitted its findings in March 1850,

16. Ibid, 47; Howe, *Political Culture of the American Whigs*, 20–21; George C. Herring, *From Colony to Superpower: U.S. Foreign Relations since 1776* (New York, 2008), 188–207. See also Thomas M. Allen, *A Republic in Time: Temporality and Social Imagination in Nineteenth-Century America* (Chapel Hill, NC, 2008).

17. Wayland, *Sermons*, 89–90; 313–319. On the redundancy of small colleges, see Wayland, *Thoughts on the Present Collegiate System*, 126–28. While Wayland viewed the United States positively, he was (like many other Whigs) critical of the federal government's treatment of Native Americans; *Sermons*, 279.

at the same time politicians were crafting compromises regarding the Mexican land cessions of 1848. While national politicians were accommodating spatial expansion, Wayland's proposed reforms fostered temporal expansion. The Brown Report took the ideas Wayland had articulated in 1842 and implemented them at a university located in a major industrial and commercial city (Providence was then among the twenty largest urban centers in America). The committee recommended that each student determine which courses he would study and for how long. Rather than awarding a liberal arts diploma, the university would grant a certificate in each discipline studied. Subjects included ancient and modern languages, mathematics, natural science, rhetoric, moral and mental philosophy, political economy, history, pedagogy, agriculture, engineering, and law. This so-called New System of diverse studies—an educational analogue of Clay's American System—would presumably increase the number of students at Brown and aid the university financially. It would also give each student opportunity to acquire an education that would contribute to the division of labor and thus enhance the national wealth. Its widespread imitation, said Wayland, might even preserve established colleges at a time when Americans were forming more practical institutions, such as agricultural colleges, or abandoning formal higher education altogether.[18]

Wayland's proposal, while not America's first plan for practical studies, wedded his political economy to Brown's curriculum. It also appears to have been a reaction to democratic innovations sweeping both Europe and America in the late 1840s. Around 1850, former Illinois College professor Jonathan Baldwin Turner urged the state of Illinois to create an industrial university to teach scientific agriculture and mechanical arts. This was a novel idea. True, some colleges in the 1830s west, such as upstate New York's Oneida Institute or central Illinois's Knox College, had embraced manual labor education—often based on the example of

18. Wayland, *Memoir*, 2: 79–80; Walter C. Bronson, *The History of Brown University, 1764–1914* (Providence, RI, 1914), 259; Francis Wayland, et al., *Report to the Corporation of Brown University, on Changes in the System of Collegiate Education, Read March 28, 1850* (Providence, RI, 1850), [3], 51–60. See also Rudolph, *American College*, 237–240; Davenport, *Friends of the Unrighteous Mammon*, 39–40. On Providence's size, see U.S. Census Bureau, "Population of 100 Largest Urban Places: 1850": http://www.census.gov/population/www/documentation/twps0027/tab08.txt (accessed Sept. 29, 2011).

Johann Heinrich Pestalozzi's Hofwyl school in Switzerland—as a way to prevent class stratification; but Turner suggested something else altogether. He proposed a college that would teach practical subjects to help students move up within the class hierarchy, rather than preventing a hierarchical social structure from developing.[19]

Wayland's plan resisted the implications of Turner's proposal. Influenced by Whig ideology and Christian ethics, as well as his European sojourns, Wayland hoped to turn Brown into a hybrid institution that taught practical subjects alongside more traditional ones, such as moral philosophy. Brown's New System would enable graduates to contribute to the national economy, without abandoning the idea that education also served moral and cultural purposes. Well into the decade following the introduction of this program, Wayland maintained an optimistic, Whig narrative of American economic and cultural progress. Yet his Whiggish stance could not be sustained in the decade preceding the Civil War. After 1854, Brown's enrollment dropped and student quality declined; Wayland resigned the following year.[20]

---

19. Turner's speeches are quoted extensively in Mary Turner Carriel, *The Life of Jonathan Baldwin Turner* (1911; Urbana, IL, 1961), 68–101; in particular, see "State University for the Industrial Classes," 69–72. On antebellum manual labor education, see Stephen P. Rice, *Minding the Machine: Languages of Class in Early Industrial America* (Berkeley, CA, 2004), 69–95. Earlier suggestions for practical higher education courses included Jefferson's 1818 proposal for the University of Virginia's ten European-style faculties, as well as Harvard's 1820s experiment (proposed by George Ticknor) with an elective system. On Virginia, see Jefferson, "Excerpts from the Report of the Legislature of Virginia Relative to the University of Virginia" in *Basic Writings of Thomas Jefferson*, ed. Philip Foner (New York, 1944), 403–444; Frederick Rudolph, *Curriculum: A History of the American Undergraduate Course of Study since 1636* (San Francisco, 1977), 82. On Harvard, see George Ticknor, *Remarks on Changes Lately Proposed or Adopted, in Harvard University* (Boston, 1825), 35–40; David B. Tyack, *George Ticknor and the Boston Brahmins* (Cambridge, MA, 1967), 34–35. Wayland visited Virginia before submitting the 1850 Brown Report, and he cited Ticknor's reforms in his writings on education; see Bronson, *History of Brown*, 272–73; Wayland, *Memoir*, 2: 92; Wayland, *Report to the Corporation*, 18.

20. On the failure of the New System, including Brown's decreasing enrollment, see Bronson, *History of Brown*, 289; Wayland, *Memoir*, 2: 108; Davenport, *Friends of the Unrighteous Mammon*, 39. For evidence of Wayland's Whig view of communications and transportation infrastructure, as well as their relationship to building national culture, see Wayland, *The Education Demanded by the People of the U[nited] States: A Discourse Delivered at Union College, Schenectady, July 25,*

Not long after Wayland implemented Brown's (ultimately unsuccessful) New System in 1850, Henry Tappan published his own manifesto, *University Education* (1851). This book, like Wayland's 1842 volume, can be viewed as an artifact of Whig discussions about universities' national roles. Having taught as the first mental and moral philosophy professor at the University of the City of New York in the 1830s, Tappan had prior experience instructing students in the ways of discipline as well as in contributing to a self-consciously national higher education institution. At midcentury, he said that America still needed such universities. When in November 1851 he introduced *University Education* to French philosopher Victor Cousin, who had written on the subject of German education in the 1830s, Tappan asserted that the United States was in great need of the "highest form of education."[21]

Tappan's book did not ape Wayland's reforms, but it did cite their influence, while at the same time critiquing and modifying them. Tappan, like Wayland, traced American colleges' origins to England, and he too was critical of this lineage. However, he was enamored of continental universities, which had retained their comprehensive character instead of splintering into British-style colleges, which were essentially just residential or dining halls. Tappan argued in *University Education* that America should have not mere colleges, but rather comprehensive universities. These institutions should possess extensive libraries and provide "all other material of learning," and retain renowned professors able "to lecture . . . upon every branch of human knowledge." He said that higher education should provide training for all aspects of society. Farmers, merchants, poets, architects, lawyers, physicians, teachers, and intellectuals could learn their respective trades in such an institution. After all (here he echoed Wayland's Whig political economy) the world's work required "division of labor." Tappan wrote, "From [the university] go forth men to fill every profession, to hold great offices in the State, and

1854, on the Occasion of the Fiftieth Anniversary of the Presidency of Eliphalet Nott, D.D., LL.D. (Boston, 1855), 12–18, 21.

21. Tappan to Cousin, Nov. 14, 1851, transcript in HPT, BHL. On Cousin, see Nye, *Cultural Life of the New Nation*, 166–167; Turner, "German Model," 75–76.

to lead on the advancement of civilization and refinement." A true university, in short, should serve the diverse needs of an expanding nation with a diversified economy and a budding, unique culture.[22]

If larger numbers of students were educated, Tappan predicted, America's politics, economy, and intellect would improve. The dissemination of knowledge and mental discipline would elevate society more than any other internal improvement by building the economy and culture as well as eliminating the influence of confidence men, social innovators, and selfish politicians. "Men thus worthily built up would get into all the relations of society," wrote Tappan, "and throw a new aspect over the arts, commerce, and politics, and a high-minded patriotism and philanthropy would everywhere appear." Subsequently, the nation's overabundant "penny-a-liners, stump orators, discourses upon socialism, bigots, and partisans" would yield to "sound writers, true poets, lofty and truthful orators, and profound philosophers, theologians, and statesmen." America, said Tappan, "should have a pure national literature, and a proud national character." The spread of education might help Americans replace dubious tricksters with deep thinkers who could create the type of culture promoted by founding-era nationalists like Rush, Freneau, and Webster.[23]

In Tappan's mind, the United States already possessed the materials and intellect to create a national character. But first, Americans would have to consolidate their resources. Echoing Wayland, Tappan argued in 1851 that the nation should concentrate its efforts on a few large universities. A good place for a national university would be the city of New York. In this cosmopolitan metropolis, students could congregate alongside existing libraries, museums, and arts: "We should thus have a fully appointed national Institution where the bonds of our nationality would be strengthened by the loftiest form of education, the sympathy of scholars, and the noblest productions of literature." Until 1857, in fact, Tap-

---

22. Henry Philip Tappan, *University Education* (New York, 1851), 43, 15, 22, 5–10, 31–34, 54–63; see also Tappan, *A Discourse Delivered by Henry P. Tappan, D.D. at Ann Arbor, Mich., on the Occasion of His Inauguration as Chancellor of the University of Michigan, December 21st, 1852* (Detroit, MI, 1852), 23–24; Perry, *Henry Philip Tappan*, 84–87.

23. Tappan, *University Education*, 66–67. On antebellum fears of confidence men, see Karen Halttunen, *Confidence Men and Painted Women: A Study of Middle-Class Culture in America, 1830–1870* (New Haven, CT, 1982).

pan remained a vocal proponent of founding a university of national importance—not just an urban university for a single metropolis—in New York City.[24]

Tappan's vision was reinforced by his European travels. His accounts of these sojourns underscored his love not just of German universities, but of all European universities that served as intellectual focal points for cohesive (or cohering) nations. In June 1851, he departed from New York, with his wife and daughter, aboard the steamship *Washington*. In the next four months, Tappan visited England, Scotland, the Netherlands, the German states, Switzerland, and Belgium; in France, he met with Tocqueville. This tour gave Tappan a chance to reflect upon the ways America did and did not resemble Europe. At virtually every step of the way, he admired some aspects of European civilization while criticizing others. Although the voyage was by no means a systematic study of educational institutions, Tappan visited multiple universities. Upon seeing these significant centers of learning, he often commented on the role of higher education in national life. Even though he had critiqued English collegiate structure in *University Education*, for example, he admired the social and political role of England's universities. In Oxford (a "great seat of learning" once a mere "*ford* for oxen"), Tappan admired the bountiful collections of the Bodleian Library. Such facilities did not just benefit the students of Oxford's colleges, he contended. Rather, such a great university and its intellectual assets served all of society. In each nation possessing "great institutions of learning" one always found "a learned and literary class" capable of perpetually "advancing the national literature."[25]

After Oxford, Tappan and his family stopped in London's Hyde Park to visit the 1851 Great Exhibition and the magnificent displays of the Crystal Palace. This world's fair embodied the spirit of national striving that filled Tappan's writings. As Thomas Bender notes, "[such] fairs were entertainments, prompts to tourism, and theaters of consumerism, but they also modeled a world of international competition, or competitive nationalism." After experiencing the fair, the travelers went to Scotland. Although he bypassed Cambridge, Tappan did visit the university

24. Tappan, *University Education*, 67–70, 88–89; Bender, *New York Intellect*, 111–14; Rudolph, *American College*, 235.

25. Tappan, *Step from the New World to the Old*, 1: 137–138, 146, 20.

cities of Glasgow and Edinburgh. He compared Glasgow to New York, noting that in the past fifty years both cities had grown tremendously: Glasgow from 77,000 to nearly 370,000; New York from 60,000 to 500,000. Even though the Scottish industrial city may not have been as grand as the American metropolis, Tappan was clearly envious. America could learn an important lesson from Glasgow, which "prove[d] that a commercial and manufacturing city can possess a great and flourishing institution of learning." He likely had his former employer in mind: Although the University of Glasgow enrolled over a thousand students in 1851, the University of the City of New York was still a relatively modest institution that had never quite realized the lofty ambitions of its founders.[26]

After Edinburgh, Tappan went to the continent. Even though he had admired the great universities of the United Kingdom, Germany's universities were among the highlights of his trip. Even while recounting his visit to Oxford, he affirmed that "[t]he best idea of a modern university . . . may be gained from considering the German universities—the most perfect institutions of this class in the world." Tappan admired the nascent nationalism of the German states as much as he revered their intellectual heritage. He enthusiastically inspected the University of Bonn and praised its 150,000-volume library, which served Prussia as a central repository of knowledge the way the Bodleian served Britain. Universities like those at Bonn and Berlin supported many scholars, said Tappan, consolidating them in one place and thus making their labors more useful. But even though Prussia had a glorious educational system capped by impressive universities superior to America's colleges, Tappan cautioned that Prussia was a monarchy ruled by despots. The United States, he said, should also have eminent institutions of learning that would prove the virtue and intellectual competence of a republican society. The justification for monarchy could only be overturned by showing "that a republic, too, can create and foster the noblest institutions of learning, can patronize the arts and artists, and learning and learned men." Although commerce and industry were important, they were not neces-

26. Bender, *Nation among Nations*, 131; Tappan, *Step from the New World to the Old*, 1: 236–237. By 1853, NYU had graduated a total of only 455 students (in twenty years); see J. W. Draper, *The Indebtedness of the City of New York to its University: An Address to the Alumni of the University of the City of New-York, at their Twenty-First Anniversary, 28th June, 1853* (New York, 1853), 9–10.

sarily society's highest achievements. It was not adequate for Americans merely to prove that they possessed "the fairest opportunities for material accumulation"; they also had to show that they could cultivate "the grandest forms of humanity itself." The United States, in short, needed universities of national stature to produce and augment the "national culture."[27]

Education and culture were matters of national pride, said Tappan, in which American democracy could not afford to be surpassed by European kingdoms. By creating major universities, the United States could prove that democracy was not culturally deficient compared to monarchy. He wrote in *University Education* how Americans needed to prove "that the spirit of a free people is mightier to the production of everything that can elevate and adorn humanity than the will of princes." The United States should have "at least one great institution of learning that may vie with the best of the old world." After all, "Have we not the means in abundance? Shall the little principalities of Germany surpass these wealthy and powerful States?" Tappan was writing at a point when the 1848 revolutions, once seen as the springtime of Europe, were being harshly repressed, especially in Prussia. This anti-democratic spirit made the superiority of German educational institutions even more galling to a believer in the promise of the republic.[28]

Tappan sought expansion over time, not just space. It was the only way for the American nation to build and consolidate itself while simultaneously preserving its exceptional character in the face of mid-1800s social and political turmoil. Sounding like Tocqueville, Tappan worried that Americans did "not form strong local attachments." Rather, they were "never remaining long enough anywhere to perfect civilization; but always pressing onward to the boundaries of civilization to fell new trees, and to make new beginnings." Was it Americans' destiny "to be mere pioneers over this great continent"? "[M]ust it be left to other generations to found, in beauty and grandeur, the institutions of a high civilization?" Unlike Democrats who placed the nation's manifest destiny in territorial expansion, Tappan and many other Whig politicians or thinkers located that destiny in disciplined intellect, arts, and science. All of

27. Tappan, *Step from the New World to the Old*, 1: 143; 2: 63–65; 1: 245.

28. Tappan, *University Education*, 99, 79–80; Jonathan Sperber, *The European Revolutions, 1848–1851*, 2nd ed. (Cambridge, UK, 2005), 252–57.

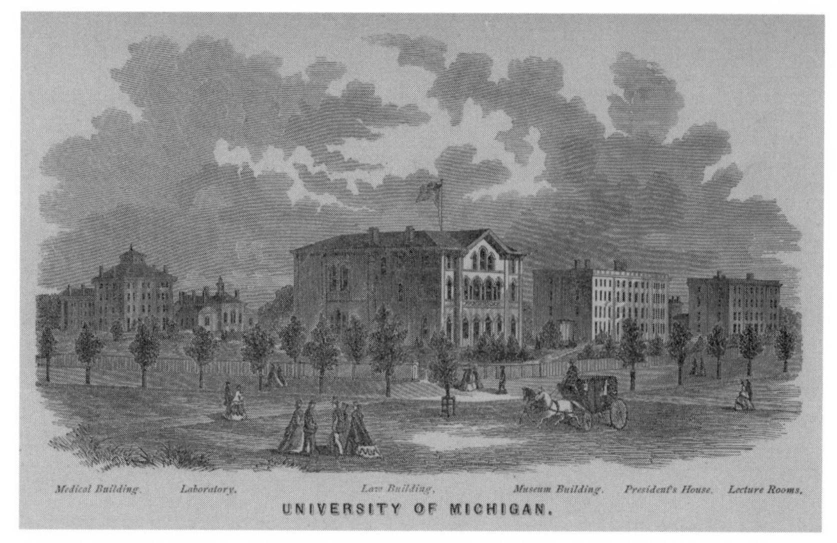

Figure 2: The University of Michigan campus around the time of the Civil War. Credit: BL001931, Bentley Historical Library, University of Michigan.

these things could be cultivated by comprehensive universities. But Tappan still feared the reality that Americans embraced geographical growth at the expense of cultural growth.[29]

Soon after returning from Europe, Henry Tappan gained a chance to shape an American university—albeit one in the west. In 1852, he was appointed president of the University of Michigan upon the recommendation of George Bancroft, who had declined that position. In December, Tappan delivered an inaugural oration that explained his vision for American higher education, as well as his plan for the state-funded university located at Ann Arbor (see Figure 2). Essentially, he rhetorically appropriated the cultural authority he had once claimed for an institution of higher education in the nation's metropolis and entrusted it to a budding institution in a state located on the fringes of America's expanding frontier. Tappan argued that by "demanding the highest institutions of learning" Americans were calling for the creation of universities that prioritized "literary and scientific pursuits." Such universities could house

29. Henry Philip Tappan, *The Growth of Cities: A Discourse Delivered before the New York Geographical Society, on the Evening of March 15th, 1855* (New York, 1855), 29–30.

or cultivate a surfeit of "books, fine arts, mechanical inventions, and improvements in the useful arts; thus creating not only, important and indispensible commodities in trade, but providing also, the very springs of all industry and trade, of all civilization and human improvement, of all national wealth[,] power and greatness." A university was a place of learning and culture, where national spirit could be consolidated and strengthened. It was also an engine of economic progress, a place where knowledge could be harnessed and channeled into growth. Although the University of Michigan was *not* a national university, it might serve many of the same purposes as an avowedly national institution. After all, Michigan's "central and accessible position would enable it to attract students from the surrounding, and even from the more distant States."[30]

Although Tappan maintained a Whiggish orientation toward economic development, it is possible to see that as the American nation expanded westward, so did his vision. He still harbored a belief in temporal development, but circumstances pushed him to accommodate the realities of spatial expansion. Although Ann Arbor was neither New York nor the District of Columbia, the University of Michigan could serve as a state-funded internal improvement, similar to the Erie Canal or the Maysville Road, which would build the nation by facilitating economic and cultural improvements. It is not surprising that a Whig thinker such as Tappan, who had once advocated an urban, national university in New York City, transferred his vision to Michigan after 1850. Like Wayland, he saw that a major university not located in the nation's capital or primary metropolis could still serve as a university of national economic and cultural importance. Even though the raw frontier town of Ann Arbor represented the fruits of territorial expansion, it might be a place where temporal development could take root. As historian Adam Arenson has recently shown, a similar desire motivated the early 1850s Whig founders of Washington University in St. Louis. Men like William Greenleaf Eliot saw that university as an institution of national importance that could help St. Louis win what Arenson calls a "cultural civil war" fought between northerners, southerners, and westerners.[31]

30. Tappan, *Discourse Delivered . . . on the Occasion of his Inauguration*, 8, 46.
31. Arenson, *Great Heart of the Republic*, 55–57.

When historians examine midcentury university leaders such as Tappan and Wayland, we should think not just of curricular innovation based on German models. Rather, we should understand the nationalistic importance of university education for midcentury Americans. Like previous generations, these thinkers argued that Americans would benefit by having universities serve as focal points for learning, letters, and economic development. This was particularly important in the era of 1848, when revolutions swept through Europe and many Americans supported a nation-building based on western expansion. Whig writers like Tappan and Wayland drew both inspiration and warnings for their nationalistic vision from their European sojourns. While they looked to comprehensive universities like those they saw in Britain or Germany or France as a way to consolidate the nation, they also wanted to avoid European monarchy as well as the revolutionary temptation to begin society anew continuously.[32]

Such an analysis, which focuses on the needs and desires of midcentury Americans rather than a teleological view that prioritizes the origins of late-1800s research universities, can help us see that university leaders were not merely trying to import German curriculum or intellect to America. The trans-Atlantic journeys and writings of Tappan and Wayland—viewed in light of their Whig political ideology in an era of European revolutions and American western expansion—reveal their belief that comprehensive universities could raise the United States to European standards of development while at the same time tying the nation together and cultivating a uniquely moderate and democratic national character that relied on temporal (not territorial) expansion. Mid-1800s thought regarding higher education, in other words, was the product of both internal needs and international influences in an era of globally competitive nationalism. Considering their historical context, it should not be surprising that university leaders traveled "From the New World to the Old" to determine what kind of education Americans needed—and then crafted a unique type of university upon their return.

---

32. On national consolidation in the Civil War era, see Bender, *Nation among Nations*, 150–75; Stephen Mihm, *A Nation of Counterfeiters: Capitalists, Con Men, and the Making of the United States* (Cambridge, MA, 2007), 18–19, 361–64; Melinda Lawson, *Patriot Fires: Forging a New American Nationalism in the Civil War North* (Lawrence, KS, 2002), 2–4, 184–85. The Library of Congress was even transformed into a national library after the war; see Ostrowski, *Books, Maps, and Politics*, 210–211.

EDITOR'S PAGE

We've moved! It's been a long time coming, but the editorial office can now be found on the eighth floor of Gladfelter Hall on Temple University's main campus. Temple's History Department has gone out of its way to provide support for *the Journal of the Early Republic.*

July, 2012, marked the official end of my tenure as editor. Adios with best wishes to all and gratitude for the support of a vibrant academic community as well as Temple University's Department of History, SHEAR, the McNeil Center for Early American Studies, and Penn Press.

The editorship now passes to the recent *JER* book review editors David Waldstreicher and Jonathan Daniel Wells. Happily, Andrew Burstein and Nancy Isenberg have agreed to assume the book review editorship. The journal will be in excellent hands. In addition, Kate Tyler Wall continues to serve as a meticulous managing editor, both organized and astute.

Brenna Holland and Patrick Grossi have served ably as editorial interns. Thanks to both! Aaron Sullivan will be taking over to work with the new editors.

Ralph D. Gray Article Prize for 2011—Report of the Prize Committee

It was a privilege and a pleasure to serve on the committee charged with selecting the winner of the Ralph D. Gray Article Prize for Vol. 31 (2011) of the *Journal of the Early Republic.* After a great deal of consideration, the committee has chosen to award the prize to Thomas N. Baker, for his painstakingly-researched and compellingly-presented article, "'An Attack Well Directed': Aaron Burr Intrigues for the Presidency." In uncovering Burr's "stealth campaign to compass the presidency for himself" (556) during the election crisis of 1800, Baker not only provides a significant contribution to our understanding of the election and its aftermath, but also offers a sharp contrast with recent scholarly depictions of Burr as "the consummate gentleman whose

Journal of the Early Republic, 32 (Winter 2012)

pledge of honor to Jefferson and his fellow Republicans in 1800 will not allow him to gratify his ambitions to be president" (557). The force of these arguments rests on the impressive breadth and depth of Baker's research in both archival and published sources and on his finely grained and creative interpretations of often vague and circumstantial evidence. Baker's rediscovery of unknown, unused, and previously misinterpreted materials, combined with his careful parsing of the extensive evidence he has compiled and his clear grasp of the political scenes at the national and certain local levels, allows him to confirm a long-standing suspicion while exposing how many contemporary actors and later historians came to accept Burr's cover-up. Indeed, in many ways this article is as much about the creation, preservation, and organization of manuscript evidence and the production of history as it is about Aaron Burr and the election of 1800. Ultimately, the essay shows that meticulous archival work, coupled with the rereading (and re-rereading) of published sources, can yield new insights on even the most well-known of stories. Thus, it offers a strong affirmation of the fact that no history is completely settled, and that the search for new information and attempts at reinterpretation are worthwhile endeavors.

Our deepest congratulations to Dr. Baker.

Laura Keenan Spero (chair), Karim Tiro, and Sean P. Harvey (winner for 2010).

Editorial Board

Christopher Olsen, Indiana State University
Juliana Barr, University of Florida
Reeve Huston, Duke University
Bethel Saler, Haverford College

Thanks to all the Board members, both the old and the new, for your willingness to serve.

Reviewers

We have been delighted with the responses from reviewers, who overwhelmingly respond "yes" to our pleas to review . . . and then completed the reviews with alacrity. We deeply appreciate their thoughtful and detailed comments on submissions that help maintain the high quality of the *JER* even in this age of larger classes, more committee work, and other pressures on faculty and public historians. Thanks to all.

Susan Klepp, Editor 2009-2012

S.C.
P
M.
N.J.
N.Y.
N.E.
Unite and Conquer

REVIEWS

EDITED BY DAVID WALDSTREICHER AND JONATHAN DANIEL WELLS

***Unnatural Rebellion: Loyalists in New York City during the Revolution*.** By Ruma Chopra. (Charlottesville: University of Virginia Press, 2011. Pp. 320. Cloth, $35.00.)

Reviewed by Serena Zabin

Ruma Chopra's study of New York loyalists does her subjects the honor of taking them seriously. Chopra views loyalists not as heads-in-the-sand reactionaries incapable of seeing the value of radical change but as men who wanted to preserve a system that worked for them and, they believed, for others. In order to reconstruct this perspective, Chopra manages to bring together political thought and material experience—in particular, the experience of military occupation—in ways that are both thoughtful and persuasive.

Chopra's central contention is that the introduction of the British army into New York both supported and undermined loyalist politics of persuasion. Although the loyalists initially welcomed the British troops, seeing them as the facilitators of reunion, their enthusiasm for an occupied city did not last long. Most loyalists did not expect to live under martial law; they wanted a return to civil government as soon as possible so they could again enjoy the benefits of the British empire. Their arguments for an attachment to the empire depended on claims to civil liberties and the British constitution, none of which could be enjoyed in a city under military rule. As Chopra writes, "They believed just and balanced civil governance in New York City would win the hearts and minds of wavering colonists" (79). Yet it was hard to make an argument to nonloyalists for the superiority of the British system when New Yorkers faced military assaults on their borders and undisciplined soldiers at home. Loyalists hoped to use New York as a persuasive model for living under imperial rule; it turned instead into a warning against capitulation to imperial power.

This is an interesting reworking of the arguments by John Shy and Sung Bok Kim (although Chopra does not acknowledge either) that the presence of troops had a notable impact on civilian populations. In 1973, Shy argued that the forced participation of adult men in the militia as well as the outrages committed by the British Army led to an increased politicization of Americans as they became committed to the Whig cause. Kim, by contrast, argued twenty years later that the same processes, at least in Westchester County, led to the opposite outcome of apathy and depoliticization. By asking what impact British troops, and particularly military rule, had on the loyalist political strategy, Chopra excavates a troubling paradox for New York loyalists.[1]

Chopra describes the Revolution in loyalist terms as an "unnatural rebellion." In their eyes, New Yorkers had no reason to become radical; in the mid eighteenth century, they saw themselves happily connected to the British empire through trade and culture. The city's elites bickered over local political power, but for the most part they agreed that they were a part of an empire that had some appropriate control over them. Apparently, enfranchised New Yorkers agreed with them, for they regularly returned members of both the Delancey and Livingston factions to office. The city's heterogeneity, Chopra argues, meant that New Yorkers rarely formed clear political blocs based on class or ethnicity. The early revolutionary conflicts—Stamp Act riots, Quartering Act conflicts, soldiers chopping down the Liberty Tree, even the "Battle of Golden Hill"—seemed to produce more internal factionalism in New York City than it did loyalism or hostility to the British Empire itself.

Chopra suggests that no New Yorkers moved toward separation with Britain until the passage of the Coercion Acts against Boston in 1774. Benjamin Carp has recently argued that the Boston Tea Party of 1773 was in part the Bostonians' attempt to prove to their radical neighbors in New York (and elsewhere) that they were committed to some form of

1. John Shy, "The American Revolution: The Military Conflict Considered as a Revolutionary War" in *Essays on the American Revolution*, ed. Stephen G. Kurtz and James H. Hutson (Chapel Hill, NC, 1973), 121–56; Sung Bok Kim, "The Limits of Politicization in the American Revolution: The Experience of Westchester County, New York," *Journal of American History* 80 (Dec. 1993), 868–89.

resistance; it would have been helpful to know what sense Chopra made of the non-importation movement in New York in the late 1760s and early 1770s. Does she interpret it as something different from "rebellion"? Chopra is more interested, however, in the clear ruptures in Massachusetts between 1774 and 1776 as explanations for New Yorkers' increasing sense of urgency that something had to be done about the imperial relationship. Given New York City's strategic importance for the mid-Atlantic and for access to Canada, both sides made the city a focus of their military plans, and the hardline attitudes of Continental Army generals like Charles Lee soon pushed moderates and loyalists out of the city. Loyalists longed for the British army to protect them and restore the city to its profitable relationship with the rest of the empire. Their hopes, however, were misplaced.[2]

Even after taking over New York, the British army was not as effective as loyalists had hoped. Shocked by British losses in battle and the French alliance, loyalists nonetheless did not give up on Britain even two years into the war. Still, they wondered, with some peevishness, how to convince the British army that loyalists should be partners, not dependents walled up in an occupied city.

Different loyalists had competing desires for their British alliance. Hawks frequently petitioned for more firepower, while moderate merchants pleaded to resume trade. The desires of non-elites are harder to ascertain. Refugees to the occupied city, for example, were often black, female, poor, or otherwise undesirable in the eyes of loyalist or army elites. Chopra effectively establishes their presence, but they do little to advance her story of loyalist frustration with the British military. Divided all along, moderates and hardliners fought not only about the role of loyalist military units, but also about political power. Poorer refugees suffered between the military abuses and loyalist politics.

Although the book is both chronological and thematic, the chapters seem to force the two strategies together awkwardly. Changes of heart (and minds) did not take place solely within three- or four-month periods, and Chopra is sometimes forced to abandon the chronology in order to explain loyalist sentiments. This route may be intellectually honest, but it is hard to follow.

---

2. Benjamin L. Carp, *Defiance of the Patriots: The Boston Tea Party and the Making of America* (New Haven, CT, 2010).

The most disappointing gap in the book is the lack of explicit engagement with the rich historiography on New York's loyalists, in particular Judith Van Buskirk's *Generous Enemies: Patriots and Loyalists in Revolutionary New York* (Philadelphia, 2002). Van Buskirk argued that the clear lines between loyalist and patriot were often muddied by personal and familial ties in and around the occupied city. Chopra, by contrast, claims that the presence of the army "locked" in political allegiance (44). Moreover, because the arguments of Chopra's loyalists were so often theoretical and idealistic, rather than personal or pragmatic, she finds herself restricted to a top-down description of the loyalist community. These criticisms aside, this is a nuanced and thought-provoking study of the painful process some New Yorkers endured in order to stay loyal to the British Empire.[3]

SERENA ZABIN is an associate professor at Carleton College. She is the author of *Dangerous Economies: Commerce and Status in Imperial New York* (Philadelphia, 2009).

Clothed in Robes of Sovereignty: The Continental Congress and the People Out of Doors. By Benjamin H. Irvin. (New York: Oxford University Press, 2011. Pp. 392. Cloth, $34.95).

Reviewed by Robert Parkinson

In February 2011, hours before the game started, the Fox network began its television coverage of Super Bowl XLV with a video montage featuring current and former NFL players reciting phrases from the Declaration of Independence. Starting in the forum of the National Archives with NFL Commissioner Roger Goodell and former Secretary of State Colin Powell, players read Jefferson's words from an assortment of patriotic venues across the United States—in front of the Golden Gate Bridge, on an aircraft carrier, at the Statue of Liberty. This performance was the latest, and most direct, effort to conflate what has become America's two holiest national days, the Fourth of July and Super Bowl Sunday. After

3. Judith L. Van Buskirk, *Generous Enemies: Patriots and Loyalists in Revolutionary New York* (Philadelphia, 2003).

reading Benjamin Irvin's book, *Clothed in Robes of Sovereignty*, it is clear that had the delegates to the Continental Congress tuned in, they would have loved it. For Congress, Irvin argues, had "dedicated substantial creative energies" (281) to the exact same project of affecting American emotions and trying to inspire patriotic feeling long before Jefferson's words—now delivered by quarterbacks and former coaches—existed.

Irvin argues that the Continental Congress, through careful, strategic appeals to "emotion, passion, faith, morality, sensibility, and aesthetics," forwarded "not a volitional model of governance, but rather an affective one" (5). Irvin sets aside studies of Congress that highlight internal factions, diplomatic or military policy decisions, or the philosophical expressions of the rational Enlightenment. Instead, *Clothed in the Robes of Sovereignty* focuses on the material and ceremonial culture that the members of Congress cultivated almost incessantly throughout the Revolution: flags and insignia, anthems and songs, parades and military display, monuments and statues, holidays and commemorations. It is a contribution to the literature on how nations "invent traditions," a concept most associated with a 1983 collection of essays edited by Eric Hobsbawm and Terence Ranger.[1] That book focused on how European authorities attempted to legitimize their rule by wrapping themselves in the mantle of cultural expressions that were thought to be ancient and traditional but were in fact brand new. Irvin explains how the Continental Congress—a body without a shred of constitutional legitimacy or legal standing—began to dedicate an impressive amount of time and resources into the same cultural processes as soon as it convened in the fall of 1774. In these efforts of political culture even more than in policy statements there emerged the shape of what political leaders believed the Revolution was about, Irvin argues. He examines how Congress tried to police public morals in the Continental Association, how they crafted a currency that projected "appropriate" values, and how they approved medals and fast days to solidify unity.

The motivation undergirding all this work was readily apparent, according to Irvin. Although historians have given short shrift to their efforts to mold an American political culture, delegates to Congress understood that many Americans were paying attention. Public trust was

1. Eric Hobsbawm and Terence Ranger, eds., *The Invention of Tradition* (Cambridge, UK, 1983).

in the balance. How the American people responded to their efforts of cultural suasion was critical to whether or not the *resolutions* passed by Congress would be followed. Martial resistance, the legitimacy of independence, the promotion of a national identity, the support of public morale: All these depended on how Congress won the battle of political culture.

To illuminate how the public received these efforts, Irvin focuses on the local context of Congress—i.e., how Philadelphians "embraced, rejected, or reconfigured Congress's offerings as it pleased them" (283). Irvin's discussions of contested reception are among the best parts of *Clothed in Robes*, for Congress had many competitors limiting its efforts to establish cultural legitimacy. The first, of course, was "Congress." That body was never "of a single mind" (282) and fought internally about what constituted proper modes of cultural expenditure. Another competing interest was "the people out-of-doors." When, for example, Congress decided to sidestep its own rules prohibiting conspicuous display to throw a gala for Martha Washington, Philadelphians called them to account, threatening to destroy City Tavern if they went ahead with their hypocrisy. Later on, the people voiced their own ideas about how to commemorate American independence or how to chastise Benedict Arnold for his apostasy, in expressions often more radical and violent than those the delegates to Congress preferred. Other competitors included Loyalist writers who impugned their masculinity and questioned their sanity. And, as the war progressed, Continental Army officers labored to develop their own ceremonial culture, while French diplomatic agents also forwarded a court culture incongruent with the republican values Congress attempted to establish. The second half of *Clothed in Robes* is a catalog of how Congress, bankrupt and divided, was increasingly upstaged if not outright ignored.

Irvin's emphasis on the material and cultural aspects of Congress's effort to carve out a political legitimacy for itself—to earn *sovereignty* not via declarations of independence but by the maxims on currency or the issuance of a commemorative sword—is at once an important contribution to the political historiography of the Revolution and a somewhat embarrassing one. Irvin's contribution is long overdue, but this is hardly his fault. His findings bring to mind what historians familiar with European studies of political culture have known for nearly a generation. Their work on "invented traditions," on the role ritual plays in the acceptance of political authority, and how the people shape these efforts to match their own agendas, and on the formulation of a national identity are all on display in this work, a grounding that makes *Clothed in Robes* seem a bit dated. But yet the problems that faced Hobsbawm and his ilk have not vanished, especially on the question of fostering a collective sense of national identity. Irvin spends a great part of *Clothed in Robes* undercutting Congress's efforts, describing how it failed far more than it succeeded. This leaves the reader wondering just how important all these efforts to shape American affection toward their government really were. What were the stakes? Had they not spent such "energies" on cultural matters, would the Revolution have turned out differently? Did these rituals—all the medals struck, feast days proclaimed, and statues dedicated—make people *feel* more American in 1776? Did they inspire loyalty to the Revolution in 1780? Do they on Super Bowl Sunday? Does it turn out that affective tableau (like backdrops of aircraft carriers, suspension bridges, or football players) mean more than the words announcing independence?

ROBERT G. PARKINSON holds the Roy and Madeline Johnston Chair of American History and is associate professor at Shepherd University. His book, *The Common Cause: Race, Nation, and the Consequences of Unity in the American Revolution*, is forthcoming.

***James Madison: A Son of Virginia and a Founder of the Nation*.** By Jeff Broadwater. (Chapel Hill: University of North Carolina Press, 2012. Pp. 266 + xviii. Cloth, $30.00.)

Reviewed by Kevin R. C. Gutzman

Jeff Broadwater, author of a George Mason biography, here turns his attention to Mason's even more august Virginia contemporary. Recognizing that James Madison has been the object of numerous scholars' attention these past several decades, he begins by denying any intention to improve upon their work. Rather, he says he has "focused on those aspects of Madison's life that are apt to be of the most enduring interest to the most readers" (xv).

Madison deserves attention, according to Broadwater, because he was second among the Founders only to George Washington in indispensability. Broadwater seemingly contradicts this evaluation in lamenting that many historians have found Madison's role in writing the U.S. Constitution and *The Federalist* far more significant than the rest of his life, "including his two terms as a supposedly mediocre president" (xi).

Broadwater will not focus, then, on Madison as constitution-writer. What he delivers instead is a brief, introductory biographical survey with particular attention to church–state relations, slavery, the Virginia Dynasty, and Dolley Madison's political role. Nearly one-third of the book's 210 pages are given over to an account of Madison's sixteen-year tenure first as Thomas Jefferson's secretary of state and subsequently as president in his own right.

An appraisal of Broadwater's work may thus fairly ask both whether focusing on Madison's role as constitution-writer would be inappropriate and whether Broadwater proves Madison to have been something other than a mediocre president. In regard to the first, it seems that if we are to accept Broadwater's assertion that Madison ranks second to Washington, the reason must be Madison's leading role in convening the Philadelphia Convention, drafting the Constitution, and winning its ratification. One might therefore have wished for greater attention to this portion of Madison's career than Broadwater provides. So little interested is Broadwater in Madison's record as a constitutional draftsman that he says essentially nothing about the writing of the Virginia Constitution of 1776, the first written constitution adopted by the people's representatives in the history of the world, other than to note Madison's presence on the committee that drafted it.

An even greater difficulty comes in squaring Broadwater's account of Madison's presidency with his implication that his subject somehow excelled the run of chief executives. Broadwater follows Ralph Ketcham in asserting that Madison's lack of Hamiltonian energy as a wartime president, his tendency to defer to Congress to a fault, amounted to republican (certainly Republican) virtue. True or false, this argument does not strike your reviewer as a case for Madison's excellence. A Jeffersonian appraisal must be that in implementing Congress's rather half-baked war policies without insinuating himself into a policymaking process the Constitution assigned to Congress, Madison acted precisely as a president ought. Far from elevating Madison above the "mediocre" category, this amounts to indicting our contemporary tendency to expect the president to lead despite the Congress. There is much to be said for this Jeffersonian position, but let us recognize that if the Jeffersonians had their way, mediocrity—lack of self-assertion—is what we would learn to hope for. Broadwater might have said that President Madison's mediocrity was itself a virtue.

Broadwater saves his attention to the matter of slavery for the end of the book, where he is critical of Madison on that score. In the Virginia Constitutional Convention of 1829–30, Broadwater faults his subject for having worked for a compromise between Tidewater conservatives and western reformers by which the growing west gained far more power in the General Assembly than it had had before, but not one man, one vote. What Madison should have done, Broadwater implies, is make a principled stand in behalf of the whole loaf—which would have risked gaining nothing at all. It would be surprising if the James Madison who had in the name of the greater good accepted an apportionment scheme for the U.S. Senate against which he had railed throughout the summer of 1787 had become an uncompromising doctrinaire by 1829–30.

Throughout the book, Broadwater relies extensively on the secondary literature, particularly the biographies of Irving Brant, Ralph Ketcham, Garry Wills, and Jack Rakove and the more focused studies of Ketcham, Lance Banning, Catherine Allgor, and Drew McCoy. Besides, it is at times unclear where Broadwater ends and Madison begins. For example, in Broadwater's description of Madison's response to the Nullification Crisis, he says that the Constitution was not a compact among the states (as Madison had said it was in calling ratification a "federal" act in *The Federalist* #39, and as his fellow leading Federalist spokesmen had assured during the Richmond Ratification Convention), but a compact among one people (which would have been "national" ratification, *pace* Madison-Publius) (203). One wishes Broadwater had confronted Madison's tergiversations head on, even while recognizing that avoiding the issue has become the standard approach.[1]

Broadwater takes issue with the standard view here and there, as in denying that Napoleon bamboozled Madison on one notable occasion (158), but in general he lives up to his promise not to try to improve on or correct the Madison historiography.

KEVIN R. C. GUTZMAN, Western Connecticut State University, is the author of *James Madison and the Making of America* (New York, 2012).

1. For a full exploration of these issues, see Kevin R. C. Gutzman, *James Madison and the Making of America* (New York, 2012).

A Town In-Between: Carlisle, Pennsylvania, and the Early Mid-Atlantic Interior. By Judith Ridner. (Philadelphia: University of Pennsylvania Press, 2010. Pp. 287. Cloth, $49.95.)

Reviewed by Gabrielle M. Lanier

The interior town of Carlisle, Pennsylvania was always, according to Judith Ridner, "a town in-between." Geographically, it was an urban place in a rural area, situated between the urban east and the agrarian west. Culturally, it constituted a migration gateway to the interior, at times accommodating multiple and sometimes competing groups including Native Americans, English Quakers, Germans, and Scots–Irish. Economically, it formed the hub of the colonial fur trade. Militarily, it became a staging and supply ground during two major wars. This between-ness rendered Carlisle "a contested space between east and west, north and south, Europe and America, and Euro-American and Native American" (3–4). The region had always represented a geography of possibilities: for the first Native Americans who situated their villages there, for Thomas Penn and his officials who sought control of the area because it promised access to Philadelphia and the Native communities to the west, for the Scots–Irish colonists who risked hardship to gain personal and material success, for Congress and the Continental Army who used the town to hold prisoners and supply arms, and for the founders of Dickinson College who sought to create an educated citizenry in a major interior town.

A Town In-Between is a rich and deeply researched microhistory of Carlisle in the eighteenth century. The author draws from a wide range of evidence including letters, account books, wills, deed abstracts, personal papers, newspapers, and census records. Ridner's stated goal is to reconceptualize the roles of such towns in developing the early American interior. She succeeds. Building on the contributions of other scholars including John Reps, Lisa Tolbert, John Frederick Martin, William Wyckoff, Christopher E. Hendricks, Gregory Nobles, and Richard C. Wade, Ridner argues that towns like Carlisle were more than just, as Wade maintains, spearheads of the urban frontier because of their utility and growth potential. While town founding doubtless played a role in colonizing the interior, Ridner argues that Carlisle's between-ness rendered it more of a hub than a spearhead. As such, Carlisle was "both unique and representative" (10), and her study suggests that towns like it were critical "to the adaptation of republican politics, metropolitan cultural standards, and proto-capitalist economic practices across the early American interior" (205).

The book includes an introduction and six chronologically organized chapters that cover the town's founding in 1751; subsequent boundary negotiations; changes prompted by the Seven Years' War and American Revolution; the founding of Dickinson College and concurrent changes to the regional economy; and economic, political, and social conditions at the close of the eighteenth century. Because they extended proprietary government, served as vehicles for cultural assimilation, and promoted commercial interests, towns like Carlisle were important tools of British colonization. Carlisle was intended to serve as an interior commercial center midway between Philadelphia and the Ohio country. Thus, Carlisle's founders superimposed its urban grid plan on a rural landscape that had long stood as a place in-between. While the presence of the Susquehanna River had governed early Native American settlement patterns, the area also constituted a major intersection of prehistoric travel routes. Yet Carlisle also represented a series of compromises between the proprietor's vision and the diverse objectives and cultures of its early inhabitants. Immigration to Pennsylvania and the growing consumer economy connected Carlisle to the surrounding region and the broader British Atlantic world. Major roads such as the Great Road brought colonists into Carlisle and the interior beyond, defining the town as a county hub that linked farmers, markets, meetinghouses, producers, merchants, and consumers.

Carlisle also formed an essential link in the fur trade, which created conflict. The Seven Years' War brought war-related service activities and people to the town, and population and economic growth ensued. Carlisle became a staging ground as well as a supply and provisioning center during the war. The Revolution fueled a dramatic decline in Carlisle's fur and skin trade, but new opportunities arose when the town became a holding site for prisoners and an important supply and arms manufacturing depot for the Continental Army.

In 1787, the public denunciation by anti-Federalists of the new Constitution confirmed the town's heritage as a contested space, lending it heightened national importance because of Shays's Rebellion and other similar acts of popular resistance (152). The town also experienced post-Revolutionary cultural and economic change. The founding of Dickinson College, part of a broader push to sustain the republic by creating an educated citizenry, occurred at a time when the fur trade was dwindling and wartime supply functions had ceased, but the grain trade, which helped to knit urban and rural parts of the economy together, was expanding. Carlisle soon became the place where grain was brought to be transported to Philadelphia and Baltimore markets.

By 1800, Carlisle had become the fifth largest Pennsylvania town. Although it no longer resembled the coarse colonial village it had once seemed, and economic inequality was increasing, Carlisle retained significant continuities with its past: It still remained a crossroads between regions as well as a contested place. In fact, Carlisle was one of two interior towns where tensions over the whiskey tax surged enough to create major disturbances. The town's protests over whiskey mirrored "wider struggles over access to economic and cultural privilege in a town where wealth and status gaps were growing" (194–95).

The book's first few chapters are particularly strong. But while the organizing idea of a place in-between works well when the focus is Carlisle's founding, the regional significance of the fur trade, and the effects of war and revolution, it is less effective for the later periods Ridner discusses. Similarly, the author's contention that Carlisle was representative of other towns, and that "Carlisle's settlement and political-economic patterns model how other interior towns functioned and how their inhabitants experienced a life in-between others" (4) is insufficiently demonstrated and remains less convincing. Still, Ridner's highly readable study makes a significant contribution to our understanding of the role of towns in the early American interior.

Gabrielle M. Lanier is a professor of history at James Madison University. She is the author of *The Delaware Valley in the Early Republic: Architecture, Landscape, and Regional Identity* (Baltimore, 2005) and coauthor, with Bernard L. Herman, of *Everyday Architecture of the Mid-Atlantic: Looking at Buildings and Landscapes* (Baltimore, 1997).

Common Bondage: Slavery as Metaphor in Revolutionary America. By Peter Dorsey. (Knoxville: University of Tennessee Press, 2009. Pp. xviii + 276. Cloth, $43.95.)

Reviewed by François Furstenberg

Eighteenth-century British North Americans, who benefited from some of the highest standards of living and greatest political and religious freedoms in the Atlantic world, found themselves, in the 1770s, sitting in coffee houses, sipping tea infused with sugar, smoking pipes of tobacco, wearing indigo-dyed clothes—and denouncing "slavery." By that term they did not mean the real slavery of some half-million people of African descent on the North American mainland, but rather a metaphoric slavery that, in their fevered imaginations, threatened the political liberties of people of European descent.

The spectacle has long fascinated and repelled observers. From Samuel Johnson's famous quip in the 1770s to the great scholarship in the late 1960s and 1970s by Edmund Morgan, David Brion Davis, Winthrop Jordan, and others, these slave drivers yelping for liberty have generated penetrating commentary. The literary scholar Peter Dorsey now launches himself into the mix with a stimulating and frustrating study, the most detailed exploration to date of what he calls "the slavery metaphor" in British North America.

Dorsey makes a strong case for a venerable historical interpretation: that the Revolution undermined slavery. The slavery metaphor—by its own internal logic—pulled down the barriers between political and chattel slavery, between slavery as figure of speech and slavery as coerced labor, and led, almost inevitably, to abolition in the North and a wave of emancipation in the South. Dorsey shows how this process worked, in part, through the operation of language itself. Drawing on theories of metaphor, he recruits an array of thinkers—from Hobbes and Locke in seventeenth century to Wayne Booth, Jacques Derrida, George Lakoff, Paul Ricoeur, Toni Morrison, Richard Rorty, and Hayden White (among others) in the twentieth—to argue that metaphor can "bring about a semantic change or a redescription of reality" (24). Which is precisely what the slavery metaphor accomplished: It "altered the reality of eighteenth-century white Americans," provoking them "to imagine themselves as slaves" (25). It thus "merged revolutionary goals and antislavery activism," and "altered the way patriots spoke about slavery" (28, 111).

Anchored in the rhetoric of colonial resistance, the slavery metaphor made Whigs vulnerable to charges of "hypocrisy" (85, passim). Loyalists, pushing full-bore into the ideological breach, adopted an increasingly antislavery position to highlight their opponents' liability. In response, Whigs had no choice but to embrace the cause. Abolitionists then jumped through this "rhetorical opening," using the Whigs' metaphoric language against the institution of slavery (156). "White abolitionists, African Americans, as well as Royalists, repeatedly and forcefully challenged Whig writers to live up to their words" (108). It all resulted in "growing antislavery convictions" across the colonies (110). "Patriots," Dorsey argues, "increasingly believed that eliminating slavery was the price they were going to have to pay for independence" (113). So far did antislavery sentiment go, it gave rise to the terrifying specter of total race war—a 180-degree turn of Fortune's wheel—leading black writers like Phillis Wheatley to "assuage the widespread racial fears ignited by the Revolution" and its militant live-free-or-die language by emphasizing benevolent, Christian virtues that ultimately undermined the struggle for abolition itself (173). Despite this turn, however, "the patriots' antislavery sentiments continued to shape the consciences of American," and, in the long run, "would continue to remind white Americans that chattel slavery self-evidently conflicted with their founding ideals" (217–18).

But Dorsey is not content with a simple linear account; his book pushes in many directions along the way. The slavery metaphor was, as Dorsey shows, "ever flexible," employed by a variety of actors to a variety of ends (72). Even as it drove white Americans toward antislavery, it also promoted "contempt" for slaves and stimulated "great racial differentiation . . . [by] suggesting that those who have already submitted to slavery were unworthy of freedom" (30). The slavery metaphor also "altered the era's understanding of gender" by opposing "the virtuous manhood of American Whigs and the effeminate corruption of Royalists" (56). Even as it denigrated feminized traits, however, it opened a space for women as political actors and "enabled white women to participate in the construction of republican and egalitarian values" (72). Racial views, likewise, were "complex and sometimes contradictory" (140). Phillis Wheatley's poetry moved "the experience of slavery from the margins of American society into the center" rather than, as Whig rhetoric did, "separate the issue of chattel bondage and political freedom"—although readers of earlier chapters might be forgiven for thinking that Whig rhetoric did something else (169). So, too, "Black Atlantic" writers abandoned revolutionary rhetoric in favor of a Christian paternalism: an interpretation based on a very narrow reading of African American (not to speak of Black Atlantic) literature and a total erasure of (for instance) the Haitian Revolution and its great influence in the United States.

Dorsey has a wonderfully fertile mind. Some of his observations are arresting in their originality; others border on the clichéd. Some of the quotations he presents are remarkable and fresh; others among the hoariest and most familiar. (I, for one, would love to see a discussion of these issues that does not come to a climax with Jefferson.) Perhaps this is inevitable. The slavery metaphor, after all, was a "crucial and fluid concept . . . applied to a wide variety of events and values and was constantly being defined and redefined" (xi). Still, by the end of the book, with my thoughts provoked but my head spinning, I was put less in mind of Jefferson and more of that great lyricist, Katy Perry: "You're yes then you're no/ You're in then you're out/ You're up then you're down."

Like any important concept, the slavery metaphor was indeed complex and contradictory, fluid and malleable, ambiguous and multivalent, defined and redefined. That language always gets heads nodding in seminar rooms, needless to say, but as scholarly argument (or as song lyric for that matter), it leaves me wanting more. I realize this is probably an unpopular position among historians rightly wary of simplification, or scholars appropriately imbued with postmodern instincts, but it seems to me that authors should not just elaborate the complex and contradictory nature of things, but should also try to impart, however imperfectly or even wrongly, greater coherence to the fascinating ideas they work so hard, and with so much benefit to readers, to unearth.

François Furstenberg is the author of *In the Name of the Father: Washington's Legacy, Slavery, and the Making of a Nation* (New York, 2006); he is currently at work on a book connecting French and U.S. history in the late eighteenth century.

The Trial of Frederick Eberle: Language, Patriotism, and Citizenship in Philadelphia's German Community, 1790 to 1830. By Friederike Baer. (New York: New York University Press, 2008. Pp. viii + 272. Cloth, $48.00.)

Reviewed by Wolfgang Splitter

In her book on a militant conflict about the use of English in early nineteenth-century Philadelphia's German Lutheran congregation, Friederike Baer tells the intriguing story of a community that was bitterly torn between fidelity to German culture and the Lutheran creed on the one hand and the inevitable need to adapt to Anglo American society with its promises of social advancement, political participation, and economic independence on the other. After the 1806 secession of numerous reputable families and individuals, this conflict culminated in July of 1816 when the state of Pennsylvania tried 59 proponents of the exclusive use of German in the church on charges of conspiracy and rioting for beating several champions of English as the second language for preaching. Eventually, the court convicted the defendants, who received relatively mild sentences.

Caught in an aporetic battle that held out little more than a Pyrrhic victory to the winner, both sides could justly claim a deep-felt commitment to their ancestral heritage and to the ideals of the American republic. Whereas the so-called German party insisted that the essence of the Lutheran teachings were captured best in the original German and therefore should be handed down to posterity in no language other than Martin Luther's mother tongue, the English party was concerned that more and more young Americans of German descent, socialized in an English-speaking society, would no longer be able to follow a Sunday sermon or understand Luther's catechism and hence were likely to leave the Lutheran church sooner or later. While the German party pleaded the right of American citizens strictly to abide by the language of their forefathers—which was not at stake here anyway—and to regulate all church matters free from encroachment by the authorities, the English party protested that their opponents not only put the survival of the congregation at risk by causing a mass exodus of young parishioners but also attempted to curtail their property rights by driving them out of a church to which they and their forebears had made substantial contributions. In addition, they emphasized the great benefits of moving with the times by cautiously yielding to the predominant influence of English.

Based on her intimate knowledge of the relevant primary sources and secondary literature, Friederike Baer convincingly shows in her clearly structured work that this fierce and protracted controversy was much more than a family feud antagonizing recent arrivals and long-established Americans, German speakers and English speakers, "true" Lutherans and "sham" Lutherans. In analyzing this passionate as much as self-destructive struggle, her analysis unfolds a complex interplay of historical, cultural, social, economic, and political factors that, in a similar setting, also troubled Reformed and Catholic Christians of German extraction.

If there is anything at all that Baer's insightful book leaves to be desired, one might think of three points. First, since the author rightly stresses the importance of the protagonists' socioeconomic background, it would have been useful to find the scattered biographic information that she actually provides for certain individuals (especially in chapters 3 and 4) briefly summarized in a table listing age, date of immigration, profession, taxes paid, place of residence in Philadelphia, and membership in other German organizations. Such a table would have corroborated her arguments even more pointedly by facilitating the collation of the respective data for the two parties.

Second, although Baer touches on marriage patterns of the English party in passing (139–40), she generally pays scant attention to intermarriage between German Americans and non-German Americans, European-born and American-born persons, Lutherans and non-Lutherans. Since marriage patterns are a crucial indicator of social cohesion, it would have been interesting to know more about both groups in this respect. After all, with German immigration slowing down markedly during and after the Revolution, members of the two parties are likely to have increasingly married American-born spouses whose persuasion may not always have been Lutheran, as was already the case in the late colonial era when German pastors lamented the weakening of confessional bonds by marriages of Lutherans to Reformed or even "sectarian" Protestants.

Third, in her investigation of the German party's motives for steadfastly rejecting all offers of compromise regarding the introduction of English, Baer clearly gives the protection of Germanness preference over the preservation of Lutheran identity. By all appearances, however, the confessional issue ranked at the top of the various reasons she mentions (all of which are no doubt valid). Any native German speaker familiar with Luther's translation of the Bible who attentively reads an English rendering of the Old and New Testaments will easily notice differences in connotation when coming across the English words for Lutheran key notions such as *Anfechtung* (temptation, trial), *Beruf* (calling, vocation), *Obrigkeit* (authority, rule), *Ordnung* (order, arrangement), *Treue* (loyalty, fidelity, faithfulness), and many more. Moreover, one does not need to be a linguist to imagine that certain passages of the Bible import slightly different meanings in German with its frequent use of nominalizations, impersonal expressions, and passive-voice phrases, than in English, which prefers verbalization, personal expressions, and active-voice clauses. Romans 13:1–4, the *locus classicus* of Luther's doctrine of authority and obedience, may serve as an instructive example. Against this background, the German party's apprehensions of losing their forebears' language and, with it, the distinctive spiritual foundations of their creed seem less irrational than the author suggests.

Friederike Baer has written a conclusive and well-conceived study that truly deserves a broad readership among scholars and students of many stripes. This fine piece of research demonstrates the great potential of community studies to elucidate general developments in politics, society, or religion by carefully investigating competing social, economic, political, and cultural interests with small, manageable groups of people at the local level.

WOLFGANG SPLITTER is a research fellow with the Center for United States Studies at Martin Luther University in Halle, Germany. He is the author of *Pastors, People, Politics: German Lutherans in Pennsylvania, 1740–1790* (Trier, 1998) and currently is working on a biography of Henry Melchior Muhlenberg.

Thomas Jefferson's Haitian Policy: Myths and Realities. By Arthur Scherr. (Lanham, MD: Lexington Books, 2011. Pp. 714. Cloth, $120.00.)

Reviewed by Wendy H. Wong

Did Thomas Jefferson hate the Haitian Revolution to the point of seeking to destroy it? In *Thomas Jefferson's Haitian Policy*, Arthur Scherr argues that no, he did not. Instead, he argues that historians, particularly American historians, need to read Jefferson on the Haitian Revolution more carefully. In aiming to write a "revaluation of values relating to Thomas Jefferson and the political, social, and cultural history of the United States in the Long Eighteenth Century" (ix), he challenges historical interpretations, both older and more recent, that commonly claim that Jefferson so wished to destroy the Haitian Revolution out of fear and hatred for blacks that he cooperated with France in embargoing trade with Haiti, to say nothing of how the Federalists were far more progressive than their Republican counterparts in their treatment of the emerging black republic.

Far from simply being a racist who sought to do little more than to crush and starve Haiti to assuage his own paranoia, Jefferson's position was far more nuanced: The founding father was actually sympathetic to the Haitian Revolution for various reasons. Slave revolt did not surprise Jefferson, and indeed, he saw it as justified in the face of the brutal injustice of slavery. Furthermore, Haiti was a potential solution to the young republic's slavery problem. In accordance with his earlier thoughts in *Notes on the State of Virginia*, Haiti was potentially a place where the United States could send its freed slaves and free African Americans. White and black could not hope to live in harmony due to the latter being a captive nation that resented their servitude, and slavery ultimately degraded southern whites. Therefore, manumission and subsequent deportation would prevent sectionalism and race warfare on American soil. Jefferson's complex feelings about slavery notwithstanding, some of which continue to grate on modern sensibilities for their presumption of a United States where African Americans had no place, Scherr argues that it did not necessarily follow that Jefferson wished to crush Haiti either directly or indirectly. Thus, Jefferson's policy toward Haiti was far from malevolent.

Scherr's purpose is to examine what historians have said about Jefferson and Haiti, what Jefferson *actually* said about slave revolts in general and Haiti, as well as his views and policies toward Haiti and its slave insurrection. His focus is largely one of diplomatic power politics, laying out the tenuous triangular relationship between France, the United States, and the emerging independent republic of Haiti. The picture of Jefferson that emerges is that he was well acquainted with power politics and was no mere idealist: Between 1793 and 1799, Jefferson linked the slave revolt on St. Domingue, the foreign policy of the Franco-American Alliance, and the French Revolution (87–88). In his strategic calculus, Atlantic isolation plus proximity to vulnerable and valuable European colonies would afford the United States military supremacy in the Western hemisphere. The foreign policy of the Jefferson administration was not subservient to French influence and power, and Jefferson was not sympathetic to Napoleon's efforts to crush the Haitian insurrection. Rather, the French complained bitterly about American hostilities to French interests, given that American merchants aided and supplied the Haitians (346, 354). Furthermore, it was mostly northern Federalists who harbored fears of a joint Haitian-French invasion of the southern states; southerners like Jefferson and Madison were largely indifferent (304). Also, it was a Pennsylvania Republican, George Logan, who initiated the embargo, and not Jefferson (483), and it was those who had no trading interests who advocated for its stricter enforcement.

This book builds on builds on earlier work the Haitian Revolution and slavery in the United States, such as Rayford Logan's *The Diplomatic Relations of the United States with Haiti* (Chapel Hill, NC, 2011), Winthrop Jordan's *White Over Black: American Attitudes Toward the Negro, 1550–1812* (Chapel Hill, NC, 1968), and Laurent Dubois's *Avengers of the New World: The Story of the Haitian Revolution* (Cambridge, MA, 2005) while addressing the work of Peter Onuf, Tim Matthewson, Robin Blackburn, and Douglas Egerton, among others. In so doing, Scherr foregrounds the contingencies of international diplomacy: Haiti and Haitians are actors in their own right, and not just passively acted upon by the United States and the great European powers, or merely reduced to the issue of race. Furthermore, he brings work in Haitian history into conversation with the history of the early American republic and its troubled relationship with France. Much of the value of this book lies in its meticulous scholarship. In his close reading of his sources—namely letters, diplomatic documents and periodicals—he has done some intricate detective work, not just in terms of Franco-American-Haitian relations, but in terms of what evidence exists that suggests the options and motives of key players such as Jefferson and Madison in both diplomacy and domestic politics. Thus, the book also reflects how closely intertwined the foreign and the domestic were.

Stylistically, however, the monograph is convoluted in places, given its length, and repetitive, due to the author's admitted purpose of serving up "history with a hammer" (ix). As a result, his larger arguments and their significance risk getting lost in a plethora of detail, intriguing as those details are. In addition, occasional snide asides referring to historical actors such as John Adams (14) and to historians who, the author argues, are misguided or careless in their scholarship are unhelpful and unnecessarily distracting. Still, this is an amply researched book, and Scherr's work suggests future work that may be done on trade between the United States and Haiti, in addition to the strides historians have made recently to integrate foreign relations with Haiti into the political culture and political economy of the early republic.

WENDY H. WONG is a PhD candidate at Temple University. She is currently at work on a dissertation entitled "Diplomatic Subtleties and Frank Overtures: Publicity, Diplomacy, and Neutrality in the Early American Republic, 1793–1801."

Empires of the Imagination: Transatlantic Histories of the Louisiana Purchase. Edited by Peter J. Kastor and François Weil. (Charlottesville, VA: University of Virginia Press, 2009. Pp. 376. Cloth, $40.00.)

Reviewed by Marise Bachand

The Louisiana Purchase came as a surprise on both sides of the Atlantic, the authors of *Empires of the Imagination* remind us. The last addition to a series of studies that commemorates the bicentennial of what the French call *la vente de la Louisiane*, this collection strives to revise the "Anglocentric vision of the North American West" (17). In synch with the theme of "imagination," well-established scholars explore the mental constructs of people involved or affected by the Purchase—including the geopolitical imagination of Jefferson (Peter Onuf), the prerevolutionary categories of Napoleon (Laurent Dubois), or the conceptions of power of the Choctaw Indians (Cécile Vidal). The essays are organized in three parts, respectively entitled Empire, Identity, and Memory. To get a good grasp on the historiography, however, the very last essay of the collection, written by Jacques Portes and Marie-Jeanne Rossignol, should be read first. Besides giving a sense of the very different treatment of the Purchase in American and French historiographical traditions, the two historians acutely pose the problem of distance between academic knowledge and public celebration of historical events.

Empires of the Imagination grants a significant place to diplomatic and political history, yet several essays examine the Purchase from the bottom up, trying to understand how it changed life in Louisiana. Opening the first part of the book, Richard White argues that life did not change much for several decades in the *pays d'en haut*, a haven for outlaws. In an inspired essay, White insists on "the fictions of empire," presenting diplomacy as "a form of pornography" and the Louisiana Purchase as a historical event that blended, "violence, desire, imaginary possession, and illicit sale" (38). Building on the work of White and other historians of Upper Louisiana, Cécile Vidal rejects the cultural interpretations that have long lauded the "colonial genius" of France when it came to dealing with the Indians. Laurent Dubois moves the narrative in the French Atlantic, uncovering the unpaid debts of the United States to the former slaves of Saint-Domingue. Dubois takes up the argument of Robert L. Paquette and writes that Napoleon was forced to abandon his western design (and thus to sell Louisiana), since he was unwilling to accept the end of slavery in the Pearl of the Caribbean.[1] While France was trying to deal with the insurgents, things were not easy in Washington. Spain's retrocession of Louisiana to France created great insecurities in the early republic, notes James Lewis. While the Federalists wanted to solve the crisis by taking to arms, Jefferson chose to adopt a diplomatic and peaceful course, animated by fears for a still fragile union between the states.

The second part of the book is concerned with questions of identity, mostly in Lower Louisiana. With his usual demographic approach, Paul Lachance examines the censuses produced in the decades surrounding the Purchase to convey how successive authorities constructed and categorized the people of Louisiana. Jean-Pierre Le Glaunec also looks at numbers in an essay on slave migration, refuting the long-standing argument on the scarcity of sources. Importing slaves by the thousands in the early American period, planters transformed Louisiana from a society with slaves into a slave society. Since territorial authorities were slow to implement a structure of control, however, the slave community was able to create a cartography of resistance. The Catholic Church in New Orleans was one of these sites of resistance for its mainly black and female congregation, argues Emily Clark, although she shows that it also "served as a site for the rehearsal of white male republican authority" (181). Clark downplays the confessional divide between Catholics and Protestants to insist instead on the shared political culture of Creoles and Americans.

As with religion, language proved not to be such a great barrier in the inclusion of the *ancienne population* in the American republic according to Peter Kastor. As long as they were white, Frenchmen "could become Americans," which was not the case for French-speaking slaves and free people of color who remained "fixed in their identities" (240). Mark Fernandez highlights the fluidity of identities at the time of the Purchase, describing Americanization as a heterogeneous process. Fernandez follows the unusual trajectory of Edward Livingston, claiming that the politician and lawyer "should probably be best remembered as the catalyst for the emergence of a stronger French identity in Louisiana" (294).

1. Robert Paquette, "Saint-Domingue and the Making of Territorial Louisiana," in *A Turbulent Time: The French Revolution and the Greater Caribbean*, ed. David Barry Gaspar and David Geggus (Bloomington, IN, 1997), 204–25.

Similarly, in the last and shortest part of the book dedicated to memory, François Weil locates after 1803 the creation of a Gallic identity in Louisiana, thanks to the arrival of dynamic migrants from Saint-Domingue and France. In light of the vivid tableaux of colonial Louisiana offered recently by Sophie White or Shannon Lee Dawdy, the conclusions of both Fernandez and Weil somewhat overstate the cultural and political apathy of the *ancienne population*. French Louisiana was not invented in the nineteenth century.

As it is expected of the genre, the essays here are unequal. The greatest weakness of this collection, however, lies in the repetitive nature of some contributions, published in parts elsewhere. This criticism aside, these essays collectively achieve their goals of inscribing "France in the cultural history of North America" (18). More than bringing a French twist to a teleological narrative of westward expansion, *Empires of the Imagination* mirrors the formidable vitality of research on Louisiana and the French Atlantic in the last two decades. In itself, this is another trans-Atlantic history worth telling.

Marise Bachand is a professeure régulière at the Université du Québec in Trois-Rivières. She is currently researching how white Creole women experienced the Americanization of Louisiana.

A Slave in the White House: Paul Jennings and the Madisons. By Elizabeth Dowling Taylor. (New York: Palgrave Macmillan, 2012. Pp. 296. Cloth, $28.00.)

Reviewed by Felicia Bell

In 1865, Paul Jennings, the enslaved personal manservant of President James Madison, published a memoir of his life experiences called *A Colored Man's Reminiscences of James Madison*. Although *A Slave in the White House* is based on Jennings's *Reminiscences*, Elizabeth Dowling Taylor cleverly offers the reader a more candid and intimate account of life in Madison's White House and private home, Montpelier. Having plowed through family records, oral histories, and numerous other primary sources, she has provided a robust story of the cruelty of slavery and the struggle for freedom from the perspective of the enslaved people who worked closely with the Madisons.

Aside from the narratives of enslaved people, we often learn about the details of slavery from owners' diaries, letters, and bills of sale or auction notices, runaway advertisements, and slave schedules. We long to know more about the details of the labor of enslaved people, both agricultural and nonagricultural, and how labor affected their lives and the lives of their family members. Sometimes the circumstances of their labor had its advantages, such as quietly learning how to read and write while serving the owner's children as they were tutored. At other times the labor took its toll emotionally, as enslaved people were often separated from their family members for extended periods.

Scholars of slavery will appreciate how Dowling Taylor provides insight on the methods and skills required for labor in and around the owner's house. She is careful to include snapshots of the lives of other enslaved people who worked directly with Jennings for the Madisons or at homes nearby. She explains their skills in culinary arts, as butlers and ladies' maids, and as coachmen. Like Jennings, these "trusty" (119) servants astutely used their skills and circumstances to gain the confidence of their owners and, eventually, access to individuals who would help them gain their freedom.

Not only are readers given the particulars about the daily life of the Madisons at their country estate but also they are introduced to their White House home and the thriving city of Washington, DC in the early nineteenth century. The political hotbed of the nation's capital finds Jennings as the proverbial "fly on the wall," the ever-present servant quietly listening as Madison and his contemporaries discuss compromises, manumission, abolition, colonization, and gradual emancipation. Through the author's delightfully descriptive writing, we get vivid images of Jennings carefully maneuvering through the intricacies of urban slavery with its black people (both enslaved and free) and, consequently, its black codes.

While Dowling Taylor identifies historical events and Jennings's connection to or involvement in them, she should allow readers to draw their own conclusions about what Jennings must have felt or thought. For instance, she explains that Jennings was hired out by Dolley Madison to President Polk at the White House. She writes that Jennings must have been "gratified" (154) to see George Washington's portrait hanging (thanks to his saving it from British invasion during the War of 1812). Perhaps Jennings looked at Washington in disgust—as another owner of enslaved people who kept his brethren oppressed. He saved the portrait because his owner *ordered* him to do so, perhaps not because of his love or admiration for George Washington. In addition, the author should have been more careful not to use negative historical language to make contemporary assertions. For example, a visitor to Montpelier described Jennings as "well-bred" (79). The author affirmed this description using the same words. Perhaps animals could be perceived as "well-bred," whereas people are *raised*.

Despite these acute shortcomings, Dowling Taylor gives attention to the details of Jennings's surroundings and the people in his life (beyond the Madisons). She adds layers, dimension, and depth to anything we may have previously read in *Reminiscences* or in the Madisons' papers. *A Slave in the White House* successfully creates a more accurate historical memory of not only Paul Jennings but also of the Madisons and the other enslaved people they owned.

FELICIA BELL is an assistant professor of history at Savannah State University. She is currently revising her book manuscript about the enslaved craftsmen who constructed the United States Capitol.

Among the Powers of the Earth: The American Revolution and the Making of a New World Empire. By Eliga H. Gould. (Cambridge, MA: Harvard University Press, 2012. Pp. 301. Cloth, $45.00.)

Reviewed by Elizabeth M. Covart

In the Declaration of Independence, Americans articulated their desire to make the United States a sovereign nation "to assume among the powers of the earth, the separate and equal station to which the Law of Nature and of Nature's God entitle them." Borrowing the title for his latest work from this preamble, Eliga H. Gould argues that the United States' drive for European acceptance as an equal nation "played a role in making the American republic at least as important as the liberal and republican ideologies that have framed scholarship on the American Revolution since the Second World War." Gould asserts that "the revolutionaries' emphasis on peace through treaty-worthiness explains why Americans ultimately opted for a national union that could represent the 'one people' in the Declaration of Independence over a looser association" (11) under the Articles of Confederation.

Gould defines the characteristics of a "treaty-worthy" nation and chronicles the long journey of the United States to achieve that status throughout his six chapters. In the eighteenth and nineteenth centuries, the law of nations represented a system of treaties whereby the secular leaders of Europe and the Roman Catholic Church agreed that the governments under their authority would recognize the rights and liberties of other European nations. To be "treaty-worthy," a sovereign had to participate in treaties and be able to enforce the provisions of those it signed. Treaty-worthy nations had the right to expect that other nations would respect their borders and trade rights in times of peace and would treat their citizens humanely in times of war. In theory, the law of nations applied to the overseas possessions and citizens of treaty-worthy nations. In actuality, all of the American colonies stood barely within the reach of the law of nations.

According to Gould, the American Revolution occurred in part because Great Britain tried to place its North American colonies firmly within the jurisdiction of the law of nations. London officials saw America as a lawless land, a place where smugglers and pirates ruled the Atlantic waves and where backcountry Indian traders incited rebellion. Britain sought to stabilize governance in North America by imposing "a series of sweeping reforms" (91) to rid the continent of its multiple legalities. Great Britain strengthened its naval forces, admiralty courts, and customs collectors to rid American waters of lawless sailors. Additionally, the empire stationed ten thousand regulars in the trans-Appalachian west to check the power of seditious Indian traders. Gould contends that while Americans "accepted the ends that Britain's reforms were meant to serve" (6, 107), they rejected the imposition of Parliamentary taxes to pay for them. Rather than submit to taxation without direct Parliamentary representation, many American colonists opted to declare independence and try to "replicate the order that Britain was attempting to produce" (6–7) on their own terms.

Gould takes a long view of the American Revolution. He begins his narrative near the onset of the French and Indian War (1755) and concludes it with the Monroe Doctrine (1823). Gould sees the Revolution as an intellectual movement and expands the interpretation by asserting that "the American Revolution was never just a struggle for the right of Americans to govern themselves . . . it was also a struggle for dominion over others" (4). He insists that the Americans' right to self-government and their prerogative to assert dominion over others came from entanglement with Europe, not independence. Only when European sovereigns saw the United States as an equal did the law of nations protect American affairs from European interference.

Obtaining equality with Europe did not prove easy. European countries gave little consideration to forging long-term peace and trade alliances with the Americans until after 1793. Before 1793, Europeans believed as Lord Sheffield: "No treaty can be made with the American states that can be binding on the whole" (126). The Articles of Confederation proved too weak to enforce treaties among its member states. Excluded from the law of nations, Americans stood barred from trade in the British West Indies and had their sovereign rights violated by the British military presence in the frontier. To obtain redress the United States needed to form a treaty-worthy government, which they did under the Constitution in 1787. In 1793, President George Washington flexed the muscles of the new government to stifle the Whiskey Rebellion and to bring law and order to the frontier. After Washington displayed the powers of the Constitution, Great Britain negotiated the Jay Treaty (1795), which opened British West Indian markets to American shippers and cleared America's frontier posts of British soldiers.

Gould asserts that even after the ratification of the Jay Treaty U.S. membership in the law of nations remained conditional. After 1795, Great Britain and France continued to meddle in American affairs. Using war as a pretext, the two nations confiscated American ships and cargo and impressed American sailors. Neither country wanted the United States trading with their enemy. Gould claims that the United States remained a probationary member of the law of nations until the end of the Napoleonic Wars and the War of 1812. Peace in Europe brought the law of nations into full effect. European nations had no excuse for interfering in American shipping or internal affairs while at peace. Gould provides proof of American equality with Europe by analyzing the outcome of the First Seminole War (ca. 1814–1819).

Gould presents a solid political history, a feat owed to his cogent argument and his well-balanced contextualization of the experiences of Americans in the United States with those of Americans in Canada and the Caribbean and with Europeans and Africans. Although Gould relies on international treaties to make his case, he omits their typically dry minutiae and captivates readers with his discussions of how and why European powers made and respected them. Political historians will consider assigning Gould's work in their upper-division undergraduate and graduate courses because of its accessibility and because it adds a new, diplomatic angle to the intellectual interpretation of American independence. However, social historians will think twice before assigning Gould's narrative.

Social historians will find weakness in Gould's imbalance of historical voices that favors elite, white men. Concerned with how Europeans conceived of the law of nations and how a nation became treaty-worthy, Gould does not differentiate between the many and varied African American and Native American populations. He refers to them as single, unified polities. To his credit, Gould tries to get at how those polities viewed the law of nations and its protections, but to do so he uses the experiences of multicultural, and exceptional, outliers such as Paul Cuffe and Milly Francis to speak for the viewpoints of all African Americans and Native Americans. The discrimination faced by Paul Cuffee, master of the Massachusetts-brig *Traveller*, more closely resembled that encountered by poorer whites than by slaves or free African Americans, who did not have the opportunities to captain their own ship or meet members of Parliament (172).

Moreover, as a political historian Gould does not examine social constructs in the detail of a social historian. For example, Gould contends that Europeans refused to admit slaves and Native Americans to the protections of the law of nations because they lacked the "moral sentiment" that underpinned "the reciprocity upon which Europe's treaty law depended" (200). Gould defines "moral sentiment" by examining how Europeans excluded Native Americans from the law of nations; they perceived Native American war tactics as too violent (200). Gould does not offer a counterpoint to this discussion. He does not explore how Native Americans viewed morality, whether they understood the Europeans' conception of it, or how they viewed the law of nations and their exclusion from it. For social historians, Gould over simplifies the history of European–Non-European interactions. However, if readers can look past Gould's reduction of social groups and constructs, they will find his political argument convincing and his Atlantic interpretation of the Revolution refreshing.

Elizabeth M. Covart completed her doctorate at the University of California, Davis in 2011. Her dissertation, "Collision on the Hudson:

Identity, Migration, and the Improvement of Albany, New York, 1750–1830," examines identity creation and adaptation in early America.

Whispers of Rebellion: Narrating Gabriel's Conspiracy. By Michael L. Nicholls. (Charlottesville: University of Virginia Press, 2012. Pp. 248. Cloth, $42.50.)

Reviewed by Douglas R. Egerton

Compared with other slave conspiracies and rebellions around the Americas, the Virginia plot orchestrated by the blacksmith Gabriel in the summer of 1800 generated but a modest collection of documents for later generations to interpret. Unlike Nat Turner, Gabriel evidently did not speak at length to a court-appointed attorney. Nor did the many blacks and whites familiar with the proceedings and participants write lengthy accounts in later years, as was the case with the Vesey affair. (Most of the relevant documents, however, will soon be published by the historian Philip J. Schwarz and the University of Virginia Press.) As a result, scholars can interpret these meager documents in a variety of ways, teasing out tantalizing references that may hold clues to the dreams and goals of the conspirators.

The latest scholar to explore the events of that contentious year is Michael L. Nicholls, a professor emeritus at Utah State University and the author of a number of articles on the early national Chesapeake. Where James Sidbury emphasized that some of Gabriel's men regarded themselves as God's chosen people, and this reviewer suggested that the enslaved smithy and his chief lieutenants drew inspiration from artisan republicanism, Nicholls shifts his story away from Richmond and into the area around the Prosser plantation and Upham Brook. Although the presidential election of 1800 and its implications for Virginia here receive an early cameo, Nicholls is far more interested in re-creating life around the plantation blacksmith shop. Gabriel's brother Solomon was also a blacksmith, and, unlike earlier writers who tend to dismiss the importance of their older brother Martin, Nicholls demonstrates that as Martin had a son named Frank who labored in neighboring Goochland County as a blacksmith. So it is possible that their elder sibling "once wielded a hammer too" (26). Unfortunately, Nicholls is no more successful than previous scholars in discovering the owner of Gabriel's wife Nanny or her fate and even whether she bore him any children; she remains a shadowy figure in this study as in others, as perhaps she always will. Nicholls argues that her presence at Brookfield on the eve of the intended rising indicates that she was "fully aware and supportive of the enterprise," and he is probably correct. Yet he does not effectively challenge those writers who highlighted "the maleness" of the conspiracy (44) by elaborating on this point.

By situating the conspiracy around the brook, Nicholls loses the larger Atlantic rhythms of the age of revolution, particularly the impact of the 1791 uprising in Saint Domingue and the gradual emancipation of blacks in northern states. (Prosser's fiancé was from New York, and her father's slaves promptly tried to run away upon arriving in Virginia.) But he also gains a good deal by downsizing his story, and Nicholls skillfully draws rural life along the Stage Road as it meandered north from Richmond. Influenced by Anthony E. Kaye's groundbreaking scholarship on slave localities, Nicholls shows how the interconnected lives of the whites and blacks who gathered at Gregory's Tavern to talk business or at Young's Spring to drink grog shaped the conspiracy. Those environs, ironically, also shaped the aftermath, since some of the rebels were hanged at Prosser's Tavern rather than in the city, "to serve as a deterrent to any slaves still contemplating rebellion" (100). Despite his best efforts to keep the focus on the countryside, Nicholls eventually returns the story to Richmond, as capturing the ill-guarded capital and magazine meant the difference between success and failure when it came to the rebels bargaining for their freedom and an end to slavery in Virginia.

In his 2007 *Journal of the Early Republic* essay, "Neighborhoods and Nat Turner: The Making of a Slave Rebel and the Unmaking of a Slave Rebellion," Kaye suggested that Turner's leadership faltered once the rebels moved beyond his plantation district, and Nicholls agrees that as "recruiting spread geographically and increased numerically," the ability of the brook leadership to control events essentially vanished (43). Unlike Turner, who was to inform a very few lieutenants of his plans, Gabriel's recruiters talked openly and so discovered the problem of maintaining secrecy as word spread beyond Richmond and down the James River. The need for large numbers of recruits, even in heavily black Henrico County, increased the potential for disaster.

As do previous scholars, Nicholls also details Thomas Jefferson's response to the plot, and once again, the vice president does not fare terribly well. Although Jefferson did warn James Monroe, then the state governor, that "there has been hanging enough," he otherwise fell silent when both his protégé and minister Rufus King peppered him with requests for further advice on the prospect of colonizing accused bondmen in Sierra Leone (87–88). Monroe, by comparison, is depicted as demonstrating "political sensitivity" to those who might question mass executions for "a crisis that had not physically materialized" (79). Interestingly, Nicholls's characterization of a grieving Monroe, whose son died the night after a captured Gabriel was returned to Richmond, is more sympathetic than that provided by biographer Harlow Unger in his *The Last Founding Father: James Monroe and a Nation's Call to Greatness* (New York, 2009), who depicts the governor as overly vengeful.

Nicholls moves his narrative along at a brisk pace with clear prose that is wonderfully free of jargon. His research, both archival and secondary, is impressive, and as he observes, researching early Virginia from distant Utah is no simple task. Regrettably, his lengthy if oddly combative notes appear only at the end of the text.

DOUGLAS R. EGERTON is professor of history at Le Moyne College and the 2011–2012 Mary Ball Washington Professor at University College Dublin. His books include *Death or Liberty: African Americans and Revolutionary America* (New York, 2009) and *Year of Meteors: Stephen Douglas, Abraham Lincoln, and the Election That Brought on the Civil War* (New York, 2010).

Empires, Nations, and Families: A History of the North American West, 1800–1860. By Anne F. Hyde. (Lincoln: University of Nebraska Press, 2011. Pp. 648. Cloth, $45.00.)

Reviewed by R. Douglas Hurt

This book is significant because it provides a new and important interpretation of the history of the North American West during the first half of the nineteenth century. It does so by focusing on family relationships, cultural practices, and state polities. Tracing change over time by using family continuity and state transformation to understand the history of the North American West seems so sensible, clear, and obvious that one can only wonder why no one had thought of this organizational and interruptive construct before. The answer to that question is such a book can be written only when a historian has thought deeply about the subject, using extensive original research to bring new insights.

Anne Hyde begins her study in 1804 by analyzing the importance of family connections to the fur trade. She emphasizes St. Louis and the Chateaus, Santa Fe and the Sublettes, the Arkansas River Region and the Bents, and the Pacific coast with the Vallejo family, among others, as well as native nations such as the Osages, Comanches, Cheyennes, and Nez Perces. She argues that families gave form and function to the fur trade; business influenced, if not determined, family relationships. Hyde's reconstructed world conveys the importance of isolation, ethnic negotiation, and government power, the latter driven by changing concepts of race. To craft her narrative, Hyde traces several families during a specific chronological period. She makes the important observation that each family and cultural group had its own ideas about how trade networks functioned and how they had to be maintained and expanded. The fur trade is the structural foundation upon which she links families and places. At first, these families influenced the outside world more than others affected them, but that relationship changed dramatically in little more than a half a century. Hyde tells penetrating stories about stability and a lack of change "by looking at the way people make families and do business in a region where no one knew who would win" (17). Most of her geographical territory lies outside the United States in both reality and law.

Hyde divides her study into three parts: The first is "Replacing a State: The Continental Web of Family Trade." Part II, titled "Americans All: The Mixed World of Indian Country," deals with the Native American response to the fur trade, war, and removal. Here, she emphasizes the importance of the mixed-race people who proved essential for business, politics, and diplomacy, and whose importance rapidly diminished as race increasingly shaped relationships with the arrival of the Euro Americans. Part III, titled "From Nations to Nation: Imposing a State, 1840–1865," emphasizes conquest and the ways in which concepts of race and imperial power changed the North American West as new groups arrived. By the Civil War, she concludes, the West had become "a place that called itself one nation but that seemed poorer for the loss of those many nations" (24).

Cogently Hyde emphasizes stability over time, family continuity, and business affairs built on personal relationships. Economic stability meant mutual trust, family reliability, and the use of military power when diplomacy failed. Kinship protected families against change and helped them adapt to it. Marriages, partnerships, and friendships gave system and order to the world, bridged cultural gaps, and facilitated peace, trade, and linkages with the outside world. The North American West was a world of disparate but not yet desperate peoples. People customarily and easily crossed racial and cultural boundaries, but those days were numbered. The great distances of the North American West that had provided cultural protection began to erode with the arrival of the Euro Americans. Slowly, then swiftly and overwhelmingly, racial distinctions and prejudices became more important than military power. The people of mixed races were the first losers. Whites imposed inflexible racial boundaries in a world where cultural flexibility had prevailed. The control of land, not the fur or hide trade, created new meaning for concepts of power and empire. Anglo American expansion and national unity did not include the accommodation of accommodating cultures.

The Mexican War introduced the matter of citizenship and identity, the latter invariably determined by race. Racially mixed families now became a liability for individual and family success or domination. In the past, nations did not matter much to the people who negotiated the North American West. Now nation-states mattered a great deal because the United States government wanted more than trade. The old traditions of war, diplomacy, and trade would not drive squatters away. War and violence now dominated relationships as Anglo Americans imposed new values about what it meant to be Indian or white and to claim, conquer, and organize the land. Mixed families now confronted even more hostility and discrimination than Indian families. Racial, particularly mixed, branding now defined many families and limited their ability to live with dignity and respect. To be a Bent, for example, no longer meant membership in a respected and prestigious family, but rather designation as a "half-breed" without voice and influence.

This study merits the attention of any historian interested in the North American West. It is smart, engaging, and gracefully written. It is, however, occasionally overwritten as Hyde covers well-trod ground in stories about the Austins in Texas, the Shawnees in the Old Northwest, the Minnesota Sioux outbreak, and Sand Creek. In this sense the text easily could have been reduced without loss. Even so, this book merits reading and rereading so rich is the detail and interpretation. It is a masterful book.

R. DOUGLAS HURT is Head of the Department of History at Purdue University. He is the author of *The Ohio Frontier: Crucible of the Old Northwest 1720–1830* (Bloomington, IN, 1998), *The Indian Frontier, 1763–1846* (Albuquerque, NM, 2002), *The Great Plains during World War II* (Lincoln, NE, 2010), and *The Big Empty: The Great Plains during the Twentieth Century* (Tucson, AZ, 2011).

The People of the Standing Stone: The Oneida Nation from the Revolution through the Era of Removal. By Karim M. Tiro. (Amherst, MA: University of Massachusetts Press, 2011. Pp. 256. Cloth, $80.00. Paper, $26.95.)

Reviewed by David J. Silverman

Karim Tiro's study of the Oneida Indians between the mid eighteenth and mid nineteenth century is a welcome contribution to an increasingly crowded field of study. Drawing on a wide source base of missionary correspondence, Oneida petitions, government reports, and treaty minutes, Tiro traces the Oneidas' struggles with the American Revolution and its aftermath. The Oneidas' transformation from a military, political, and territorial power in what is now upstate New York to a people scattered among tiny reservations in Wisconsin, Canada, Kansas, and the Empire State in the space of just eighty years is, Tiro notes, testament to the forceful determination of the early republic to dispossess even its Indian allies. He adds that the Oneidas' survival as a distinct people defensive of their rights is equal evidence of their refusal to cave in to this power.

Portions of this story have been told recently by a number of scholars, such as Alan Taylor, David J. Norton, Lawrence Hauptman, and Joseph T. Glatthaar and James Kirby Martin, among others, yet Tiro advances the conversation in several respects. Whereas the aforementioned scholars either treat the Iroquois as a whole or focus on the years of the Revolution, Tiro narrows in on the Oneidas but over the course of a century. What this perspective sacrifices in terms of contextual breadth, it makes up in terms of ethnographic detail and time depth. Tiro is particularly attuned to shifting factions within the Oneida community and how those divisions influenced land cessions and migration. Likewise, he provides a sensitive reading of the dynamic role of Christianity in Oneida spiritual and political life. Even as Tiro explores divisions within the Oneidas and the Iroquois as a whole, he makes a powerful argument that the Iroquois behaved rather civilly toward each other during their so-called civil wars of the Revolution and War of 1812. By this he means that the Patriot Oneidas made every effort to avoid engaging Loyalist Iroquois and to warn them when trouble was coming. Tiro also joins a growing chorus of historians who emphasize that Indian removal took place in the North as well as the South and, in the case of New York, under state auspices. Not the least of all, Tiro traces Oneida land loss in compelling detail, including the underhanded methods of New York and United State officials, the Oneidas who sometimes colluded with them, and the many Oneidas who protested them. Thus, though Tiro is reluctant to place his study in historiographical context, his contributions are significant. *People of the Standing Stone* is the best account of the Oneidas during the long era of the Revolution.

This is not a simple story of either loss or persistence or of either victimhood or subaltern agency. *People of the Standing Stone* acknowledges the real toll the Oneidas suffered because of white grasping, internal factionalism, alcohol abuse, and landed dispossession. At the same time, Tiro is sensitive to the ways in which the Oneidas made their cultural traditions relevant in the face of these steep challenges. Along similar lines, Tiro sees the Oneidas as important actors in this dark chapter in their history without denying that American colonialism put serious restrictions on their options. Tiro is to be applauded for this balance and nuance.

DAVID J. SILVERMAN, George Washington University, is the author of *Red Brethren: The Brothertown and Stockbridge Indians and the Problem of Race in Early America* (Ithaca, NY, 2010).

Fatal Self-Deception: Slaveholding Paternalism in the Old South. By Eugene D. Genovese and Elizabeth Fox-Genovese. (New York: Cambridge University Press, 2011. Pp. 232. Paper, $26.99.)

Reviewed by Staughton Lynd

In the first paragraph of their Introduction, the authors say they have been led to a conclusion "that some readers will find unpalatable." What is that conclusion? It is that the paternalism of slaveholders before the Civil War was a belief system entertained in good faith. Employers of slave labor, it is contended, sincerely considered "Christian slavery" to be "the most humane, compassionate, and generous of social systems" (1).

But if by "unpalatable" is meant "untrue," why would any reader doubt this central conclusion? Most perpetrators of evil throughout history sincerely have believed that they were doing good. Surely the more interesting question is whether southern slavery was in fact a humane social system. Indeed the title of this volume makes plain that the authors themselves concede that the paternalism slaveholding employers ascribed to themselves amounted, at least in part, to "self-deception."

I do not make these comments as a condescending outsider to the phenomena described by Genovese and Fox-Genovese. My mother-in-law was a Howard of Virginia who passed on family traditions about white women who went to the slave cabins when a child was ill. She also told of a relative, Edward Coles, secretary to James Madison and later governor of Illinois, who traveled with his slaves across the Ohio River, and how, when he told the slaves that they were free, they asked if they might stay nearby. *Fatal Self-Deception* presents a number of similar instances.[1]

Also, my father grew up in Louisville and, despite all his life singing songs and telling jokes that I came to consider racist, was unfailingly kind to African Americans he encountered. In both respects he closely resembled another white man from the Upper South, Abraham Lincoln.

Moreover, Eugene Genovese and Elizabeth Fox-Genovese are not the only distinguished American historians to have questioned the mainstream narrative about the slave South and the Civil War. William Appleman Williams denounced Lincoln's refusal to let the South depart in peace, claimed that an independent southern nation might have abolished slavery on its own initiative, and implausibly presented the Earl of Shaftesbury as an exemplar of communal values.

However, there is a problem. Although assuming the posture of describing an ideology rather than facts on the ground, the authors of

1. The authors of this book and Eric Foner agree that Coles "settled" his former slaves on farms of their own: *Fatal Self-Deception*, 98; Eric Foner, *The Fiery Trial: Abraham Lincoln and American Slavery* (New York, 2010), 7.

this book say in the second paragraph of their Introduction that "The westward movement of planter households . . . strengthened relations between masters and slaves" (1). Really? This is not a description of an ideology but an allegation of fact. Economic historian Gene Dattel writes of the "internal migration into the new cotton states—Alabama, Mississippi, Louisiana, Arkansas, and Texas" that for slaves "the hardship was manifest and the separation of slave families devastating." Dattel offers examples of more and less paternalistic behavior by settlers in "the western reaches of cotton country." John Steele, a Virginia planter, at first urged his brother to provide warm clothing for his slaves back home. "Eventually Steele's paternalism succumbed to 'cotton fever' as he frantically pressed his brother to sell property in Richmond in exchange for 'two Negroes. . . . They would sell here for 1000 or 1,200 . . . [per slave] this year.'" Steele's personal obligations extended only to his personal slave, George, whose family he felt bound to hold together. At the other extreme was the Wade Hampton family of South Carolina, among the largest slaveholders in the antebellum South. Genovese and Fox-Genovese say of Wade Hampton II that he "managed his nine hundred slaves competently" (36) and of Wade Hampton III that he "appealed for white-black friendship" (122). They say nothing about the patriarch, Wade Hampton I, who helped to put down the German Coast slave uprising of 1811. Charles Deslondes, the supposed leader of the rebellion, had his hands chopped off and before he died was put in a bundle of straw and roasted. Another eighteen slaves were executed and their heads displayed on pikes.[2] Nor do the authors of *Fatal Self-Deception* add about Wade Hampton III that he was an original proponent of the Lost Cause movement and a leading opponent of Radical Reconstruction who was especially angered by the arrival of black troops in South Carolina.

The foregoing is an initial instance of how the authors repeatedly drift from describing a paternalistic ideology to alleging facts consistent with that paternalistic self-image. These ambiguities recur throughout the book.

Consider northern racism. We find in this volume a stinging description (112–19). I do not question its accuracy. But what about the experi-

2. Gene Dattel, *Cotton and Race in the Making of America: The Human Costs of Economic Power* (Chicago, 2009), 31, 40, 47.

ence of Union soldiers in the Civil War? In a setting of what Howard Zinn called "equal status contact," white soldiers underwent "a broad evolution of opinion" toward African Americans, Eric Foner writes.[3]

The difficulty with the methodology of *Fatal Self-Deception* is not that it states facts that are untrue, but that it states only some of the facts.

No doubt the fundamental arena in which the battle of historians must be fought out involves the attitude of slaves toward their owners. In a chapter entitled "Loyal and Loving Slaves" and in a final chapter called "Devotion unto Death," Genovese and Fox-Genovese present varied and contrasting contemporary evaluations of such questions as how slaves would act if their masters were to arm them.

The two great truths about the loyalty and resistance of slaves in the United States, it appears to this reviewer, are, first, that slave insurrections were relatively rare, and second, that slaves endlessly took advantage of opportunities to flee. I used to discuss why this was so with African American students at Spelman College in the 1960s. Why, I would ask them, was there no Haiti in the American South?

The answer seemed to follow from the demographics. In Haiti, slaves outnumbered whites by a ratio of something like 10 to 1. In the United States, in contrast, only in South Carolina and Mississippi were the numbers of blacks and whites relatively equal. Coupled with the certainty that in any situation of armed conflict the national government would side with the whites, as at Harpers Ferry, these facts prompted a rebellious but intelligent slave like Frederick Douglass to opt for flight rather than insurrection. W. E. B. DuBois presented a slightly different version of the same hypothesis. The "difference between the slave revolts in the West Indies, and the lack of effective revolt in the Southern United States," DuBois suggested, had to do with the presence of five million poor whites who acted as a "special police force." In fact there were "more white people to police the slaves than there were slaves." DuBois, like myself and my students, also emphasized the possibility of flight to the North. He called it "the Safety Valve of Slavery; the chance which a vigorous and determined slave had to run away to freedom" (although conceding that one "cannot know the real facts concerning the number of fugitives").[4] Genovese and Fox-Genovese, while recognizing that slaves

3. Foner, *The Fiery Trial*, 251–53.

4. W. E. B. DuBois, *Black Reconstruction: An Essay Toward a History of the Part which Black Folk Played in the Attempt to Reconstruct Democracy in America, 1860–1880* (New York, 1935), 12–13.

"deserted when Union troops approached, and seized opportunities for freedom" (146), arguably gives too little attention to the flight of slaves to the North.

The professional lifetimes that these authors have devoted to the slave South leave one with the question: Why?

I did not have the opportunity of meeting Elizabeth Fox-Genovese. However, I knew Gene Genovese when he was a graduate student at Columbia where I, too, received my master's and doctoral degrees. He was at the time a Marxist and, I believe, an editor of the Marxist journal *Science and Society*. We both became editors of *Studies on the Left* along with James Weinstein, Stanley Aronowitz, Norman Fruchter, and Tom Hayden. I can recall sitting with Gene at the Chattanooga airport and discussing the possibility of nuclear war between the United States and Soviet Union. I was present at the teach-in against the Vietnam war at Rutgers University when Professor Genovese declared that he hoped for victory of the National Liberation Front of South Vietnam, a courageous statement that cost him the possibility of academic employment in the United States, at least in the short run. And the only conversation I ever had with the greatest historian writing in the English language during any of our lifetimes, Edward Thompson, took place at Eugene Genovese's Manhattan apartment in the mid-1960s.

Thinking of that conversation with Genovese and Thompson, it seems to me that each of us sought in a particular way to keep alive awareness of the limitations of capitalist society. Thompson lost his early confidence that a transition to socialism was at hand in Great Britain and retreated to the customs in common of the eighteenth century. I left academia altogether and, as a lawyer as well as an historian, have spent decades sampling the solidarity of manual workers and high-security prisoners. Eugene Genovese, I suggest, never abandoned the hostility he shared with Thompson and myself to "commodity production requir[-ing] profit maximization" (2), and found his alternative in the patriarchal households of the slave South.

STAUGHTON LYND is the author of, among many works, *Class Conflict, Slavery, and the U.S. Constitution* (2nd ed. New York, 2009), *Intellectual Origins of American Radicalism* (2nd ed. New York, 2009), and "Free Trade, Soverignty, and Slavery: Toward an Economic Intepretation of American Independence," *William and Mary Quarterly* 68 (Oct. 2011), 597–630.

Illinois in the War of 1812. By Gillum Ferguson. (Urbana: University of Illinois Press, 2012. Pp. xiii, 349. Cloth, $34.95.)

Reviewed by Robert M. Owens

Occasionally the notice of a forthcoming history is met with an audible sigh of relief, perhaps alloyed with an array of giddy smiles. Historians of the War of 1812, as well as scholars of the Midwest, have spent years bemoaning the lack of a modern, comprehensive treatment of Illinois' role in that conflict. Many others, especially outside of academia, would question whether Illinois played any role in that war at all. Into this void steps Gillum Ferguson, an attorney and amateur historian. One says "amateur" in this context with some caution, as Ferguson has published a number of articles on the subject, and in general the research and writing compare favorably with any professional treatment imaginable.

Part of the reason historians have ignored Illinois' role in the War of 1812—a war that itself has been comparatively neglected—is the fact that there was little activity by British regular troops in the region. In Illinois, the fighting was primarily between Indians loosely allied to Britain and the citizenry of Illinois and the surrounding territories—Wisconsin, Indiana, and Missouri. Ferguson rightly begins with an assessment of the difficulties faced by Illinoisans when the conflict began. As the few Federal troops available were stationed elsewhere, the Illinois Territory's militia—"every white man between the ages of eighteen and forty-five"—would bear the brunt of the war. They risked more than life and limb to do so. They were required to provide their own arms, which was surprisingly difficult, as firearms were relatively scarce and therefore strikingly expensive in this frontier region. Ferguson notes that, from a strictly financial standpoint, militia service could be debilitating. "Nearly every man called from his farm into active military service was the sole support of himself and his family, and extended service in the field could severely disrupt his ability to meet the unforgiving rhythm of the growing season" (10). The fact that their payment from the Federal government might take months, years, or infinity only made things worse.

Because the war took the form of a frontier "Indian war," there were few large set-piece battles, but rather a seemingly endless string of raids and counterraids. One of Ferguson's great achievements, for which we are truly indebted to him, is the painstaking way he compiles and chronicles—from a broad array of sources—these nearly innumerable incidents.

He also introduces the primary characters in this drama, from the Potawatomi chief Gomo, who labored to maintain his people's neutrality even when they were attacked indiscriminately by Illinois settlers, to the Whiteside family's two generations of famed frontier fighters. One of the more intriguing characters is Illinois' appointed territorial governor, Ninian Edwards of Virginia. Edwards comes off quite well in the narrative, painted as a man who put duty above personal gain and strove, with little encouragement or even acknowledgement from Washington, to protect his citizenry. Secretary of War John Armstrong literally would not even answer Edwards's letters, except to demote his role in military defense. Still, Edwards soldiered on.

The majority of the region's Indians who took sides fought against the United States, inspired by Tenskwatawa, the Shawnee Prophet, and his brother Tecumseh. Ferguson notes that most of the Prophet's warriors at the battle of Tippecanoe (Nov. 7, 1811) were actually from Illinois tribes. Many of these warriors returned to Illinois after the battle to preach "the gospel of resistance among their own tribes" (41). The fierce Potawatomi warrior-prophet Main Poc and the Sauk warrior Black Hawk, who later became a much larger figure in a much smaller war, also make appearances. The years 1812 and 1813 proved difficult for Illinoisans. Terrifying attacks from warriors of the Kickapoo, Sauk, Fox, Winnebago, Menominee, and Potawatomi nations rained down on settlers, as well as neutral and allied nations. Ferguson is careful to note that the Illinoisans' position was made far more tenuous by Federal neglect and local foolishness, including the murders of allied Indian hunting parties. "When violence did occur [between whites and Indians], it was the fault of the Americans" (116).

Through the efforts of Governor Edwards and the militia, as well as chiefs like Gomo who tried to maintain neutrality, by the summer of 1814 Illinois was fairly secure along the Mississippi River. But reverses in Wisconsin Territory, including the British-Indian retaking of Prairie du Chien, threatened to reverse that trend. By Christmas Eve of 1814, the public were so angry that the Illinois territorial legislature passed a bounty for the killing of Indian warriors and the capture of Indian women and children. (The law did specify that the Indians were to be from "hostile" groups,[1] but the fog of war would have definitely put

---

1. See Francis L. Philbrick, ed., *Pope's Digest 1815*, vol. I. *Collections of the Illinois State Historical Library* 28 (Springfield, IL, 1938), 306–308.

"friendly" Indians at risk.) As Ferguson notes, by this time the majority of enemy Indians were beyond the reach of Illinoisans. Further, some tribes, like the Kaskaskias, had been guaranteed protection under Federal treaty, yet suffered not only from attacks but also from the lack of promised supplies.

Word of the final peace from Ghent took months, and many tribes continued to fight, as they had been neither defeated nor consulted. The last real battle took place in Missouri in May of 1815, five months after the treaty was signed. The Menominees did not make peace until 1817, and at least one group of Winnebagos never officially made peace. Edwards and others opted for a relaxed policy toward Indians over the next several years, guessing correctly that Indian removal would be much easier (for the Americans) later on.

Illinois in the War of 1812 is a thorough, engaging, and extremely useful narrative analysis. The only substantial criticism would be semantic, perhaps tonal, in nature. Ferguson takes pains to point out that white Illinoisans were often to blame for frontier deaths, and is perfectly correct to note the deliberate brutality of Indian attacks, which were of course terrifying by design. Yet words like "savage" and "massacre" creep up with a disturbing frequency. And a reference to the U.S.-allied Kaskaskia Indians as "tame" (116) is particularly cringe-inducing. Yet even with these qualms, Ferguson deserves our thanks and commendation for his remarkable achievement.

ROBERT M. OWENS teaches history at Wichita State University and is the author of *Mr. Jefferson's Hammer: William Henry Harrison and the Origins of American Indian Policy* (Norman, OK, 2007).

Kentucky Rising: Democracy, Slavery, and Culture from the Early Republic to the Civil War. By James A. Ramage and Andrea S. Watkins. (Lexington, KY: The University Press of Kentucky, 2011. Pp. 445. Cloth, $40.00.)

Reviewed by William A. Stone

In *Kentucky Rising*, James A. Ramage and Andrea S. Watkins present a well-crafted and diverse overview of Kentucky from the late eighteenth century through the 1860s. The authors assert that the state strove for "greatness in a global sense" (336) from its inception. Through an analysis of culture, politics, and society, they document how Kentuckians came to be a leading nationalist force in the early West and in the antebellum United States. After the Civil War, Kentucky became thoroughly identified with the Lost Cause ethos, despite never officially joining the Confederacy. Ramage and Watkins point to Henry Clay's theory of Union, wherein only states had the constitutional right to legislate slavery internally, as the cause behind this phenomenon. When the Union was not restored "as it was" and the federal government outlawed slavery completely, many in the state felt betrayed and sympathized with the defeated Confederacy. Ramage and Watkins rely mainly on the vast array of existing secondary literature, while only occasionally using primary resources, mostly newspapers, to enhance the narrative. The reader is often alerted to previous historians' arguments, but these are rarely challenged. This lack of contention is not necessarily a weakness; it is simply not the authors' objective. Instead, they focus on presenting a diversity of topics to demonstrate the forward-looking culture that existed in antebellum Kentucky and the effects of slavery and Civil War on the state's perception of its place within the nation.

A variety of detailed chapters on cultural and social development support the argument that Kentuckians actively worked toward a "rising globally oriented society" (16). In particular, many accomplished artists and architects provided Kentucky's upper class with quality pieces of work. Portrait painter Matthew Harris Jouett, wildlife artist John James Audubon, and the renowned architect Benjamin Latrobe are just a few individuals highlighted to show the demand for artistic cultivation in the state. The fostering of education, science, and medicine is central to the theme of advancement put forth by Ramage and Watkins. In the first half of the nineteenth century, Ephraim McDowell and Benjamin W. Dudley were pioneers in surgery, while medical botanist Constantine Samuel Rafinesque roamed the wilderness identifying plants still used in medicine to this day. Transylvania University, with its Medical Department, became the West's premier institute under the tutelage of Horace Holley, and even eastern families sent their sons west to be educated.

Ramage and Watkins also examine popular culture and society through the lens of everyday citizens in Kentucky. The growing diffusion of newspapers and stump speaking marked a growth of participatory politics in the state. The increased presence of theatres, musical troupes, and the fascination with steamboat racing show the full range of entertainment pursued by Kentuckians of all classes. Social stratification itself, the authors maintain, was softened in this environment but not eliminated. They argue that economic opportunity was available in this West, but Atlantic desires and mindsets were brought and reestablished in Kentucky. This frontier was a democratizing force, not because class was eliminated, but because of the economic policies pursued by its leaders. On this point Ramage and Watkins disagree with historian Stephen Aron's thesis that the West was "lost" for the poor laborer because of Henry Clay's American System for Kentucky. In particular, they assert that it was through Clay's system of internal improvements that "the West was found" (90), because all Kentuckians benefited from greater access to national and international markets created by improved transportation infrastructure.

Henry Clay's political theories on the Union and slavery tie the early republic and Civil War era together in this study. For Ramage and Watkins, these ideas ultimately led to the alienation and discontent that pushed Kentucky into the ideological fold of the Lost Cause. The state suffered its own internal Civil War, which was characterized by the guerilla campaigns of Confederate General John Hunt Morgan and the pacification policies of Union General Stephen Gano Burbridge. The authors argue Clay's steadfast devotion to the Union and his theory that only states could legislate regarding slavery were "the lodestar that guided Kentucky through the Civil War" (17). Initially, these principles kept the state from seceding as many believed that Abraham Lincoln was committed to restoring the Union as it was prior to the war, leaving slavery purely a state issue. The Emancipation Proclamation and enlistment of black soldiers into the Union army tested loyal Kentuckians and pushed some over the brink. This increased the harshness of pacification and led to political manipulation that kept the crucial border state within the Union.

After the war, the authors conclude, Lincoln's betrayal of Clay's vision of the Union and slavery convinced Kentuckians that they too had lost in the monumental struggle. The evidence for this is hard to ignore. Kentucky was the last state to ratify the Thirteenth, Fourteenth, and Fifteenth Amendments, resisting until the bitter end. Finally, a statue of Confederate General John Hunt Morgan was erected at the Fayette County courthouse in Lexington, the symbolic heart of the bluegrass. Ramage and Watkins close with the deterioration of the previously discussed institutions of art, education, and entertainment that were the means to early Kentuckians' goal of global greatness. In the end, the message seems to be that the commitment to slavery and the outcome of the Civil War stymied Kentucky's antebellum rise in cultural and political prominence as it underwent its own Reconstruction.

This book is a welcome contribution to the literature on early Kentucky history. Its chronological breadth and topical diversity provide a compromise between the more focused, specialized studies and the standard survey histories of the state. The variety of subjects discussed and the nature of certain chapters to stand on their own produces a disjointed flow at times, but the chapters are brought together nicely in the conclusions. Regardless, the wealth of secondary research within this work provides a fantastic resource for any student of Kentucky and antebellum America. By far the greatest contribution is the authors' connection of the early republic to the state's post-Civil War historical trajectory.

WILLIAM A. STONE is a PhD candidate at the University of Kentucky. He is currently writing his dissertation on Kentucky politics in the early republic.

Celebrating the Republic: Presidential Ceremony and Popular Sovereignty, from Washington to Monroe. By Sandra Moats. (DeKalb: Northern Illinois University Press, 2010. Pp. 255. Cloth, $36.00.)

Reviewed by Ronald J. Zboray and Mary Saracino Zboray

During the past two decades, scholarship on the vital roles that public celebrations, memorials, and rituals have played during the early American republic has broadened our understanding of the inextricable intersections between government, the body politic, and cultural life. Studies by Simon P. Newman, Sarah J. Purcell, Len Travers, and David Waldstreicher have explored the ways politicos and common people alike constructed political cultures, civic memory, and, indeed, nationalism itself, out of, for example, George Washington's birthday fetes, Bunker Hill commemorations, and Independence Day processions. These historians have also located meaning-making contests among varied groups within public festivity, from partisan politicos jockeying for power to disfranchised women and free African Americans struggling to achieve a sense of agency. In this study, an expansion of her 2001 dissertation about President Monroe's 1817–1819 national tours, Sandra Moats brings to this ongoing conversation a focus on the positions that the first five presidents—particularly George Washington, Thomas Jefferson, and James Monroe—assumed within this world of political spectacle.[1]

Celebrating the Republic "tells the story," according to Moats, "of how our first presidents invented the American political culture that endures today by employing the symbols and rituals they believed best illustrated republican principles to an American citizenry who now possessed sovereign authority over this new national government" (3). The five-chapter-long story reconstructed from published presidents' papers, congressional documents, and newspapers, is based upon the premise that popular sovereignty was not a " 'fiction,' " and that this "governing principle had to be activated for the new government to succeed" (6). The first two chapters are devoted to Washington, who, beginning with his pre-inaugural procession that approximated a "royal progress" through triumphal arches, appropriated monarchial traditions for republican ends—to reach the sovereign citizenry. His 1789–1791 national tours, graced by receptions, toasting, and speechifying, as well as his open houses, levees, and dinner parties at the capital, provided accessibility, but smacked of aristocratic pretension according to critics. Republicans pounced—none more relentlessly and covertly than Thomas Jefferson, according to Moats—on regal presidential ceremony, even as John Adams was strategically lowering its register during his administration. Assaults upon Federalist-fashioned pomp hardened under Jefferson—the subject of chapter 3—who "adopted an intentionally unadorned public style" (83) that at times made his official hostess, Dolley Madison, flinch. Jefferson's dismantling of formality, however, "introduced a new generation of voters to a new way of honoring republicanism" (88). While James and Dolley Madison brought back some of the bygone elegance, it was James Monroe who revived Washington's ceremonial tours—albeit without some of their fussiness and on a larger, more

1. Simon P. Newman, *Parades and the Politics of the Street: Festive Culture in the Early American Republic* (Philadelphia, 1997); Sarah J. Purcell, *Sealed with Blood: War, Sacrifice, and Memory in Revolutionary America* (Philadelphia, 2002); Len Travers, *Celebrating the Fourth: Independence Day and the Rites of Nationalism in the Early Republic* (Amherst, MA, 1997); David Waldstreicher, *In the Midst of Perpetual Fetes: The Making of American Nationalism, 1776–1820* (Chapel Hill, NC, 1997).

regionally defined stage that lent distinct local flavor to the proceedings. Chapters 4 and 5 show that although Monroe's nonpartisan tours were meant to celebrate national unity, they invited last-gasp Federalist rallying in the Northeast, unleashed election-minded Republican horn-tooting in the South and West, and engendered newspaper attacks all around. Moats concludes that the architects of the Second Party System refashioned political ceremony in more democratic ways, but with the same end in mind as their predecessors, namely "putting sovereign citizens in contact with their government" (171).

What is best about this book is that it tells a story, and a well-written, coherent, and entertaining one it is, that plumbs mundane details for their greater significance while revealing the everyday mechanisms behind life in high places. While early-republic historians will recognize some of these anecdotes, Moats weaves them together with new emphasis. Washington's 1789 oddly endearing questionnaire asking officials' advice on conducting dinner parties and visiting hours, becomes, in Moats's hands, a "ceremonial blueprint for his two terms in office" (37). Jefferson's greeting guests in "slippers and shabby clothing" before formal dinners, signifies a tribute to "republican simplicity" (85). That Monroe mysteriously "'disappeared'" (157) in Georgia's hinterland, according to confounded newsmen hot on his trail, reveals his dogged determination to reach a secluded Indian missionary school during his 1819 tour. By attending to the particulars of lived experience such as household routines, travel arrangements, and entertaining, Moats cuts room in her narrative for white women who, as ordinary participants in public fetes, or as political wives at the scene of government, performed the work of nation building. But while Martha Washington is given her just due for helping George "reach . . . a wider audience than he could have alone" as president (46), and Elizabeth Monroe is credited, at least, with convincing James to sit during his presidential tour for a Gilbert Stuart portrait, Abigail Adams, to whom John delegated official entertainment responsibilities during his administration, comes and goes in a blink (as does her husband for that matter). Propertyless men, free African Americans, and the enslaved as historical actors also seem to have vanished, notwithstanding Moat's insightful rendering of southern planters' modes of celebration that were infused with the "rituals and hierarchy of the slave culture" (144). So, despite its concern with popular sovereignty—indeed, perhaps because of its too-easy acceptance of the concept's realization in the early republic—the book remains a top-down presidential history in which contestation arises mainly from partisan factions within the governing class, and not "the people." Nonetheless, *Celebrating the Republic* remains a welcome contribution to the study of political ritual that inspires us to rethink the category of presidential duty to include the invention and restyling of national icons. It also urges us to contemplate how, even now, the project of devising and reinterpreting presidential ceremonies, is still evolving.

RONALD J. ZBORAY is a professor of communication and affiliate faculty in women's studies and cultural studies at the University of Pittsburgh, where MARY SARACINO ZBORAY is a visiting scholar. They are coauthors of *Voices Without Votes: Women and Politics in Antebellum New England* (Lebanon, NH, 2010). Their current project, "The Bullet in the Book," which examines cultures of reading during the Civil War, is being funded by a 2012 National Endowment for the Humanities Fellowship.

Thoreau the Land Surveyor. By Patrick Chura. (Gainesville: University Press of Florida, 2010. Pp. 212. Cloth, $34.95.)

Reviewed by Dominique Zino

Scholars of Henry David Thoreau have tended to dismiss the ways in which Thoreau earned his living—selling and making pencils, teaching occasionally, buying a rundown farm, and surveying—ultimately leaving undisturbed the assumption that Thoreau's books are the main expression of his philosophy. Lawrence Buell has claimed that while Thoreau "took pride in his skill and success at [surveying],"such work forced him to "anesthetize his proper sensitivities."[1] Patrick Chura's book, however, thoroughly complicates this neat opposition between politics and vocation, and between literature and life. Rather than explain Thoreau's "higher laws" as superseding or apologizing for the rest of his life's work, *Thoreau the Land Surveyor* proposes that Thoreau's ideas about possession, property, duty, and nature are cultivated through the one hundred

1. Lawrence Buell, *The Environmental Imagination* (Cambridge, MA, 1995), 478n64.

and sixty-five surveys he conducted in and around Concord from 1840 through 1861.

Chura places himself, literally, behind the surveyor's compass, using the practice of surveying as a way into the historical conflict over territory that is central to our national relationship to ownership. The cross-fertilization of geography, surveying history, and textual scholarship in this study demonstrates that not only might Thoreau's ethics be in conversation with his fieldnotes but, more interestingly, his fieldnotes and surveys can lend us access to a view of nature that underlies his Transcendentalist beliefs. Making the surveyor's work his own, Chura attempts to redraw the boundaries of historical and literary fields, resituating a range of texts, including *A Week on the Concord and Merrimack Rivers* (1849), *Walden* (1854), "A Plea for Captain John Brown" (1859), and "Life without Principle" (1863), in relation to the fieldnotes.

Thoreau the Land Surveyor begins by offering various accounts of the significance of the surveying profession during some of the earliest moments in American literature, history, and mythology, reminding us that George Washington's first career was as a surveyor in Virginia County. Noting the surveyor's complicity in reinforcing the hierarchical order of the colonial aristocracy, Chura provides a sense of the complexity of the concept of possession within an American ideology plagued by an ambiguous relation to property, both human and territorial. With regard to Thoreau, he identifies the various ways in which the surveying profession forces the writer and naturalist to compromise his own "anti-institutional" persona. *Walden* and *Cape Cod* are read in light of the U.S. Coast Survey, the rhetoric of which linked scientific advancement, national responsibility, and a belief in Manifest Destiny in antebellum America, particularly in the decade leading up to the publication of *Walden* (47, 49). Chura proceeds to highlight the merger of Thoreau's manual and intellectual labor, providing a compelling analysis of the ways in which his 1846 survey of Walden Pond subverts professional surveying standards in favor of higher ideals, often ignoring personal property lines. Chura is bold in his claim that the surveying notes of Walden Pond may have in fact preceded *Walden* itself and thus might be "an urtext of Thoreau's masterpiece" (41).

New students of Thoreau often feel scandalized when their teachers reveal that the Fitchberg Railroad ran less than fifty feet from Walden Pond and suggest that the text itself is an effort to regain the kind of freedom and autonomy that the landscape lacks. Yet Chura's sixth chapter, "The Science of the Fieldnotes," presents a way of recontextualizing the pond–railroad dichotomy through a reading of the surveying notes that allows us to imagine how the geographical position of the pond might empower rather than disrupt the book Thoreau began to ponder there.

Perhaps most wide-ranging in its argument for the relevance of surveying, not only in shaping Thoreau's sensibilities but as a political tool in wars over territory, is the discussion of Thoreau's relationship to "that other Kansas surveyor," John Brown. One of Chura's aims, offered with a concision and clarity that characterizes his writing, is "to explain how Thoreau's fieldwork was closer to Brown's than to Washington's—how the best surveyor in Concord often managed to combine civil engineering with civil disobedience" (21). In the midst of this discussion, however, a reader might notice that while attention is devoted to the ways in which surveying is used by both Thoreau and Brown to combat the usurpation of Native American land, there is a notable silence surrounding the identity of Thoreau's "Irish helper" (likely an immigrant displaced from his own land). The helper is obviously crucial to the surveying effort but is apparently referenced by Thoreau only vaguely in his journals. Though the fact that surveying is a multiperson effort mentioned repeatedly in *Thoreau the Land Surveyor*, the ironic position of this unnamed assistant is left untouched by Chura.

Despite such moments of silence, Chura's book is a provocative and productive enactment of Thoreau's own concluding sentiment in "Life without Principle" that our lives are not as much a forgetting as a remembering. What Chura has remembered here is something that even Emerson overlooked when he eulogized his friend Henry: Thoreau's mode of earning a living was not a distraction from his study of higher laws but an expression of a broader Transcendentalist position—the "ability to intuitively derive ethics from physics" (150). Moreover, considering the author's fluid integration of political and philosophical facts with physical ones, it is not surprising that Chura's scholarship is informed by his *own* lived experience. While writing his manuscript, he enrolled in a course in historical surveying through the Surveying and Mapping Department at his home campus. These experiences infuse the explanations of surveying with a dexterity and sensitivity to the material and phenomenological aspects of the work that could not have been replicated by a researcher limited to studying the drafts of Thoreau's surveys in a library. Chura's project, in short, is a refreshing reminder that theory and practice depend upon one another.

DOMINIQUE ZINO is a PhD candidate in English at the CUNY Graduate Center working on a dissertation about developments in nineteenth-century physiological optics and visual culture and their relationship to the aesthetics of Ralph Waldo Emerson, Emily Dickinson, and William and Henry James.

Common Sense: A Political History. By Sophia Rosenfeld. (Cambridge, MA: Harvard University Press, 2011. Pp. 337. Cloth, $29.95.)

Reviewed by Nathan Perl-Rosenthal

Is common sense revolutionary? Sophia Rosenfeld's rich intellectual history argues that it was in the eighteenth century and indeed may still be so. The career of the concept, as she presents it, also helps us understand one of the central dramas of early U.S. history: how a revolution led by a minority and marked by coercion and violence could so quickly become the basis for republican politics that eschewed internal violence and assumed that legitimacy flowed from the assent of the majority.

Rosenfeld's story begins in the seventeenth and early eighteenth centuries, when common sense assumed two incommensurate meanings. In one version, advanced primarily by thinkers in Francophone Europe including Denis Diderot and the Baron d'Holbach, common sense referred to a practice of radical critical inquiry that entailed questioning all forms of received wisdom up to and including the sacrality of monarchy. Its proponents, aware that this skeptical stance was seditious and unpopular, framed critical common sense as primarily the province of the enlightened and initiated. Around the same time, a group of thinkers based in the Scottish provincial city of Aberdeen developed a very different account. For them, common sense meant that widely accepted propositions were virtually self-evident: Common sense thus actually affirmed the authority of kings, the existence of god, and many of the other ideas that were primary targets for the radicals. Seen in this way, of course, common sense was not only accessible to a wide public but actually derived from their shared beliefs.

Thomas Paine, Rosenfeld argues, effected a brilliant fusion between these two seemingly opposed traditions. In *Common Sense*, he agreed with the Aberdonians that the essence of common sense was giving assent to universally accepted propositions. Yet in the manner of the radicals, he believed that these inherently true statements in fact called into question much that was common believed. The two most important targets of his pamphlet, Britain's rule over its North American colonies and the principle of monarchy, both fell before this logic. Monarchy made no sense because why should the descendant of a long-ago hero be especially suited to rule? And the seemingly self-evident principle that a small thing should never rule over a large thing, in his view, made American independence inevitable.

In addition to contributing materially to the coming of American independence, this synthesis may also have marked an important step in the creation of modern politics. Rosenfeld argues that Paine's approach was original in the sense that it permitted anyone, not merely the educated and instructed, to use folk maxims and logic to attack British government. American independence may have been the program of a relatively small group of elite gentlemen in 1776, but Paine's argument grounded the decision to break away from Britain on principles and argumentation that were accessible to everyone. In this sense, the logic of *Common Sense*, by making political arguments subject to the judgment of all, may have opened one of the first theoretical paths toward the development of a modern, critical, and democratic public.

The final two chapters of Rosenfeld's study briefly sketch the tragic history of common sense from the French Revolution through the twentieth century. Once the first steps had been taken away from the traditional order, she shows, the same searing appeal to first principles that revolutionaries had used so effectively to attack the old regime could be readily adapted into weapons of right-wing, counterrevolutionary, or conservative populism. Right-wing thinkers turned the folk logic of common sense against the revolutionaries themselves. That same critical, skeptical attitude could be used to attack the new "received wisdom" of kingless government and democratic politics. Common sense, Rosenfeld argues, thus encoded an uncomfortable paradox right in the heart of democratic politics: The same principles of critical engagement that are its foundation can also be used to undermine it from within.

Rosenfeld's juxtaposition of the American and French Revolutions is one of the most valuable recent additions to the venerable but today much diminished comparative history of the revolutionary era. Scholars have long debated which revolution "invented" modern politics: After decades in which the French Revolution reigned supreme as the Big Bang of politics, the past decade has seen a slew of studies that give equal or greater credit to the American Revolution.[1] Rosenfeld shows that each revolution made a necessary contribution. One crucial innovation, the combination of the two conceptions of common sense, took place during the American Revolution. But it was only during the French Revolution that this innovation was adopted by the right as well, marking the moment when populist common sense came of age as a political paradigm, employed by right and left alike.

Rosenfeld's argument should get us thinking anew about the relationship between Europe and the early American republic. For one thing, *Common Sense: A Political History* is unusual in arguing for a direct role for Continental political thought in the American founding. Most scholars see Continental traditions arriving in early America primarily after decades of being filtered, Anglicized, and transformed in Britain. By recasting *Common Sense* as a direct juncture of British and Continental strands of political thought, Rosenfeld places the Continent right at the heart of the Revolution. Still, paradox reasserts itself here as well: Even though *Common Sense* represented a junction (or even a summa) of multiple lines of European radical thought, it never had much of a life beyond the United States. Though reprinted and translated several times in Europe during the 1770s and again in the 1790s, *Common Sense* had little visible impact. Paine's European reputation rested instead on his European writings, especially *The Rights of Man*. The book that repre-

1. See especially David Armitage, *The Declaration of Independence: A Global History* (Cambridge, MA, 2008). Wim Klooster, *Revolutions in the Atlantic World: A Comparative History* (New York, 2009), similarly emphasizes the desire to achieve sovereignty as a characteristic feature of the first age of revolutions (ca. 1760–1804). This theme of a struggle for "home rule" is native to the historiography of the American, not the French, Revolution. Even recent work by French scholars on the age of revolutions displays the relative resurgence of the American Revolution: Compare, for instance, the attention given to the American case in Marcel Dorigny, *Révoltes et révolutions en Europe et aux Amériques (1773–1802)* (Paris, 2004), to the cursory treatment in Jacques Godechot, *Les révolutions, (1770–1799)* (Paris, 1963). Of course, a growing number of historians also name the Haitian Revolution as an origin point of modern politics; whether this is a revalorization of the French Revolution or not depends on one's view of the relationship between events in metropolitan France and the Caribbean.

sented a crucial juncture between two strands of common sense thought thus had a largely provincial afterlife.

There is also a larger message here for historians of the early republic. As Paine's experience demonstrates, and many dreamers and utopians would later find, the United States was a place where European radical visions could be made into reality. In Paine's case, it was the lack of press censorship and the turbulent political moment that allowed him to openly avow radical precepts that would have merited him severe punishment in most European countries. Yet as the fate of *Common Sense* also suggests, radical visions enacted in the United States did not necessarily find much of an echo on the other side of the Atlantic. Rosenfeld's book reminds us that the early United States, paradoxically, lay both on the margins of European politics and at the center of many of its political imaginings.

NATHAN PERL-ROSENTHAL is assistant professor of history at the University of Southern California. He is currently at work on a book about cosmopolitan American seamen and the state in the revolutionary world, ca. 1760–1815.

INDEX—VOLUME 32, 2012

ARTICLES

REVIEW ESSAYS

REVIEWS

Journal of the Early Republic

VOLUME 32, 2012

The *Journal of the Early Republic* is published quarterly by the University of Pennsylvania Press for the Society for the Historians of the Early American Republic

S.C.
P
M.
NJ.
N.E.

Journal of the Early Republic

VOLUME 32, 2012

CONTENTS